GROWING ORGANIC

Vegetables

West of the Cascades

GROWING ORGANIC

Vegetables

West of the Cascades

BY STEVE SOLOMON

Pacific Search Press

Pacific Search Press, 222 Dexter Avenue North
    Seattle, Washington 98109
© 1985 by Steve Solomon. All rights reserved
Printed in the United States of America

First edition published in 1981 as *The Complete Guide to Organic Gardening
    West of the Cascades*
Second printing 1982
Third printing 1983

Edited by Marlene Blessing
Designed by Judy Petry

Library of Congress Cataloging in Publication Data

Solomon, Steve.
    Growing organic vegetables west of the Cascades.

    Updated ed. of: The complete guide to organic
gardening west of the Cascades. c1981.
    Includes bibliographies and index.
    1. Vegetable gardening—Northwest coast of North
America. 2. Organic gardening—Northwest coast of North
America. I. Solomon, Steve. Complete guide to organic
gardening west of the Cascades. II. Title.
SB324.3.S67 1985 635'.0484'09795 84-22635
ISBN 0-914718-95-9

Contents

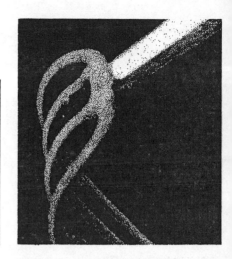

Introduction

In the northern United States, temperatures vary from extreme heat in summer to extreme cold in winter. But on the west coasts of continents, air masses have their usual extremes moderated by currents of tropical water moving close offshore, creating what is called a maritime climate.

Maritime climates are not widespread. England has one. So do coastal southern Chile and a bit of southern New Zealand. The tip of Africa would have one if the continent extended another thousand miles into the Antarctic Ocean. In our own maritime Northwest, it is the Japanese current that brings tropical warmth in winter and that cools our summer flow of air. Farther inland, the Cascades block this sea-influenced airflow, so summers are blazing hot and winters freezing cold.

Cooling as they rise over the land, maritime-influenced air masses dump their moisture load. Winter rainfalls are very heavy, particularly along the lower slopes of mountain ranges. Some places in the Coast Ranges and along the Cascades experience eighty inches of rainfall each winter, while along the particularly steep slopes of the Olympics, some microclimates get nearly two hundred inches a year, resulting in temperate rain forests. In summer, the westward-moving, moisture-laden air systems move north, bringing several months of California-like, stable, dry airflow. Though sunny, this air is still strongly sea-influenced and not "California hot." Residents of the maritime Northwest complain when temperatures exceed eighty-five degrees.

Growing vegetables in the maritime Northwest is not always easy. First of all, though our mild springs permit growth of early vegetables by March/April, the soil is almost always too wet to till before May. Some particularly rainy springs delay planting until Memorial Day. Even then, late frosts often take tender transplants. June weather is rarely sunny and warm. Cool, cloudy, and showery conditions spoil germination, retard the growth of heat-loving vegetables, and give melons and cucumbers powdery mildew. The sunny, mild days of July/August, coupled with cool nights, make the maritime Northwest a recreation paradise. However, days in the seventies and nights in the low fifties do not grow crops the same way hot days and warm nights do. Little heat causes late harvests, and many years the tomatoes barely begin to ripen before the rains return and frosts end their season. Surprisingly, only the earliest heat-loving varieties will perform in a region that may have as many as two hundred fifty frost-free growing days.

Mild fall weather goes on and on—often into December. But early maturing cole crops split, rot, or otherwise fall apart before winter comes. Though many winters are so warm that celery and chard often survive unprotected, few gardens have more than an occasional forgotten plant nestled in the weeds after November. The maritime garden, like its eastern relative, usually produces food only from July through October with what seem to us more weather problems than experienced by most.

Not only is our climate difficult, but the seeds we buy don't perform for us as described in the eastern seed catalogs. Corn that matures in seventy-five hot, humid eastern days might begin to tassel out after one hundred twenty cool, dry maritime summer days—which are all we have at best. Tomatoes described as main season never ripen at all; midseason varieties are very late; and only the early types produce much before the end of August, unless heroic measures are used to force and pamper the plants. Many of the region's gardeners have learned that it is far wiser to buy local seeds and bedding plant varieties that have proven themselves over time.

The region's smarter gardeners are realizing that our particular climate has more potential than would first appear to someone from the East. Rainy, mild winters permit something called winter gardening, which permits twelve months of fresh harvest. The promise of fresh garden fare year-round makes up for the woefully short few weeks of vine-ripened fresh tomatoes.

Our unique maritime climate requires specialized gardening techniques. For example, Ruth Stout's famous mulching method may work wonders in Connecticut, but in a land where soil fails to freeze in winter, mulch provides an ideal, year-round breeding ground for slugs, sowbugs, and earwigs. Mulched soils also warm up too slowly to produce good early summer growth. Another eastern strategy that doesn't apply to gardening in the maritime Northwest is planning a garden with the idea that winter ends food production. Most maritime winters allow the abundant harvesting of salads and other greens, while root crops can be dug from unfrozen earth until March.

Soil management cannot be done by a single prescription. What works in Pennsylvania may be much less effective in Oregon. Our cool, damp conditions produce fairly high levels of soil organic matter, which decomposes slowly. Similarly, low soil temperatures decrease the rate of nutrient release, and consequently, though common manures may produce excellent results in hot, active soils, when it rots slowly in cool earth, fertilizers may be needed, too.

In the maritime Northwest, cold frame design requires more attention to low winter light levels, with less attention to insulation and weather stripping. Our summer rainfall is so low as to be useless from mid-June through mid-September most years. However, most gardeners do not understand the principles of irrigation. They need to in order to avoid leaching. Our low summer temperatures require careful attention to varietal choices when buying garden seed. Some of the varieties essential for winter gardening are available only from a few companies at this time.

I wrote this book to serve as a complete guide for the maritime Northwest gardener, covering soil improvement and fertility, irrigation, planning for year-round food production, insect control, and providing full cultural information to grow all types of vegetable crops. I want the novice to be able to use the sections on gardening basics as a springboard for solving garden difficulties so that he or she will no longer be dependent on the advice of "experts," but will in fact become his or her own expert. The hope I harbor that underlies all of this is that many more people in the maritime Northwest will produce a larger percentage of their own food year-round and will thus enjoy better health and greater economic security.

Gardening Basics

One of my hats at Territorial Seed Company is "extension agent," so most of the questions arriving in the mail end up in my in-basket. Many times a questioner needs information easily supplied. Occasionally, however, a query betrays an unfamiliarity with basics so profound that I must begin answering by explaining the physiology of plants.

A complete review of botany and soil science is far beyond the scope of any single gardening guide. However, by highlighting some of the most pertinent aspects of botany in a manner that must seem impertinent to any true expert in the field, I hope to focus the reader's attention on the most critical processes of plant life so that he or she can understand the phenomena faced daily in the garden.

Here is an example of how such basic understanding can be essential to solving garden problems. An organic gardener phoned me one day to request aid. Symphylans were ruining her peppers and the only solution (according to the Extension Service) was an unacceptable (to her) pesticide. Symphylans are a root-nibbling soil dweller common to all soils and gardens in the maritime Northwest. Now, this incident occurred during the exceptionally cloudy, cool summer of 1983 with low temperatures and low light levels. Being tropical plants, peppers were barely able to stay alive, much less grow rapidly that year. The symphylans were most likely no worse than normal, but their effects were more noticeable because the peppers weren't producing ten times the amount of root being eaten off. Even if pesticides eradicated the symphylans, the peppers would have hardly grown.

Though I tried long and hard to explain this, the questioner couldn't get past the idea that there *were* symphylans, and *they* were eating root tips, and consequently the plants were stunted. The connnection between sunlight and root growth eluded her.

Botany "101"

Most garden plants begin with a seed, which is a small container filled with food that holds a tiny plant or embryo within. The embryo is dormant—living, breathing, and eating at a very low rate. The seed possesses a certain potential to grow and develop, a potential contained within the specific genetic makeup of the embryo and limited by the vigor of the seed itself. Genes determine the kind and quality of the plant and contain a program for its development and changes. Genes tell a seed how to sprout, tell the seedlings how to grow, how to protect themselves from environmental menaces, how to make use of opportunities, and when to reproduce. The gardener needs to understand what the efforts of the organism are and what can be done to assist, train, shape, and control these efforts.

Not all seeds within a packet have the same genetic program, despite the best efforts of plant breeders and seed technology. Some hybrid varieties are remarkably uniform; others have a range of types that are similar but quite distinct from one another when closely examined. Additionally, not all lots of the same variety of seed possess the same vigor.

Seed Vigor

It is easy to see vigor, but hard to measure it exactly. At Territorial Seed Company, we observe vigor on a daily basis in the germination lab. Vigor expresses itself in rapidity of sprouting and growth. When testing seed, we sprout many types of similar seed simultaneously. Ten varieties of red cabbage or several different years' production of a single variety will sprout differently. Some lots come up in the shortest possible time for that type. Other lots take more days to emerge. The quick-sprouting lots usually have thick stems, big leaves, and begin growing immediately. Vigorous seeds rarely succumb to damping-off disease during the first week of growth and proceed to develop into large, healthy plants as quickly as conditions permit. Slow sprouting, nonvigorous seeds have thin stems, small leaves, and grow slowly after emergence, often succumbing to diseases. In the field, weak seeds will not develop as rapidly nor make the same final size and yield.

Vigorous seed is produced by healthy parent plants that form fat, well-filled-out seeds containing large reserves of complete nutrition for the embryo within. If these seeds mature at temperatures that cause neither the degradation of the food reserves nor damage to the embryo, dry down to the correct moisture range at the correct rate, and are harvested, thrashed, cleaned, and stored under proper conditions that avoid damage or deterioration, the vigor is preserved. Bad weather at harvesttime, mechanical damage from thrashing (especially possible when harvested at the wrong moisture content), improper storage temperatures or humidity levels, all can reduce vigor. Vigor is also a product of the genetic potential of the variety itself. Some species or even particular varieties within a species are known for having high vigor—others are intrinsically weak and need careful handling, especially in the seedling stages.

Seed vigor is not a static condition. The embryo is a living thing, slowly breathing and consuming its food reserves. The food supply is itself deteriorating over time; the embryo is aging and decaying, too. Eventually, a seed declines in vigor to the point where it will no longer sprout successfully. Sowings that fail to come up may or may not be poor seed, because many external conditions can prevent emergence. But, seed that comes up and then grows very slowly or disappears shortly after sprouting is very likely poor, especially if the soil is otherwise fertile and grows other plants well.

Seed Germination

Getting seeds to germinate can be a frustrating experience that causes many gardeners to feel they must buy transplants, can grow onions only from sets, or cannot grow certain things. Seeds that sprout in one location may not sprout in another. Seeds that sprout one day may not sprout when sown a week or two later. Seeds that did not sprout will come up handily when resown a few weeks later. The novice is often frustrated by these mysteries, while the experienced one knows how to coax many types into life.

As a seedman, I've paid a lot of attention to seed germination. Every bag of seed we receive carries the result of a recent germ test, usually well in excess of the minimum standard germination level prescribed by the Federal Seed Act. But, we've found that seeds that sprout in a germination lab often will not sprout in the field. In the laboratory, a high percentage of planted seeds can be made to come up within hours of a scheduled time. In the field, lots that sprout 99 percent in the laboratory might come up at 70 percent at best, if field conditions are *ideal.* But field conditions are rarely ideal.

The gardener cannot count on having seeds so vigorous that some still sprout under extremely adverse conditions. It is the task of the gardener to create sprouting conditions good enough that seeds of only average vigor and germination ability will come up and grow well. Understanding what ideal germination conditions are enables the grower to create those conditions in the field as closely as possible.

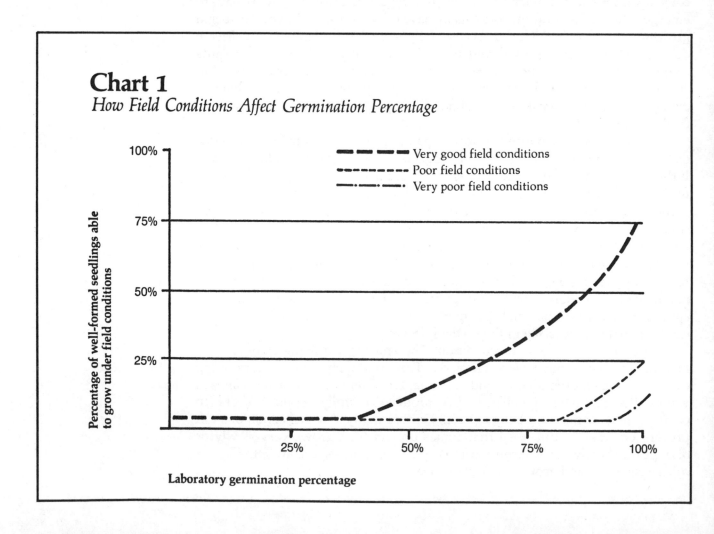

Chart 1
How Field Conditions Affect Germination Percentage

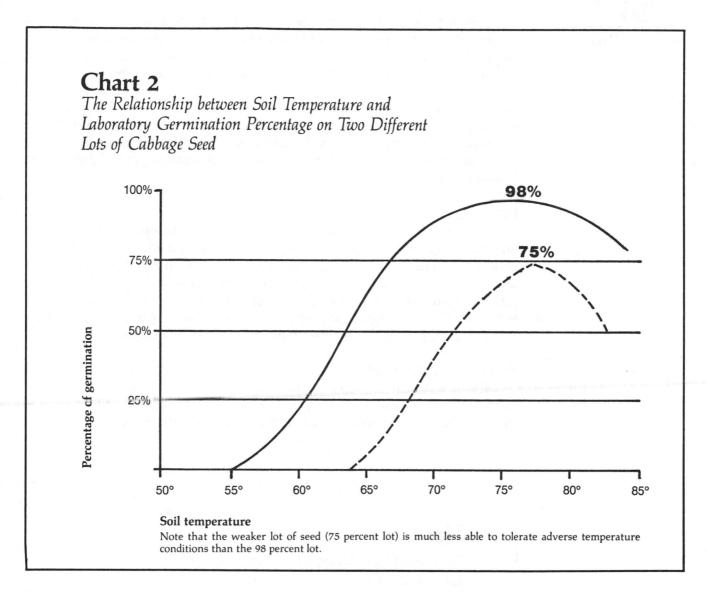

Chart 2
The Relationship between Soil Temperature and Laboratory Germination Percentage on Two Different Lots of Cabbage Seed

98%

75%

Percentage of germination

100%

75%

50%

25%

50°   55°   60°   65°   70°   75°   80°   85°

Soil temperature

Note that the weaker lot of seed (75 percent lot) is much less able to tolerate adverse temperature conditions than the 98 percent lot.

Proper Soil Moisture

In the laboratory, most vegetable seeds are sprouted in a medium that is at a specific moisture level and held at controlled temperatures. These two factors are the primary ones that control the rate of sprouting and its success or failure. Surprisingly, seed does not germinate at its highest percentage in wet soil. Soggy soils are full of damping-off disease organisms that often kill seedlings before they emerge into the light. Seed can absorb moisture from surprisingly dry soil. In fact, the way our seed testing laboratory moisturizes soil is to add water slowly to dry soil, until when a handful is squeezed hard into a ball it just barely sticks together and will easily break apart into fine particles. Laboratory soil is sealed into an airtight container when the seeds are sown, losing no moisture as it would in the field, and needing no watering until the seeds are up. In our own laboratory experiments on germination in unsterilized soils, we found that soil with low but adequate moisture levels could sprout twice the number of seedlings as soil that was exposed to air and watered every day or two.

Proper Temperature

Temperature is also a vital factor. The speed with which cellular activities occur is determined by temperature. Cold seeds sprout slowly, if at all, and all the while are prey to diseases and insects in the soil. Slow sprouting also requires consumption of much larger quantities of food, and the reserve supplies carried in the seed coat can become depleted, leaving a weak and relatively exhausted seedling trying to start out life. Most vegetable seeds sprout best at 75 to 85 degrees. Some of the tropical ones like peppers, eggplants, and melons won't sprout at all if soil temperatures fall below 70 for much time. A few types of seed sprout better at slightly cooler temperatures. Spinach, for example, sprouts best at about 55 to 60 degrees and will not sprout well at high temperatures. In the laboratory, the germination cabinet is set at the temperature optimal for the type of seed being sprouted.

Proper Sprouting Medium

The sprouting medium also plays a vital part. The emerging seedling is capable of exerting only a certain amount of force against surrounding soil particles as it pushes out roots and sends up a shoot reaching for the light. In the laboratory, the medium is often a damp blotter paper with the seeds laid on top, sealed in a small, airtight container, or a specially composed soil mix that is light textured and has fine particles, similar to those used in greenhouses. Even a delicate seedling is capable of developing under these conditions.

The Embattled Sprout

It is important to the success of the crop that the seed sprout quickly and well. Sprouting is an exhausting process to the seedling. Having a fixed food reserve that deteriorates with age, the embryo must build an entire functional plant and then supplement its food supply from the remaining reserves while the first true

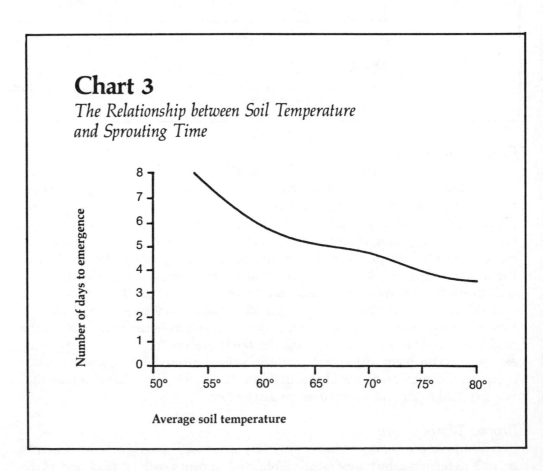

Chart 3
The Relationship between Soil Temperature and Sprouting Time

leaf is grown. Only after the first leaf has fully developed is the average seedling producing all its own food, and enough surplus to grow new plant tissues rapidly. If sprouting takes much more than the shortest possible time or if soil conditions greatly resist the seed's efforts to move root and shoot through it, the seedling may emerge with overly depleted reserves. Weakened seedlings often die shortly after sprouting or grow very slowly, have difficulty with every insect and disease that comes along, and rarely make big, healthy, productive plants unless conditions for their growth improve dramatically immediately after emergence. Old, weak, or low-germination-percentage seed often produces weak, poorly growing plants if it sprouts at all.

Corn, peas, beans, squash, and cucumbers have big, vigorously sprouting seeds. Most gardeners are successful getting these to sprout. Some small-seeded vegetables like lettuce, radishes, kale, broccoli, beets, and chard sprout quickly and strongly. These are the types purchased from seed racks in the greatest quantity. Some small-seeded vegetables require very good conditions to sprout in the field and are usually grown successfully only by more experienced gardeners. Included in this group are celery, carrots, cauliflower, cabbage, and onions. Some small-seeded vegetables can't be successfully started under field conditions in the maritime Northwest and are transplanted after being sown in a greenhouse. Included in this group are tomatoes, peppers, eggplants, and melons. Harder-to-start vegetables like cabbage are often sold to gardeners as transplants.

In the field, there are many obstacles to successful sprouting. Soil-living insects eat seed and especially eat the tender root tip and shoot while they are still in the soil. If soil texture is not uniformly fine, it becomes difficult for the seed to pick up moisture and hard for the emerging seedling to force its way to the light. Sometimes hard crusts form on the soil's surface that completely block the emergence of seedlings. Weather can cause soil to become very chilly or very hot—both conditions can inhibit germination. Hot, sunny weather can make soil dry out very fast, and if the soil dries out to the depth of the seed, it can kill the seed rapidly. However, too frequent watering of the seedbed can cause surface crust formation or damping-off diseases. The contrast between the laboratory germination percentage and the sprouting rate in the field reflects how far from ideal the field conditions were.

To sprout seed successfully, you will need to pay attention to soil temperature. Spring soil warm-up begins in February when soil temperatures may be close to forty degrees. Different soils warm up at different rates. South slopes heat up fastest. Dark-colored soils heat faster than light ones. Well-drained soils heat faster than soggy ones. Below sixty degrees, many types of seed sprout very slowly or not at all. Many maritime Northwest soils don't reach stable sixty-degree temperatures until May or early June.

Weather conditions can rapidly change soil temperature several inches down. When the sun is shining strongly, soils heat up fast and can reach eighty degrees or more near the surface. At night, these same soils can drop into the sixties on the surface. However, if the weather changes and becomes cloudy or rainy, soils can drop into the fifties and stay that way until the weather improves, particularly in May. Planting early is an invitation to failure. Ideally, sow heat-demanding vegetables just prior to a spell of hot, sunny weather. Should bad weather follow sowing and germination not happen within ten days or so, it is a safe assumption that the seeds will not sprout well. Certainly if they don't sprout within two weeks, it is time to resow them.

The soil's surface dries out fast when the sun shines and air temperatures are high. Small seeds near the surface must be kept moist. However, frequent watering tends to create crusts that can block the emergence of delicate seedlings. As a general recommendation, covering small seed with a prepared medium can greatly enhance sprouting. Sifted compost, horse manure, well-rotted sawdust, or a mixture of half soil, half sphagnum moss are all materials that hold a lot of moisture, act as a mulch, prevent moisture from escaping, remain loose and open, and permit easy emergence. We have found that small seeds covered with sifted compost may be watered every two days in hot weather, while seed covered with soil had to be watered daily.

One reason large seed is much easier to sprout is because big seed can be planted an inch or two deep where the soil doesn't dry out rapidly. Usually, if watered when sown, enough moisture remains at seed depth to sprout the seed well. In fact, large seed is better watered only once until emergence because watering lowers soil temperatures, slows germination, and encourages rot and soil diseases. However, sandy soils may dry out so fast that watering may be required every few days.

For the seed to pick up moisture, it must be in close contact with the soil. If the seedbed consists of large soil clumps or clods, many seeds may fall into air pockets and not have good seed-soil contact. Cloddy soil doesn't allow roots to penetrate well either, so seedlings may not be able to draw sufficient moisture. Rough soil may not permit leaves to emerge either. Again, big seed survives much better in rough ground because the large shoots can exert sufficient force to move aside a small clod; the massive initial root system can rapidly penetrate into deeper moist soil.

To get small seed to sprout well, it is essential to work up a fine seedbed. Low soil moisture content at the time of tillage results in a fine seedbed, while wet soil forms clods when tilled. However, waiting for soil to dry out enough to make a fine seedbed can force you to postpone planting well into June. This dilemma is one reason that commercial vegetable production is usually done on light-textured soils, which dry out rapidly.

Plant Growth

Like other life forms, plants have a drive or goal to grow. Most achieve this by creating a large sunlight-powered conversion factory (leaves) and by mining the air itself and the soil below, converting water and mineral nutrients into sugars, proteins, fats, and structural materials like cellulose. These organic materials help the plant build a larger manufacturing and mining facility, which in turn makes more nutrients and so forth.

Many people do not really appreciate the fact that plants eat, too. Every plant cell is a consumer of food in the same way an animal cell is. At least half the plant's cells do not manufacture food at all. Root and stem cells are completely dependent on the work of the food-producing areas. At night, even the cells in the leaves must eat from reserves of food stored up during the day.

Growth can only occur when energy being received and nutrients needed for new cell and food manufacture exceed the plant's survival requirements. The relationship between light and growth is integral and is especially important to understand in the light-deprived maritime garden.

Growth Rates

Plant growth is usually geometric. The pattern is easiest to observe in a plant with a rosette habit of growth, such as lettuce. A tiny lettuce seedling seems like it will never grow, but is actually doubling in size quite rapidly. A few days after emergence, the lettuce seedling is barely an eighth of an inch in diameter. After a time, the plant is twice that size. The amount of time it takes to double is called the rate of increase. For most types of lettuce growing during the period of maximum light intensity in our Northern Hemisphere (which is June/July), the rate of increase is about one week per doubling, so that the lettuce arrives at its harvest size of eight inches within six weeks.

Growth rates change seasonally in temperate climates. Sown in the chill and short days of early spring, lettuce has a very low growth rate, taking two to three weeks per doubling. For this reason, early sowings don't result in equally early harvest, though as the season advances, increasing light levels, longer days, and warmer temperatures decrease the time needed to double. In this case, sowing seven weeks later results in harvest only three weeks later. There is also a lot less trouble with slugs as well as more reliable germination from a late April sowing than from one in the chill of early spring. In fall, the rate of growth again falls off, and in winter, plants that are hardy enough to survive chill and rain can hardly grow at all from lack of solar input. Even if protected from frost and rain in a greenhouse, summertime vegetables that are adapted to intense light gradually lose leaves and deteriorate as their consumption of food exceeds their ability to make new supplies under very low light levels.

Sowing and thinning strategies can help gardeners cope with a seedling's vulnerability in a period of lessened light. Compared to the environmental menaces it faces, a seedling is a tiny and weak thing for quite a while. It is generally wise to sow several seeds for each plant desired at maturity. But in early spring when growth rates are slow, it is wise to sow ten to twenty seeds for every one desired. This allows plenty of seedlings to feed slugs, flea beetles, and damping-off diseases, while many are healthy survivors. I always advise maritime gardeners to sow thickly, thin gradually (but promptly to avoid overcrowding), and sow on the late side to minimize problems with low light levels and pests.

Mid-September is another tricky period for maritime plants. If you have

Table 1
Growth Rate of Two Different Sowings of Lettuce

Date	Doubling Rate	March 1 Sowing Size	April 21 Sowing Size
March 1	21 days	1/8 inch	
March 21	17 days	1/4 inch	
April 7	14 days	1/2 inch	
April 21	10 days	1 inch	1/8 inch
May 1	9 days	2 inches	1/4 inch
May 10	8 days	4 inches	1/2 inch
May 18	8 days	8 inches/harvest	1 inch
May 26	7 days		2 inches
June 2	7 days		4 inches
June 9	7 days		8 inches/harvest

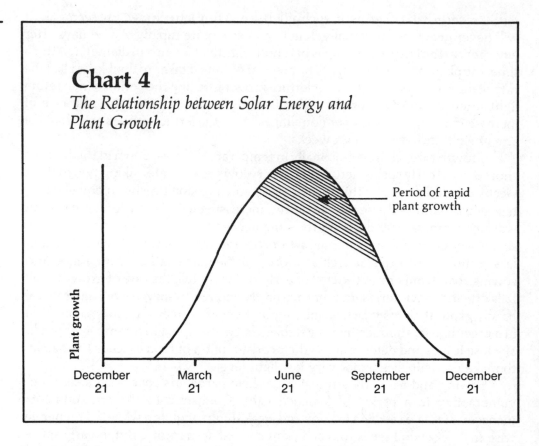

Chart 4

The Relationship between Solar Energy and Plant Growth

Period of rapid plant growth

Plant growth

December 21 · March 21 · June 21 · September 21 · December 21

been skillful enough to have harvested high-quality tomatoes prior to mid-September, you may notice that something happens to fruit flavor about then. Usually triggered by a short spell of unsettled weather, the tomatoes suddenly lose their rich, midsummer quality. What has occurred is that decreasing light levels cannot permit the manufacture of enough plant food to pack the fruits to their maximum potential. As light levels diminish further, the fruit declines in flavor, and usually, by early October, the light is so weak that the declining plants no longer can support their fruit load and begin to die. This same thing happens to other garden fruits like melons and peppers at about the same point in time.

Plant Survival Strategies

Competition for space and resources spawns a multitude of survival strategies. Some plants—trees—grow tall and strong, surviving many years, delaying reproduction in an effort to gain size and capture light. Some, like lettuce, spread broadly and thickly, quickly hiding competing seedlings from the light. Some, like carrots and vines, grow thinly, interspersed with their neighbors. Some root deeply, some shallowly. Some store water and nutrients one year and then invest them the next to shoot up a tall flower very early, thus completing their reproduction cycle before their neighbors can even begin—biennials. Each strategy has its particular beauty and harmony.

Under stiff competition, plants acquire survival traits that make them less acceptable as food sources. Wild plants tend toward thick, strong cell walls, strong stems, and tough leaves. Bitter, unpalatable flavors discourage would-be consumers. Requiring fewer nutrients allows a plant to thrive in poor soils, but forces it to develop as a smaller plant with woody composition. A grouping of many small, hard seeds is more likely to sprout before being eaten by animals than are a few fat, tender ones.

Weeds

In early agriculture, people developed vegetables from wild plants by breeding them for succulence, flavor, and nutritive value. Root systems became less extensive because vegetables were watered and fertilized. Food diverted from root development was redirected into thicker, juicier leaves, pods or stems, larger flowers, sweeter fruit. Competition was eliminated by weeding and thinning, so vegetables became larger and more succulent. Unfortunately, these weaker and less vigorous vegetables do not grow well untended by people. When put under the stress of competition, vegetables either adapt and become relatively inedible or succumb. That is why thinning and weeding are vital in the garden. More vigorous weeds will inevitably overtop vegetables and decrease or prevent their yield unless the vegetable has already densely overshadowed the weed and prevents the weed's rapid growth.

Often new gardeners doubt that vegetables need all this pampering and so permit many weeds to grow in their garden. They may even have heard of some gardeners who intentionally leave a few weeds growing for the purpose of confusing insects, and so feel there is some justification for their laziness. However, in the porous, well-fertilized, watered environment of the garden, weeds are propelled into a rush of growth they never enjoy in nature. So intrinsically vigorous are weeds that in the garden they inevitably outgrow vegetables many-fold. Fortunately, not all weeds need be removed from the garden—only most of them. The following profiles of the most common weed types are listed in order of priority for weed control:

1. *Grass.* Grasses have highly invasive root systems, and though they may not overtop vegetables and compete for light, grass roots rob the soil of most available nutrients and water, stunting any nearby vegetables. Grasses also have a strong ability to grow in even the most shaded portion of a garden. Established grasses don't pull out easily and can damage neighboring root systems when pulled, so great care must be taken in their removal. Many types of grasses multiply rapidly through underground runners, and so must be nipped in the bud if they are to be controlled.

2. *Pernicious weeds.* Certain weeds are hard to eradicate because they either regrow rapidly from their roots and/or make huge quantities of seeds. Included in this group are thistles, morning glories, and nightshade. These weeds should not be allowed to go to seed in or anywhere near the garden. Thistles have the ability to develop and mature seed after a flowering seed head has been cut off, so these should be targeted for early and frequent hoeing.

3. Any weed that reaches above neighboring vegetables begins to offer light competition, which will stunt the vegetable. Pull these when seen. A few weeds left here and there will produce aromas that confuse many kinds of destructive insects, as well as provide homes for many beneficial species. Many gardeners like to plant strong-smelling herbs and flowers here and there in the garden for the same purpose.

Thinning

Just as weeding must be done to eliminate harmful competition, thinning must be done to give each vegetable sufficient space to develop properly. When too crowded, vegetables compete with each other. The results can be big disappointments. Radishes, if not carefully and promptly thinned, will not bulb at all, producing only tops. Unthinned carrots don't develop well, unless the stock is so highly variable in vigor that some uniquely vigorous individuals crowd out their neighbors, producing good roots. Crowded bush beans make small pods; corn makes fewer well-developed ears and more culls and smalls. Crowded lettuce doesn't head.

There is no absolute rule for correct plant density. A gardener must consider many trade-offs when trying to decide how close to plant. Very dense stands, as recommended by the French intensive system, produce the highest possible yields. However, the percentage of deformed, small, or otherwise unappealing yield is also high. If the most attractive-looking and best-tasting production is desired, plants should be spaced out so they do not compete with each other for light when fully developed—but this strategy causes a drop in absolute yields. Somewhere in between produces the highest marketable yield.

When irrigation is in short supply or nonexistent, even wider spacings reduce water competition and permit growing many vegetable species that would otherwise require watering. One southern Oregonian grows an extensive vegetable garden without watering in a climate virtually rainless from May through September. His ground retains water, of course, or this would be impossible. He grows carrots twelve inches apart in rows thirty-six inches apart. It might seem foolish to space carrots this far, but he says each weighs several pounds and is as large as a rutabaga.

It is best to plant a lot of extra seeds and thin gradually. This ensures a stand of seedlings even under poor field conditions. After germination, the weaker seedlings will be rapidly thinned by damping-off diseases and insects for up to a week after emergence. The better-established survivors should then be thinned to prevent clusters of seedlings from competing. As a general rule, small seedlings should stand 1/4 to 1/2 inch apart at this point. After another week, the more vigorous plants begin to stand out and many of the now obviously weaker ones should be pulled. Another week, and a few extremely vigorous ones are showing. Surprisingly, it is usually best to pull these, too, as any off-type or outcrossed plant is liable to be bursting with hybrid vigor and outgrow its neighbors manyfold. And, of course, underlying all these steps is the idea that seedlings should not compete for light, water, or nutrients. Once small seedlings are four to six weeks old, they may be considered completely and stably established and thinned to the final desired spacing. Big seed has a much higher survival rate. When growing vegetables such as squash or beans, fewer seeds are sown and a single thinning done a week after emergence is sufficient.

Methods for Improving Plant Growth

The concept of limits is a very useful idea when considering plant growth. Most life forms will grow as rapidly as needed components are available. But if any one of these, such as light, is in short supply, growth will be reduced to that level. For example, if a plant needs fifteen different elements for tissue building and fourteen of these are abundantly available, the rate of growth will be reduced to the level permitted by the one in short supply. Often, by increasing the availability of scarce nutrients, amazing increases in growth rates can occur. A few grams of the limited nutrient can result in hundreds of grams of increased

Illustration 1
Factors that Limit Plant Growth

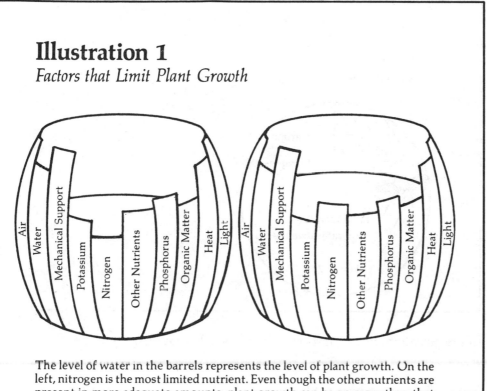

The level of water in the barrels represents the level of plant growth. On the left, nitrogen is the most limited nutrient. Even though the other nutrients are present in more adequate amounts, plant growth can be no more than that allowed by the level of nitrogen. When more nitrogen is added, the level of plant growth is controlled by the next limited nutrient—potassium.

plant weight.

When fully dried out, plants lose 75 to 90 percent of their weight. Besides water content, plants are composed of various mineral elements. Carbon is the next largest component, forming the basis of organic compounds plants use for construction and food storage. Sugars and starches are main food reserves; cellulose and lignins are the main structural building blocks. All these substances are composed of carbon, combined with hydrogen and oxygen. Plants derive carbon from carbon dioxide in the air and take hydrogen and oxygen from water. Rarely are these nutrients limited, though under stress in dry soil plants become stunted, and in greenhouses, where carbon dioxide levels can be artificially raised, growth rates can sometimes be increased dramatically.

Once carbon, oxygen, and hydrogen are deducted from the plant's mass, what remains is no less significant, though it amounts to only a percent or two. Nitrogen, phosphorus, potassium, calcium, and magnesium compose the largest part of the balance, with traces of some other nutrients such as manganese, boron, copper, and zinc no less important. Any of these can greatly limit growth. For example, nitrogen is the essential building block of protein, both in plants and animals. Phosphorus is a key factor in energy transfers within the cell. All these mineral nutrients are taken from the soil through the plant's root system.

Not all soils can supply a good balance of nutrients. Many soils are naturally deficient in one or more nutrients, and plant growth on those fields can suffer accordingly. Historically, two basic approaches have been used by growers seeking improvement of the level of nutrients available to plants—soil management

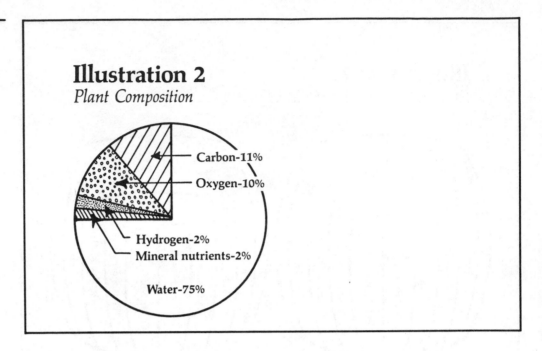

Illustration 2
Plant Composition

Carbon-11%

Oxygen-10%

Hydrogen-2%
Mineral nutrients-2%

Water-75%

and fertilization. Both approaches have their limitations.

Soil Management

Slash-and-burn agriculture is an old soil management technique, very workable on highly leached forest soils such as those in the maritime Northwest and other rain forests. The idea is to enrich soil by clearcutting a patch, burning all the slash, and returning the ash to the soil. The ash contains most of the mineral nutrients that were originally within the plant material growing on the site. Then, leaves and other organic residues naturally deposited on that site are blended with soil, greatly accelerating their decomposition. Essentially, the nutrient collection of many years of forest growth is made available at one time. Slash-and-burn fields are highly fertile for a few years, after which growth declines greatly and the patch is returned to forest for a slow rebuilding of fertility. Slash-and-burn fields can be cropped only a few years per generation.

Rotational schemes are a similar soil management approach. A field is put into grass, pasture, or cover crop for some seasons or years, while the vegetation accumulates plant nutrients. Once the sod is thick, it is plowed in, releasing several years' nutrient collection. With rotations, a field that would not produce a high-yielding food crop at all can grow one every few years. Somewhat more fertile fields can also benefit from rotations. If only one nutrient is in short supply while others are abundant, a crop can be grown one year that has little use for the deficient nutrient, or that concentrates that nutrient in a part of the plant not removed from the field at harvest, allowing the soil levels to increase. Next season, a more demanding crop is grown.

Fertilization

Fertilization is another approach. Spreading seaweed, manure, or fish wastes will increase plant nutrients for a time. Gardeners have also used leaves, dried blood, ground bones, brewer's wastes, and many other organic and inorganic substances that contain significant levels of nitrogen, phosphorus, potassium, etc. After scientific analysis of plant ash revealed (circa 1840) that NPK (nitrogen, phosphorus, and potassium) were the main elemental nutrients, growers began spreading water-soluble chemicals containing high levels of these minerals.

Organic gardeners tend to think that manures, plant wastes, composts, and other organic substances naturally contain useful amounts of all needed nutrients, and that by adding them to the garden, high yields and excellent plant health will be the inevitable result. This belief is broadly correct, but when put into practice, natural substances must be used wisely or the results will not be as good as imagined. Organic gardeners often go wrong when they confuse the nutrient requirements of field crops with those of many vegetables. A thin covering of horse or cow manure or the turning in of a well-grown clover cover crop may well sufficiently improve growth of *low*-demand crops, like corn, wheat, barley, oats, sorghum, beans, carrots, beets, and kale. Exacting vegetables, like cabbage, cauliflower, brussels sprouts, celery, head lettuce, melons, tomatoes, peppers, and squash, require nutrient levels higher than most maritime Northwest fields can consistently produce unless potent fertilizing substances are used. Before the age of chemical fertilizers, market gardeners were expert at creating high-potency composts and greedy for the purest and freshest manures unmixed with bedding (then called short manure, as opposed to long manure, and which contained bedding) to coax along the more demanding crops.

Today, most market gardeners use chemicals. High quality manures, free of sawdust or other bedding, are very hard to obtain these days, and making potent compost is an art similar to baking first-rate bread. However, where bread may be attempted daily until the cook achieves mastery (in a limited time), composting takes months per heap, and it can take many, many years to master the process. Fortunately for the organic gardener, other very concentrated natural substances are available for use as fertilizers—substances like seed meals and processed animal wastes. Though compost should be made, it is best to consider it a relatively nonnutritive organic matter (as are long manures) and use it for textural improvement of soil.

I am certain that some dedicated and well-studied organic gardeners will resent my assertion that ordinary manure or indifferently made composts will not grow many types of vegetables very successfully in the maritime Northwest. Such a statement seems to contradict what has become virtual dogma to many an organic gardener. So, before describing how to make and use natural fertilizers, I will give a brief explanation of why fertilizer is so important in the garden west of the Cascades.

Nutrients dissolve in the soil and thus become available to plants through weathering of rock particles and through breakdown of rock particles and organic matter by soil organisms. Manure has traditionally been used to add nutrients, which will be released by soil bacteria's digesting the organic matter manure contains. Manuring also increases the rate of natural nutrient release by feeding soil bacteria and fungi, as well as improving conditions for these microorganisms by increasing the amount of air and water in the soil. Manuring is broadly effective and has for centuries been a basic farming technique worldwide.

It has become a truth that all one needs do to improve a garden's performance is to incorporate lots of any sort of organic matter or compost and eventually, steadily and gradually, the soil becomes a virtual "garden of eatin'." "Our garden was not too good this year, but we're building up the soil and next year should be better," is a statement I've heard from countless folks. The main support for this practice comes from garden books published in the East by eastern garden writers. Now back in Michigan where I come from, summers are virtually tropical and soil temperatures are extremely high. Soil biological activity and the consequent rate of organic breakdown are largely a function of soil temperature. Hot soil rots a lot of manure rapidly. In California, I could hardly maintain any level of organic matter no matter how much I added, and even manures composed largely of sawdust would grow decent crops after a few weeks' wait after tillage.

However, in the maritime Northwest, soils are very slow to warm up in spring. By themselves, maritime soils will not usually release enough nutrients to grow really *demanding* vegetables until midsummer. Unless fertilizer, hot chicken manure, shrimp waste, or high-quality compost is used, corn will often not green up and grow fast until July; brassicas may well limp along, barely making more growth than the insects chew down; lettuce can be slow growing and bitter. Early sowings of even low-demanding crops may grow slower than the appetites of insects for them unless fertilizer is used. Our cool summers require the most rapid possible growth and maturation if many types of vegetables are to ripen before summer ends. After experiencing all these things myself and answering the queries of countless others having similar difficulties, I have become a believer in the need to fertilize vegetables west of the Cascades. Of course, there are exceptions to any rule, and a few coarse-textured, dark-colored, highly mineralized soils may warm up much faster than most and prove me wrong. But even the successful market gardeners who grow organically on Oregon's finest soils along the Willamette River near Eugene use chicken manure on many types of vegetables.

Banding Fertilizer

Chemical fertilizers dissolve readily. Within a few days, they are completely incorporated into the soil water and are absorbed by plants, washed out by irrigation or rain, or have recombined into insoluble compounds that plants can no longer absorb. Because they are concentrated and instantly available, chemicals in very small quantities can have very big effects.

It is dangerously easy to overuse chemicals. One teaspoonful to one tablespoonful of chemical fertilizer sprinkled around a plant can induce a maximum growth response in a large vegetable plant for three weeks or so. More might burn the roots or wilt the plant. Less is not maximally effective. So, small quantities of chemicals are usually *banded* beside or below the furrow. Banding means placing fertilizer beside or below a seed or seedling so that it is close to the tiny root systems. After a month or so, more fertilizer is added, either by sprinkling it down the row or by mixing it into irrigation water.

If banded, organic fertilizers can be more effective than chemicals. Most organics release increasing levels of nutrients over a period of three or four months. Compared to chemicals, this means a single fertilization can grow a plant to maturity without danger of damage to the plants. As the plant grows, the soil also warms up, so nutrient release increases and the plant is fed more. Organic fertilizers are used by the 1/4 cup to the pint per plant; 1/2 to 1 cup per 5 to 10 row feet. A small shovelful of fresh chicken manure will grow a big squash vine; and a light sprinkling of chicken manure in a furrow of corn seed can have amazing effect. Rich garden soils, or those built up through years of manuring, may only need a small amount of fertilizers in spring, supplementing nutrient levels until the warming of the soil releases enough nutrients by itself.

Organic fertilizers aren't usually soluble and to take effect must be blended into soil so bacteria can break them down, thus releasing their nutrient content. It is not sufficient simply to put organic fertilizer into a hole or sprinkle atop the ground. Large clumps of organic fertilizer may putrify if located below transplants. Generally, the fertilizer should be mixed into a small volume of soil so that bacteria can work on it rapidly.

When sowing seeds in rows, a deep furrow is made with a hoe or furrower and fertilizer is sprinkled along the bottom. Then the furrow is partially filled in, seeds are sown and covered. Doing this bands the somewhat dispersed fertilizer directly below the seed. When setting out transplants, a half cup or so of fertilizer is blended directly below the seedling into about a gallon of soil. When sowing types of vegetables traditionally grown in hills, such as squash, the hill is fertilized as though growing transplants, with seeds sown atop the fertilized spot.

Fertilizer placement by banding is essential. As the seed sprouts or the transplant gets established, it immediately encounters a zone of highly enriched soil, provoking rapid growth. As the roots enlarge, the fertilizer breaks down further. Irrigation moves the nutrients down, but the enlarged root system still picks them up. Then as the soil warms, it begins to release higher levels of nutrients from its own reserves and the plant becomes less dependent on the fertilizer. For this reason, midsummer sowings often do not require much fertilization at all.

Making a Balanced Fertilizer

Well-balanced, preblended organic fertilizers may be purchased for fairly high prices—especially high when compared to chemical fertilizers. But gardeners may also mix their own, to save considerable money as well as tailor fertilizer blends to the plant being grown.

The basic element of organic fertilizer is oilseed meal. Ground oilseed, after the oil has been extracted, is dried and sacked for use primarily as animal feed supplements. Various seed meals are easily available in the maritime Northwest. Cottonseed meal is usually the most inexpensive. Canola seed meal is much more readily obtainable in British Columbia. Sometimes linseed meal or soybean meal are also offered inexpensively. Over the past five years, cottonseed meal has fluctuated in price from about $175.00/ton to about $350.00/ton, rising and falling with the demand for beef and the size of the cotton crop. Fish meal (smelly) is also a good base for organic fertilizer. All these meals analyze differently, and though I would like to be able to give an NPK percentage analysis as glibly as many organic gardening books do, the individual meals also vary from lot to lot. However, most run from something like 4-2-1 (4%=2%=1%) to about 8-4-2. Primarily, seed meals are nitrogen sources, with significant, but unbalanced, amounts of phosphorus and potassium.

To make a relatively balanced all-purpose vegetable fertilizer, one starts with seed meal and then brings up the level of phosphorus and potassium so the ratio of the three basic elements is about 1:2:1. I recommend either rock phosphate or bone meal as phosphorus sources. Bone meal is more expensive than rock phosphate, but breaks down faster, and consequently less is needed. Phosphate rock gives a longer residual benefit. For potassium, by far the best source is kelp meal, which usually analyzes at about 18 percent potassium and as an additional benefit contains virtually every known trace mineral that plants could use.

This is the complete organic fertilizer mix that I have recommended for years. All measures are *by volume*, not by weight.

4 parts seed meal or fish meal
1 part dolomite lime
1 part rock phosphate *or* 1/2 part bone meal
1 part kelp meal

Lime is included because many seed meals are rather acid, and because both calcium and magnesium are essential plant nutrients. Even if the garden has been well limed and the gardener is certain that the pH is well above 6.0, I'd still advise including dolomite. Though this blend might seem to contain too much seed meal, remember that seed meals are lightweight compared to rock flours or bone meal. This fertilizer mix may be varied for special purposes and the ratios are not critical in any case. When growing legumes that can manufacture their own nitrogen, the seed meal may be left out or greatly reduced. When fertilizing in early spring when the soil is very cold, one or two parts of the seed meal or fish meal may be changed to blood meal. Blood meal is very high in nitrogen that is virtually water soluble and releases rapidly. When fertilizing in midsummer on crops intended to winter over, high nitrogen levels can result in fast-growing plants that don't harden off sufficiently to survive winter's frosts. Lower nitrogen levels are much better. In these cases, the mix may be changed to one or two parts seed meal.

There was a time not too long ago when organic fertilizers and their basic components were not easy to obtain in the maritime Northwest, but since 1980, there has been a resurgence of interest in using these materials. This has been especially true of phosphate rock. Virtually all garden centers sell lime and most sell dolomite in large quantities at moderate prices. However, many only sell seed meals and bone meal in small packages at very high prices per pound. Increasing numbers of them are responding to consumer demand and offering fifty-pound or larger sacks of these basic commodities, which is how they should be purchased by the gardener interested in economy. Seed meals, bone meal, and kelp meal are primarily used as animal food supplements and their best sources are feed and grain or farm supply stores.

Three main garden distributors of these materials in the maritime Northwest are Green Earth Organics, Puyallup, Washington; Down to Earth Distributors, Eugene, Oregon; and the Webfoot Fertilizer Company, Portland, Oregon. Webfoot sells in ton lots or wholesale only. The others sell both wholesale and retail and all will gladly give the name of a local retail store they are supplying.

Fertilizing a garden is not expensive. Dick Raymond, a famous eastern garden writer, worked out the value of his garden one year recently and discovered that each square foot of his garden produced 73¢ worth of food if taken at the wholesale value of the vegetable at the time of harvest, and if only unblemished, well-formed food was counted. It has been my experience at Lorane that a well-grown, average square foot in our long growing season can produce $1.00 in food. But if fertilizer is not used in poor ground, that square foot might produce only 20¢ worth of value. Yet it takes the same amount of work, seed, and water. A square foot of garden can be fertilized for about 5¢ with organics, and for a penny or two with chemicals.

Soil

Highly successful gardening demands an understanding of soil management far beyond simply adding water and fertilizer. Soil quality or *tilth* also is a powerful influence on seed germination, plant growth and health, and disease and insect resistance. Few garden guides devote much space to scientific soil management, and I hope my reader's patience is not unduly tested by what follows. But, like other areas of understanding, if a person comprehends the basics, apparent anomalies and mysterious events can be understood.

The Importance of Air in Soil

When considering soil/plant interactions, it helps to remember how roots develop and function. The root system is a support structure and nutrient uptake system. Root cells are not able to manufacture food and convert carbon dioxide gas into oxygen as do green cells. Food for the root system comes from leaves through the plant's vascular system. Oxygen for root cells must come from air in the soil. Consequently, development and health of the roots depend on an adequate air supply in the soil. Soil management can greatly alter the level of soil air.

Though absorption of water and nutrients is accomplished by the root system, not all roots are able to absorb water. At the very end of the root is the root tip, and protruding from the sides just behind the tip are root hairs. Only the tip and hairs are absorptive. The tip is constantly attempting to grow and new hairs are pushed out behind it. Hairs remain absorptive only a short time; then they become toughened and impervious to water and drop off. So the root system is efficient only so long as it expands, allowing new hairs to be generated. Heavy, airless soil will not permit healthy root growth, no matter how high the level of nutrients it may offer. In such soil, plants may not uptake enough nutrients, even if available.

Soil Fungi

In healthy soil, many plants develop symbiotic relationships with soil fungi, which are essential to plant health. Fully described by Sir Albert Howard in *The Soil and Health*, this symbiosis is called mycorrhizal association. What happens is that the threadlike structures of soil fungi, called hyphae, invade the plant's actively growing root tips and hairs by penetrating between cell walls. The hyphae drink from the plant's internal food supply, but return something even more valuable to the plant. Soil fungi are able to break down mineral particles by releasing weak acids and then absorbing the dissolved nutrients. These nutrients are combined into complex organic chemicals which move through the hyphae. When the aging root hairs toughen, the invading hyphae are cut off and dissolve within the plant, releasing these complex organic nutrients directly into the plant. It has been well established that plants become diseased or grow poorly if mycorrhizal associations do not develop. However, not all plants and not all vegetables develop mycorrhizal associations, though many do. Cabbage family members, for example, do not.

These helpful fungi do not derive their main food supply by robbing the plant, but eat decomposing organic matter primarily. The plant only supplies that extra something the fungi need; much as the nutrients added to the plant by the fungi are in no way its main supply, but are more like vitamins, which make the difference between robust health and slight illness. Cultural practices can have profound effects on soil organic matter, and thus on the level of soil microlife and plant health. Organic matter levels are also the main determinant of soil air levels, especially in heavier soil types. Adding manures or composts can be vital.

Soil Composition

Soil is a complex mixture of particles, water, air, and living things. Solid particles usually make up about 50 percent of soil mass; the rest is water and air. Soils are in a constant process of change. As moisture content varies, so may air supply. Periods of heavy rain fill pore spaces completely, driving out all air, except for that dissolved within the water. After draining, soil air returns. Rock particles are slowly weathering. Organic matter content may increase and decrease seasonally. Life forms change their ecology with the season, too. In native soils of the maritime Northwest, organic matter and life forms typically amount to 3 to 5 percent of weight in the top 6 to 8 inches of soil.

Soil organic matter is created by plants. When they die in uncultivated fields, the tops fall over and rot into the earth; root structures decompose, breaking up the soil. Assisted by worms and insects, which mechanically break down and digest plant material, organic matter is gradually altered into humus. Humus is well-decomposed organic matter that has become relatively resistant to further digestion. The process of creation and decay of organic matter has been named the carbon cycle. Native soils arrive at a relatively stable level of organic matter, determined by the climate and native mineralization of the soil rock particles.

Soil scientists divide soils into two basic types: "wet" and "dry" soils. Wet soils, such as are found in the maritime Northwest, are those that receive more rainfall each year than evaporates each year. Dry soils receive less rainfall than annual evaporation. Wet soils are usually forested, have high levels of organic matter if the average temperatures are low, and are made nutrient poor by the leaching action of water passing through them. Dry soils usually grow grasses or scrub, have high levels of organic matter if in sod such as prairie soils, or very low levels of organic matter if semiarid or desert, and are often very rich in nutrients that are unleached by rain. Maritime Northwest soils tend to be rather high in organic matter and badly leached of nutrients.

Mineral particles are derived from solid rock below or are transported by water (alluvial soils) or wind (loess). Through a series of weathering processes, the size of the particles is reduced and their mineral content gradually dissolved and transported to the ocean, which is why the ocean is salty. Freezing and thawing, weak acids in soil produced by soil organisms, and dissolved carbon dioxide gas—all these forces weather rock particles.

Soils are also classified according to the size of their particles. This is not merely an academic exercise. Agricultural soils vary widely in their behavior and in the kind of management they need. Understanding this and identifying the type of soil one is working with is invaluable. The largest sizes of soil particles are sand; intermediate sizes are named silts; and the finest particles are called clay.

Sand grains are tiny pieces of rock that, if examined under magnification, look like gravel or pebbles. Their edges are usually rounded with few sharp angles. Because sands usually decompose very little, their mineral reserve remains largely untapped. Silts are particles that have not only mechanically weathered smaller, but that have also undergone some chemical decomposition. Under magnification, they are less angular and more rounded than sands.

Clay particles have been fully broken down from sands into individual mineral crystals that have been chemically rearranged. Clays are thin, flat crystals that layer themselves like pages in a book. Slates and micas are types of rock formed from clay deposits, which were heated under high pressure and fracture

Table 2
Relative Particle Sizes for Different Soil Types

Soil Type	Particle Size
sand	50 to 2,000 microns*
silt	2 to 50 microns
clay	under 2 microns

*Scientists describe soil particle size in a unit of measure called the micron. A micron is a millionth of a meter or 1/1,000th of a millimeter, or about 1/25,000 of an inch. As a standard of comparison, grains of table salt or white granulated sugar are approximately 50 microns.

into thin sheets similar to the clay crystals themselves. Clay particles fit tightly together and clay soils tend to be heavy and airless. Clay particles are also electrically charged. These charges make the particles stick together and cause clays to attract dissolved mineral salts, which themselves carry small electrical charges. Calcium, potassium, and other minerals that carry small positive charges when dissolved in water are called cations (pronounced cat-ions) when so dissolved. Clays stick cations to themselves, holding them strongly between layers of clay crystals.

Sand and silts also have an ability to attract cations to a degree, but through a different mechanism. Soil water will form a thin film that adheres to all soil particles, including clays. For example, a sand particle may be compared to a book firmly closed. Clay particles are like that same book with all the pages spread open. The consequence of this is that clay particles have a much higher ability to hold nutrients than do sands or silts, both from having a larger surface area and by being electrically charged.

Clay's ability to hold nutrients may not benefit the gardener. Depending on soil acidity, cations may be so strongly attached to clays that they become unavailable to plants, or clays can act like a storage battery, sticking and unsticking nutrient cations continuously, feeding the plants upon demand. Heavy winter maritime rains tend to leach cations. As soils become deficient in cations, clays become "hungry" for them and the soil will develop a low pH, becoming acid. Acid clays hold on to cations so tightly that plants cannot remove them.

Adjusting Low Soil pH

The remedy for acid soils is liming, and the amount of lime needed to correct an acid soil is determined by its clay content. Lime is finely ground calcium and/or magnesium carbonate, a very soft rock that dissolves rapidly in soil, releasing huge quantities of cations. These saturate the clay particles, reducing their acidity and allowing a freer interchange of all types of cations to occur.

It's hard to state exactly how much lime is needed to adjust the pH of a soil from one point to another, because there are several types of clays, each having different abilities to absorb cations, and most soils are only part clay. However, lime at about 1 ton per acre (50 pounds per 1,000 square feet) will change an average clayey soil about half a pH-step upward. This means that to move a clay

Chart 5
Effects of Soil pH on the Availability of Plant Nutrients

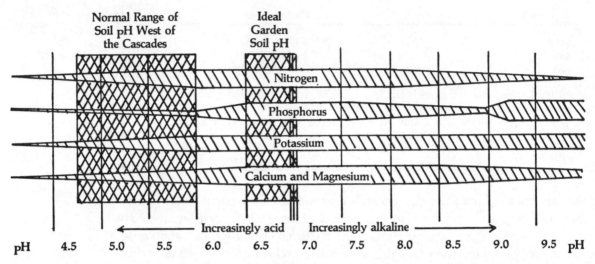

Width of the bar indicates the availability of some plant nutrients at various soil pHs. Increasing acidity below 6.5 makes nutrients more and more unavailable to plants. Simply by changing soil pH upward in the direction of 7.0, a far higher percentage of the soil's nutrients becomes available. If the soil is potentially rich, but acid, a healthy dose of agricultural lime will often turn it from an apparently poor soil to one that is quite good. In the same way, if you add nutrients to an acid soil, they only become immediately unavailable to the plants. The most basic, important step in soil improvement is adjusting the pH.

soil from 5.5 to 6.0 takes about 1 ton per acre; from 5.5 to 6.5 takes 2 tons per acre. Since virtually all maritime soils are acid to a degree, it is safe to prescribe adding a ton of lime per acre to any of them for starters. Clayey ones might take as many as 4 tons per acre. If I were gardening without a soil test, I'd apply a ton per acre per year until there seemed no more improvement in how my plants grew.

Once pH has been adjusted above 6.0, it has to be maintained. Winter rains will leach out about half a ton of lime from each maritime acre each year, except where rainfall is below 40 inches. This should be replaced every year or two, regardless of soil type.

Some gardeners believe that dolomite lime is a superior product because it contains magnesium and calcium in more or less equal parts. Both these elements are vital plant nutrients, and maritime soils tend to be highly deficient in both. Dolomite costs more. I'd use it.

Do not worry about overliming. It takes increasingly larger amounts of lime to move pH, the closer 7.0 is approached. When I started my first trial ground at Territorial Seed Company back in 1979, the heavy clayey soil tested at 4.5 and lime at 4 tons per acre was indicated. After this heavy application, it took three years for the pH finally to rise above 6.0. During these years, fertilizers did not work too well because the clay would absorb cations faster than the plants and not release them. Then, the third year, the soil began working right. So, the next time I started a new field, I attempted an experiment. Lime at 10 tons per acre, more or less, was added to that same clayey soil. Tilled in the fall, by spring pH was 7.2. It will not likely go higher than that, and within a few years should fall back to something like 6.7. Plant growth was excellent the first season.

Increasing Soil Phosphorus Levels

Besides tending toward extreme acidity, maritime soils are almost uniformly poor in phosphorus, though alluvial soils along the Cascades' river drainages and some western Washington glacial soils are somewhat better. Once I had the opportunity to study a report from the Oregon State University soil lab, which presented a compendium of soil analysis data in organized form, county by county. I discovered that hardly 1 percent of western Oregon's soils showed high enough levels of phosphorus to grow crops to their fullest. At least 70 percent were poor enough to demand improvement. Unfortunately, low levels of phosphorus are not readily identifiable by a vegetable's appearance, so many of the region's gardeners are unaware that their plants would grow a notch or three better if they had more adequate phosphorus nutrition. Incidentally, most maritime Northwest soils are very well endowed with potassium, so many gardeners waste money with the extensive additions of greensand suggested by eastern garden writers, (especially foolish when common manures and beddings are rich in potassium).

The most commonly available source of phosphorus is a chemical fertilizer called superphosphate, which is a basic ingredient in most blended complete chemical compounds. Superphosphate is simply phosphate rock (a naturally occurring mineral) that is about 30 percent phosphorus, treated with phosphoric or sulphuric acid so that the phosphate content is recombined into a water-soluble form. When incorporated into soil, superphosphate granules dissolve in a week or two. Superphosphate is used in quantities of 100 to 200 pounds per acre, usually banded directly below seeds or transplants. Seedlings will absorb excessive amounts of phosphorus without apparent damage, if it is available, and store it for later use. In many farm soils, this initial feeding of phosphorus is virtually all the plant gets until maturity. I think plants are healthier if a smaller but steadily available supply of phosphorus is present.

The organic method of increasing phosphorus is not, as one might think, manuring. Though this technique might work well in soils only slightly deficient by increasing the rate of nutrient release from phosphate reserves already present, it won't work in most maritime Northwest soils because there aren't large phosphate reserves to be activated. Additionally, most manures do not contain much phosphorus, certainly not nearly enough compared to the amounts of nitrogen and potassium they contain. (Chicken manure and shrimp wastes do contain fair amounts of phosphorus, though still rather less than optimally balanced amounts.) Organic gardeners have the option of banding natural phosphate fertilizers or of increasing the phosphate reserve of their soils, and thereby naturally increasing the amount of nutrient release. As a fertilizer, bone meal contains 20 to 39 percent phosphorus, which breaks down completely over a period of three to five months, depending on whether the meal is steamed (fast) or raw (slow). Moderate amounts of phosphate rock can be used as fertilizer, too, as it has no tendency to burn, no matter how concentrated, and a percentage of its content is readily soluble. I usually recommend banding phosphate rock instead of bone meal because after the initial release, phosphate rock becomes part of the background nutrition, gradually increasing in effect for seven years or more.

Clays have the ability to retain phosphorus well, as does the soil humus.

Table 3
Composition of Some Common Manures and Fertilizers

Type of Fertilizer*	Material	N%	P%	K%
1. Nitrogen plus humus	Steer manure	1–2.5	.4–.7	2–3
	Dairy manure	.6–2.5	.3–.5	2–3
	Horse manure	.7–1.5	.3–.6	2–3
	Compost	.4–4.0	.3–2.0	1–3
	Rabbit manure	2.5	1.5	0.5
	Goat manure	1.5	.25	1
2. Phosphorus	Rock phosphate	...	22–33	...
	Bone meal	3	20	...
3. Potassium	Kelp meal	1	...	12
	Wood ashes	...	...	10
	Granite/basalt	...	...	3–7
4. Humus	Sawdust	...	...	1–2
	Urea	42	...	...
5. Fertilizers (primarily to add nitrogen)	Urea	42	...	...
	Blood meal	12	...	...
	Hoof/horn meal	14	2	...
	Fish meal	10	6	...
	Cottonseed meal	4–8	2–3	1–2
	Chicken manure	2–4	1–2.5	1–2

Though the chemistry of phosphorus in soil is too complex for explanation in a garden book, suffice it to say that in soils of moderate clay content, phosphorus will not likely leach out. This means the gardener can afford to use enough rock phosphate to increase phosphate reserves to the highest levels, resulting in a nutrient release adequate for all vegetables at any time. Doing this will produce much healthier soil and plants. It is accomplished by spreading phosphate rock at a rate of 50 pounds per 1,000 square feet every year until no further improvement in plant growth is noticed, but not to exceed 225 pounds per 1,000 square feet total application, if potentially phytotoxic trace mineral accumulation is to be avoided.

Two hundred twenty-five pounds per 1,000 square feet (4 tons/acre) is a very heavy and expensive dusting, but it should last a lifetime and eliminate any future need for phosphorus fertilizers, except perhaps in a very early spring, when cold soils prevent rapid nutrient release.

The Importance of Organic Matter

Although organic matter comprises only a small percentage of native soils, it can have a huge effect on texture, water and nutrient retention, and the ratio of air to solids (called pore space). Some soils can be greatly improved by additions of organic matter; others are naturally well structured and will grow fine crops of vegetables without high organic matter contents.

Organic matter starts out as a complex of materials that provide food for soil bacteria. First, the bacteria consume proteins and sugars, which comprise much of the animal waste or plant residue. What remains is relatively resistant to further digestion and is called *humus.* Some types of soil lose water and nutrients rapidly, but humus is a spongy material with a high ability to hold and release both water and cations. If sand has the holding ability expressed numerically as one, silt would be three, clay ten, and humus thirty.

While digesting organic matter, soil bacteria secrete large quantities of slimes and gums, which cement soil particles into larger clumps called *aggregates.* Some heavy soils are naturally airless, restricting root development. This bad tendency can ruin vegetable growth. However, well-aggregated, heavy soils develop large spherical particles called crumbs. These crumbs do not pack tightly, allowing much more air. A well-aggregated, heavy soil is said to possess good crumb or good tilth.

Although incorporating organic matter will make light soils retain water and will lighten up heavy ones, the gardener must be cautious when adding manures, composts, and other organic materials, because one consequence can be a loss of available plant nutrients for a time. Increasing in population rapidly under the stimulus of a new food supply, soil bacteria construct their bodies of the same nutrients plants use. This condition persists until much of the organic matter has been digested into humus. Then, declining bacterial populations release nutrients

Chart 6
Soil Nutrient Levels After Addition of Crude Organic Matter

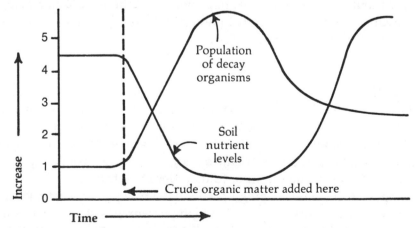

When crude, undigested organic matter is added to soil, the population of decay organisms increases rapidly. These organisms construct their bodies from the same nutrients plants use to build cells. Consequently, the level of nutrients available to plants is lowered until the decay organisms have consumed about half the organic matter. Then, their population begins to die off, the rate of decomposition slows, and as the bodies of the bacteria break down, the nutrients they contain are released for plants to use.

back to the plants from their dissolving bodies.

For this reason, it is helpful to know exactly how much of what kind of organic matter is really needed and when best to apply it to reduce the likelihood of nutrients being tied up in the bodies of microorganisms rather than being available to plants. As a general rule, large quantities of organic matter that are tilled in during autumn will be broken down by late spring. Smaller additions of organic matter can be digested in a few weeks when the soil is warm. Fortunately, most soils do not require large additions of organic matter, and even those that need great additions of organic matter to grow vegetables do not need it more than one time if regular, smaller additions are made thereafter.

Although I've already mentioned the differences in manure quality, noted that chicken manure should be considered fertilizer, not a source of organic matter, and have included a table showing the range of nutrient content of various manures, I think a fuller discussion of the nature and properties of manures and compost might well be in order.

Cow and Horse Manure

If unmixed with bedding, collected frequently, and composted immediately, cow or horse manure makes excellent compost, which doesn't tie up soil nutrients, begins fertilizing immediately, and has an NPK in the vicinity of 2:½:2. If phosphate fertilizer is included in the composting process, it rots very rapidly and becomes a balanced fertilizer rich in humus. However, when mixed with equal quantities of sawdust or straw, horse or cow manure takes twelve to eighteen months of careful composting to rot enough so that soil nutrients will not be tied up when tilled in. And if the pile is not turned frequently, dries out, or becomes leached out by forty to eighty inches of winter rain, composting virtually ceases. For these reasons, horse and cow manure are best considered sources of organic matter to be turned into humus by spreading in fall, tilling, and allowing soil bacteria to work on the crude organic matter until late spring. This procedure is called sheet composting and is an effective method of increasing soil organic matter, without interfering with plant growth. As little as a 3/4-inch-deep covering of sawdust manure can greatly inhibit plant growth for a month after being tilled in, even if the plants are fertilized.

Compost

Please glance back at Chart 6. What composting accomplishes is to conduct the primary digestion of organic matter in a heap instead of in the soil. When properly made compost is blended into soil, great increases in soil bacterial population do not occur. Soil nutrients do not get diverted from the plants, while the compost itself can add significant quantities of nutrients.

Compost is made by heaping up sawdust, straw, plant waste, leaves, bark, etc., blended with materials containing high percentages of nitrogen—like fresh horse manure, chicken manure, garbage, blood, or even chemical nitrate fertilizer. Large bacterial populations quickly develop, especially if consideration is given to the inclusion of other nutrients like phosphorus and calcium, and if the pile is well aerated and kept moist. Bacterial activity becomes so intense that the pile can reach temperatures in excess of one hundred sixty degrees. When most of the crude organic matter has been digested, the pile cools. What remains can be anything from relatively nutrientless predigested organic matter to highly fertile humus, depending on the skill of the composter and the quality of the raw materials used. Expertly made compost looks like crumbly, rich black soil, is sweet smelling, and can have NPK levels in excess of 3:3:3. The process is so complex that entire texts have been written on the subject. Rodale Press issues several, from backyard level to a massive text for the professional industrial composter.

I've had highly varied results from my own composting efforts. I continue to compost, because it's the easiest way to deal with garden wastes and kitchen garbage on the homestead. But I cannot rely on the nutrient content of my composts; I get wildly different growth responses from batch to batch. What I now do is to permit my compost piles to be leached out by winter rains, thus ensuring that they contain relatively nutrientless humus that can safely be spread thick in spring and tilled in without overfertilizing the bed. (If I wished to retain the nutrient content of my compost, I'd cover the pile with plastic from October to May or build a large composting shed.) Because it is fully rotted, I can use about half as much compost as compared to horse or cow manure for the purpose of maintaining soil organic matter levels.

Chicken Manure

Commercially raised chickens are primarily fed seeds or other very concentrated foods. The resulting manure is very potent. If moistened, chicken manure heats rapidly and breeds flies prolifically. It should be stored dry and not broadcast, but rather banded like fertilizer when used.

Chicken manure contains little organic matter (unless mixed with bedding, which is rarely the case when obtained from egg or meat operations) and should not be used to improve the soil's tilth, as is horse or cow manure. Not quite as potent as seed meal, a pint to half-gallon of chicken manure will produce the same growth response as a half-cup of complete organic fertilizer. Precomposted, sacked chicken manure is often sold at garden centers or supermarkets and has a lower potency than the fresh, dry material.

Steer Manure

Feedlot beef is fed high potency concentrates, and their manure is also rich and free of bedding. It is sold sacked and dried. One to two hundred pounds of sacked steer manure can fertilize a one-hundred-square-foot bed pretty well. However, the product is not handled with the grower in mind, and nutrient content varies greatly from lot to lot. It should not be considered a significant source of organic matter and is seriously low in phosphorus.

Rabbit Manure

If unleached, rabbit manure is equal to sacked steer manure in fertilizing ability. If leached, it can be little more than a source of organic matter. Forty to eighty inches of rain can leach out a lot of nutrients.

Classifying Soil Texture Types

Soil scientists recommend adding different amounts of organic matter according to the size of the soil particles. These differences are so great that it is essential to know for certain the type of soil you are dealing with before it can be managed intelligently. Rarely are soils pure sand or pure clay or pure silt. Usually, they are a blend of variously sized particles. For garden purposes, it may be enough to rub some soil between one's fingers to approximate the type. Sandy soils feel gritty. Silty ones have a talcumlike smoothness to them. Dampened clayey soils get very gooey and sticky when kneaded between the fingers.

If in doubt, the gardener can determine quite accurately the composition of a soil by performing a soil fractional analysis at home. This may well be worth doing, as much unnecessary hauling of organic matter may be avoided if the exact type of soil is known, as will be seen shortly. To perform a soil fractional analysis, first sample the desired plot. Take a tablespoon of soil from many locations in the garden at depths from the surface to 8 inches and mix all these samples together. About a quart should be taken. Dry the sample thoroughly, and when fully dry, pulverize the soil as finely as possible. At home, a rolling pin, mallet, or rounded stone can be used. Soil labs often use an old blender.

Assemble the equipment. This consists of:

1. A one-quart jar with a tight lid;
2. One cupful of finely pulverized dry soil;
3. One teaspoonful of nonsudsing dishwashing detergent;
4. A watch or clock; and
5. A crayon or grease pencil.

Fill the jar two-thirds full of water, pour in the soil and detergent, fasten the lid securely, and shake the jar vigorously for ten to fifteen minutes. Then set the jar

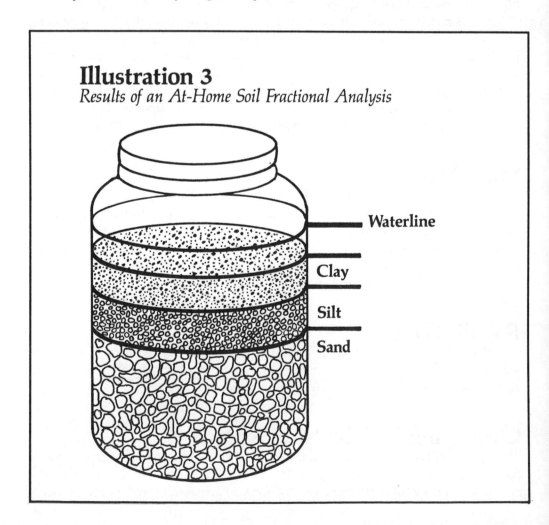

Illustration 3
Results of an At-Home Soil Fractional Analysis

Waterline

Clay

Silt

Sand

down in a place where it will be undisturbed.

The sand particles in the soil are the largest and heaviest. These settle to the bottom of the jar within one minute. At the end of one minute, mark the jar with a crayon or grease pencil to indicate the level of the sand. Silts are much smaller and require a longer time to settle out. In two hours, virtually all the silt particles will have deposited on the bottom. At this point, make a second mark on the side of the jar, indicating the level of silt. Clay particles are very small and go into suspension readily and stay there for quite a while. However, within a few days they will settle. When the water is clear, the clay has settled. Then, mark the level on the jar.

On the side of the jar is a graph of the relative amounts of each type of soil particle. If A is the thickness of the sand deposit, B the thickness of the silt deposit, C the thickness of the clay deposit, and D the thickness of all three deposits, then:

$$\text{Percent of sand} = \frac{A \times 100}{D}$$

$$\text{Percent of silt} = \frac{B \times 100}{D}$$

$$\text{Percent of clay} = \frac{C \times 100}{D}$$

One problem with this test is that certain clays can require a long time to come out of suspension. If the water has not cleared within a few days, there is a shortcut that is not quite as accurate. Repeat the test, but this time, pour only the soil into the water at first. Swirl the jar gently three or four times and let it settle. Mark the total soil level on the side of the jar now. This will become D. Then add the detergent, shake as before, record the sand and silt fractions, and then calculate the clay fraction by deducting A plus B from D.

Soil scientists divide texture classes into types. Each type responds in a predictable manner to various cultural practices such as watering, cultivation, manuring, etc. The exact type is determined by comparison of component percentages with the graph in Chart 7. Any combination of percentages can be represented by a single point on the graph. For example, a soil that would be 10 percent sand, 25 percent silt, and 65 percent clay is indicated on the graph with a large *. Another that would be 70 percent sand, 20 percent silt, and 10 percent clay is indicated with a #.

Fine Clay

This soil type is the most difficult to manage. It will absorb water only very slowly, becomes sticky when wet, dries out very slowly, and then becomes very hard when dry. Surface crusts form readily, preventing seedling emergence and shutting out air. Clay tends to shrink when drying, forming deep surface cracks. (The pattern of the cracks is similar to the shape of clay crystals.)

Composed of thoroughly leached soil particles that have fully decomposed, fine clay tends to be very mineral deficient in rainy climates such as that of the maritime Northwest. Mineral poor, clays produce little biomass and so are low in humus and do not aggregate, accentuating their bad tendencies. Plant growth can be very poor.

Fine clays are improved by improving soil aggregation. Though this principle

Chart 7
Determining Soil Type by Percentage Composition of Particle Size

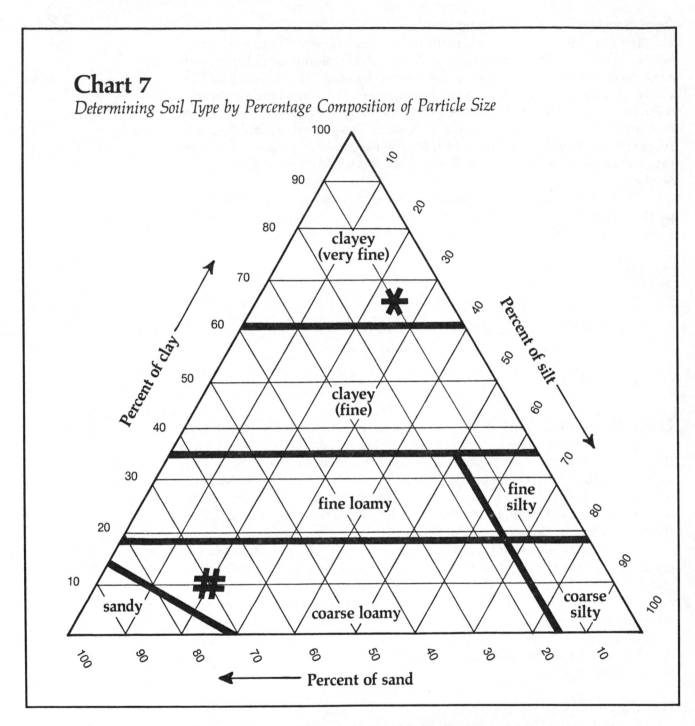

is well understood by many gardeners, in practice one must keep in mind the difference between increasing and maintaining. Initially, the object is to raise organic matter from, say, 1 or 2 percent to over 5 percent 7 or 8 inches down. Once that is achieved, it takes much less effort to maintain that higher level. An initial application of 3 to 5 inches of organic matter, preferably incorporated in late summer or early fall, followed by an annual addition of 3/4 to 1 inch of well-rotted manure or compost, will result in much better tilth in a season or two.

Because fine clays drain poorly and dry slowly, it is usually late spring before they are tillable. It is especially important to allow fine clay time to dry sufficiently before working, because its natural tendency to compact and shrink when drying makes it form clods readily. Clods can't be broken down by further tillage and only another winter will soften them sufficiently. Consequently, the best soil management program for fine clay gardens is to make raised beds after the initial spreading of organic matter and lime (and likely phosphate rock) and tillage. These raised beds are not deeply tilled again. Future additions of organic matter need be only 3/4 to 1 inch deep and are confined to the top 2 inches of these permanent raised beds, resulting in an organic matter content well over 10 percent in the surface inches. Thus the surface never develops deep cracks and crusts are much less likely to form. If the beds are not stepped on, they do not require tillage before sowing and a humusy seedbed may be worked up under relatively wet conditions. Overwintering green manures help retain a loose soil texture without tillage. (Raised beds and green manuring are discussed at length in "Planning the Garden.")

Clay

This soil type has not yet weathered fully to the finest particle sizes. It possesses many of the liabilities of fine clay soils, but has reasonably good drainage, a higher organic matter content, better aggregation, and usually a somewhat higher pH and level of fertility. However, its better structure is a very fragile thing. It should be handled like a fine clay soil, though the initial application of organic matter may be reduced to 2 to 3 inches.

Fine Loamy and Fine Silty Soils

Loamy and silty soils contain mixtures of sand, silt, and clay particles. The fine ones contain large percentages of clay. These clay crystals tend to fall between the larger silts or sands, producing a soil of great density with small pore spaces and rather poor drainage. Cultural practices should be directed at increasing soil permeability through the addition of moderate amounts of organic matter and reducing compaction through the use of raised beds. Three-quarters to 1 inch of organic matter worked in each year is more than sufficient for these and other less clayey types. Because fine soils tend to form surface crusts after heavy rains, additions of organic matter are best confined to the surface few inches. The percentage of nonweathered soil particles in these types is high, so soils of this type tend to be rather fertile.

Coarse Loamy Soil

Oh! If only I had some of that stuff. Coarse loam is a combination of sand and silt that has less than 20 percent clay. It is often the most fertile soil type, consisting of unweathered particles. Its drainage is excellent, pore spaces large, soil air capacity high, permeability excellent. Plants grow wonderfully in it. Even asparagus beds don't die out in it during our rainy winters. Usually the organic matter content is high enough for most vegetables without incorporating manures or composting extensively. However, growing row crops tends to reduce soil organic matter, though persistent attention to wintertime green manuring may replace what is lost without ever having to haul in manure. Soils of this type that have a high percentage of finer silts sometimes puddle or pack when irrigated. These should be maintained at a somewhat higher organic matter content—easily accomplished by the addition of an inch of manure or compost every few years and by green manuring whenever possible.

Sandy Soil

This contains over 70 percent sand. Sands are easy to till when wet without forming clods, have excellent drainage and large pores. However, they hold water poorly and lose nutrients readily from leaching. Chemical fertilizers have to be added frequently. Adding humus is the best way to improve soils of this type, increasing their ability to retain water and nutrients. Initially 3 to 4 inches of organic matter should be added, followed by an annual supplement of 3/4 to 1 inch. Irrigations should be frequent and light.

Further Reading

I can imagine some readers of this book reaching this point and feeling somewhat baffled by all this data. I imagine others who have found many previously acquired bits of information linked and organized in a more useful way. For readers who want to pursue studies of these subjects further, I suggest the following:

The Albrecht Papers, William Albrecht, Acres, U.S.A., St. Louis, Missouri.

Acres, U.S.A. is a radical agricultural monthly paper, published in Missouri. The group also publishes some books, among them this collection of shorter writings by William Albrecht, who for years was a vital force at the University of Missouri with his research on the interactions of soil fertility and nutrition on animal health.

The Soil and Health, Sir Albert Howard, Schocken Press, New York, New York.

The classic statement of the founder of the organic gardening and farming movement. *The Soil and Health* describes Howard's odyssey as a young research scientist assigned to cure plant diseases on tropical plantations. Inevitably, he found connections between soil that had deteriorated from poor cultural practices and plant diseases. The diseases were usually cured by increasing soil organic matter or nutrition.

The Nature and Properties of Soils, Buckman and Brady, Macmillan Publishing, London.

Having gone through many editions without substantive change, this book is the standard agriculture school text, well worth a few careful readings by any really serious gardener.

Botany, any good university-level text.

A complete understanding of gardening is not possible without a full understanding of plants. I'd buy this kind of book at a used book store.

Geography, any good university-level text.

An introductory text in geography explains the world's weather and climate patterns, as well as variations in day length in terms of planetary airflows, ocean currents, and differences in receipt of solar energy.

Planning the Garden

A lot of usable food can be wasted through poor planning. For example, twenty-four hybrid broccoli transplants may be purchased at the garden center one May day. The result? During July, twenty-four large heads of broccoli appear within a few days. If a freezer full of broccoli was not intended, this temporary abundance may be wasted. Here is another example, all too frequently seen: the garden is "put in" over one May weekend. Corn, beets, carrots, lettuce, squash, and cucumbers are sown; tomatoes, cabbage, broccoli, and cauliflower are transplanted. The result is a great abundance of food from late July through early October—so much that the vegetables can hardly be canned, frozen, or given away fast enough. This glut is followed by eight months of barren, rain-drenched soil.

North of the sunbelt and east of the maritime Northwest, winter ends vegetable gardening. With differing degrees of severity, winter weather becomes frosty and soil freezes solid for a time. In my native Michigan, the frost line might go as deep as three feet in a severe winter. Farther south, the freezing level might only be a few inches for a few weeks during the most intense storms of midwinter. In either case, freezing soil ends the life of most vegetables, though certain types of onions, spinach, and corn salad can outlast freezing soil, especially under a snow blanket. In the North, few garden vegetables still stand after Halloween, and no harvests are again possible until early summer.

Prior to the refrigerated rail transport of fresh California and Florida produce, most wintertime vegetables in the North came out of root cellars. Wintertime fare was limited to roots and a few types of coles—usually low in quality compared to freshly harvested food. Gardeners and farmers planned on harvesting all food crops safely by October and preserved them, eating from the root cellar, or from cans, or from the dryer. So, it was natural to calculate a growing cycle that began with the last usual frost date and ended by fall.

Maritime Winter Gardening

The maritime Northwest is different. Our mild winters almost never freeze the soil, and many hardy crops are capable of growing outside until November's chill and low light levels check their development, and then, of standing in good condition until harvest or resuming growth in spring if not already mature.

Twelve months of fresh vegetable harvest is possible most winters in most locations.

Winter cropping techniques and varieties were unknown to the easterners who settled western Oregon and Washington and are only just now being discovered here—after 140 years of settlement. The fact that winter gardening is a novelty is ironic. To the early settlers of the maritime Northwest, winter meant root cellars and summertime canning/drying. Even though the practice of winter cropping was well-established and had been developed to a high art in England, land of many of our forebears, we did not acquire their cropping technology or varieties until recently.

I suppose the current interest in winter cropping comes from a renewed focus on self-sufficient homesteading, the influx of new rural residents, and the increasing cost of California winter vegetables. It is not likely that winter vegetable production will attain much commercial significance as long as California's produce is available, because the mild Mediterranean winters farther south give high yields of very good-looking food in a totally different class than the rain-battered lower yields that the maritime Northwest is capable of growing. Sometimes, too, the maritime winter freezes out crops, making economic production dicey. But winter crops do have value in the home garden, something that should convince maritime Northwest residents to take up the practice as firmly as do the gardeners of England.

The Pluses of Winter Gardening

I believe in winter gardening and have spent the best part of the past five years writing and lecturing about it, researching its technology, and selling the seeds that enable a gardener to succeed at it. I also believe that eating fresh fruits and vegetables as much as possible is healthful, so I would prefer to eat brussels sprouts, cabbage, carrots, leeks, parsnips, and endive during the winter rather than subsist on canned beans and tomato sauce-flavored starches. I would like others to enjoy better health. To that end, let me offer some other convincing reasons to winter garden.

Some people prefer to live in a self-sufficient manner, something like Robinson Crusoe, but rather than an uninhabited tropical paradise, they foolishly choose the maritime Northwest. I have some sympathy for this myself. Occasionally, I dream of living a relatively cash-free life, harvesting bitter-free acorns my company has yet to breed, growing grain, raising wool, and using sheep manure to grow a garden and home orchard. Winter gardening is an essential part of this dream.

Then, there are those who garden to save money. These folks, too, are trying to attain a degree of self-sufficiency, even if they haven't defined it in those terms. At a time of year when supermarket produce is very dear and of low quality, winter gardens supply inexpensive, *fresh* food. Which leads to the next area of interest in winter gardening.

I am and have been a garden gourmet for some years now. My lustful appetites are responsible for an addiction to gardening I cannot overcome. I've outgrown many other passions, but have become hooked on gardening and can't quit unless I become rich enough to hire a first-class gardener to take my place. Why? Because I cannot buy food as good as that which comes from my garden, no matter how rich I might be. A fresh cabbage tastes better than one harvested several weeks ago, regardless of how sophisticated the climate-controlled storage system is. And a fresh cabbage bred for flavor instead of bred for good keeping qualities in a supermarket is better yet.

Summers are such a delight to my palate that I dare eat little but vegetables and fruits, lest I get fat as a blimp. I now find fresh snap beans better than meat, though if not eaten within six hours of harvest, snap beans are better composted and fresh ones picked. Beans are so rich in usable protein when consumed raw that I often feel as though I'd eaten steak. Fresh vegetables deteriorate so rapidly after harvest that within a day or two, most have lost whatever it is that sets them apart from supermarket fare. Vine-ripened tomatoes are a world apart from the stuff harvested half-ripe for sending to the market. This deterioration of produce is so marked that when I am traveling and eating from supermarket produce counters and salad bars, I find my body developing strong cravings for a "real meal" of meat and potatoes. Whatever it is that fresh, ripe, organic food has, commercial produce lacks it. During winter, my body feels much better when I eat carrots, cabbage salads, and apples instead of supermarket tomatoes and lettuce. I find English winter cabbage a superior salad green, especially when compared to California iceberg lettuce.

So there you are. Winter gardening makes one healthy, wealthy, and wise. I hope everyone takes it up.

Maritime Regions Less Suited to Winter Cropping

There are a few maritime locations that don't encourage winter gardeners. For example, folks in the very northwestern corner of Washington State can almost count on having blasts of Arctic air leak through the Cascades and freeze out much of their winter gardens most winters. Similarly, people gardening at elevations much in excess of one thousand feet may experience low temperatures, which will wipe out winter vegetables many years. Lorane, Oregon, at nine hundred-plus feet, gets frozen out about one winter in three.

The tolerance of vegetable varieties to low temperatures is limited and fluctuates somewhat from year to year. For example, the December, 1983, freeze suddenly dropped temperatures to seven degrees at our trial grounds after a mild fall. Though the temperature remained subfreezing for three and a half days, the very warm soil remained unfrozen. Varieties that in previous years had survived three-degree lows or had only 50 percent losses at six degrees were totally destroyed. Why? Because the frostless 1983 autumn had been extraordinarily mild and warm, resulting in lush, tender growth, not nearly as hardy as it might have been. Only one cabbage variety in my entire winter trials survived, and we ate supermarket salads all winter. That same winter, the Vegetable Crops Research Station at Agassiz, British Columbia, experienced much frosty autumn weather and even a bit of snow during November. Most of their winter trials survived the December freeze with somewhat colder temperatures than we had at Lorane. I suppose that Willamette Valley gardeners could count on likely winter survival five years in six; those south of Yoncalla, Oregon, and along our mild coasts are very unlikely to lose their winter gardens any year; while in frosty Washington State, increasing distance from the sea or the Sound greatly lessens the chances for winter survival.

Soil conditions may also preclude gardening once rains start up in earnest. If root systems remain waterlogged for days at a time and as a consequence are unable to take in oxygen, plants sicken and die. Poor drainage can sometimes be improved by simply making raised beds, turning paths into drainage ditches that rapidly carry away run-off. Ditching may be required in some locations. Areas with high winds are also unlikely spots, though fencing and windbreaks are not bad ideas for any garden, especially in winter.

Space Requirements for Winter Gardens

The simple facts of light and plant growth require that winter gardens have more space than summer gardens. From June through mid-September, relatively small plots will produce more food than a family can eat. For example, I am able to make a huge lettuce salad, which is a complete meal in itself, for four people every day from about 100 square feet of bed, by continuously resowing seeds as plants are cut. The same size area of tomatoes will make a meal for our family of four every day during August and September when the patch is "on." And 100 square feet devoted to cucumbers or zucchini is overwhelming. But when light levels drop and vegetables are in living cold storage outside, it's different. To make a big, family-sized cabbage salad daily from November through March means one hundred big cabbages and requires about 400 square feet. Similarly, we need several hundred square feet of carrots under straw for the winter supply, a bed of beets and rutabagas, two beds of brussels sprouts, two beds of Purple Sprouting broccoli for March/April harvest, at least a bed of overwintered cauliflowers for April/May, a bed of leeks, a bed of overwintered onions to make a bushel of sweet bulbs for summer fare, and several beds of lettuce and endive covered with cold frames for a change from the continual cabbage salad.

Successions

After all the work I've put into my garden soil, it now seems to me somewhat like a taxicab with its meter running. If I don't go somewhere, a lot of money is being wasted. The level of available nutrients is high from years of liming, additions of phosphate rock and organic fertilizers, and from annual manurings of my heavy, silty clay soil. Nitrogen levels are fairly high now, even in early spring, and consequently soil microlife is busily consuming my organic matter at a high rate. Anything I can do to retard or prevent nutrient and organic matter loss is of benefit.

Growing plants absorb mineral nutrients released by weathering and biological activity, creating new organic matter that contains the nutrients. If I keep my garden continuously green, losses are lower. I might even be able to increase soil organic matter somewhat. The most profitable way to do this is to have food crop following food crop. Since more than half the weight of the crop is residue, either in root system or trim, this creates a lot of compost and already-in-the-ground material from rotting root systems. By making the ground more productive, I can also reduce the size of the garden, needing less manure, lime, phosphate rock, fertilizer, weeding, tillage, water, and *WORK*. And, if food crop cannot follow food crop, I can grow what is called a green manure crop—some sort of fast-growing vegetation to produce quantities of mineral-rich organic matter.

So many possible successions exist that it would be foolish to attempt a complete list. Variations in sowing date and microclimate and personal taste are too great. Instead, let me mention some of the successions I've used at Lorane as illustrations. Spring sowings of peas are usually harvested by July and may be followed by transplanted brassicas (coles) that are harvested during fall/winter.

Spring sowings of spinach or other greens and overwintered onions are usually out by mid-June and can be followed by carrots, beets, parsnips, or chard. Overwintered sprouting broccoli is usually through by May, as are most overwintered cauliflowers. Their beds, after a dressing of manure or compost, are perfect locations for lettuce crops, beans, or other hot-weather crops. Beds of tomatoes, peppers, melons, cucumbers, and squash are all through by October 1 at Lorane. These are put into overwintered green manures such as clover, field peas, favas, corn salad, or tyfon. Corn salad and tyfon are also edible—a double bonus.

Beds of fall/winter-harvested coles are usually fairly bare and weedy in spring. This is a good time to add manures or compost and sow peas or favas, which are either allowed to mature or used as green manure to prepare the beds for summer crops. Early spring-sown coles are usually harvested by mid-July. These are good spots for fall root crops, late lettuce crops, or other greens. Early sowings of potatoes are often dug by mid-July, and are good spots for overwintered brassicas.

Once one starts winter gardening, crops flow into crops in a rather beautiful manner. The garden can almost become self-sufficient in organic matter, and with the high nitrogen output of favas, perhaps close to self-sufficient in this important nutrient, too.

Raised Beds

A new trend in gardening has been improving American gardens over the past ten years—the raised bed. Not a new idea at all, permanent bed culture has been used in the Orient for millennia and was a basic component of the European market garden before the age of machine cultivation. There are so many advantages to raised beds that they should be used whenever possible. Only a few crops do not fit them well—these are sweet corn and vining squash.

Although the slick home/garden/travel magazines tend to show raised beds as very tidy things neatly surrounded by long planks or railroad ties, doing this only makes them very expensive to construct and much more work to maintain. For the easiest maintenance, raised beds should be low mounds of earth with paths between. The primary reason they are raised is to delineate them as beds—a bed being something almost sacred. Raised beds should almost never be stepped on because if the soil is not compacted by foot traffic, it rarely or never again will need to be tilled deeply. Additions of organic matter, if worked into the surface few inches of soil with a sturdy hoe, will keep the top of the bed soft and friable, permitting amazingly easy weeding and usually extremely successful seed germinating and transplanting. The roots of vegetable crops and green manure crops will penetrate the uncompacted soil 18 to 24 inches down, and when these roots rot, the soil is thoroughly broken up and soft enough for the succeeding crop to root speedily and well. The only time I till my raised beds deeply is if carrots or parsnips are to be grown there. (And incidentally, my garden soil is a silty clay that tends to be airless and compacted.)

An additional benefit of the raised bed is improved drainage in winter. After only two or three rainless days, the humusy top two or three inches of soil on my beds have dried sufficiently to be worked gently with a hoe and rake, permitting sowing seeds during early spring breaks in what seems almost perpetual rain. I get several beds in during March/April, and can spring-sow green manures on beds that may have gone over the winter relatively bare for one reason or another.

Solid masses of garden peas make excellent edible green manures in this case. Even if tilled in before any peas mature, they make lots of biomass and add nitrogen. Peas also leave the surface in beautiful, fluffy condition for sowing small seeds.

It's easy to take a green manure crop off a raised bed without a rear-end rototiller. Cut down the vegetation with a scythe or lawnmower, rake it up, and compost it. Then, chop in the stubble with a hoe, wait a few days or a week, chop one more time, sow, transplant, or rake out a seedbed if sowing fine seed. If the beds do not have boards around them, any clods atop the bed may be effortlessly raked down into the paths where foot traffic will break them up. In early spring, before green manures have gotten more than a few inches tall, they may be entirely hoed into the bed's surface, where they break down rapidly. This kind of treatment does not work when the green manure is tough and strong, so I do not advise using rye or other grasses or grains as green manures. Instead, grow tender, succulent types of vegetation that are easily handled with hand tools.

It is much easier to work up an entire bed when sowing seeds or improving the soil, so gardens are best planned with a bed carrying one type of plant or a group of vegetables that will all be out of the ground more or less at one time, such as tomatoes, peppers, eggplant, cukes, and squash. This way, a bed may be made entirely bare and easily rejuvenated. It's a good idea to add organic matter to raised beds at least once per year, about one-inch thick on old, established beds, thicker on clayey or sandy plots for the first few years. These additions may tie up soil nutrients, but at least they will only do so in the surface few inches, so once the plants being grown there have rooted below the surface, they encounter relatively undisturbed soil with normal microlife activity. Whenever the beds are bare—either midsummer after spring crops are out, or in fall, after summer crops are done—I spread them an inch or so deep with compost or old horse manure/sawdust conveniently obtained from a large stable across the road. I chop this in with a hoe and sow either vegetables or green manures.

Dimensionally, raised beds should be as wide as possible to minimize wasted paths and maximize growing area, but narrow enough that one can reach to the center from the path. So the length of the weeder's arm determines the width. Most of my beds are about 4 feet wide.

Though John Jeavons (author of *the* bible of French intensive gardening, *How to Grow More Vegetables*, Ten Speed Press, Berkeley, California) and other biodynamic gardeners believe in scattering seeds on raised beds, I've found that these broadcast sowings demand too much hand weeding and thinning. Instead, I suggest planting in short rows across the bed, far enough apart to permit a hoe to slide easily through the fluffy surface. Sometimes preliminary thinning can be done with a small, sharp-pointed hoe. My own garden consists of nineteen such beds, 4 feet by 25 feet. With the exception of weeding the paths, which I now do with a power cultivator purchased for trials work, I can hand weed all my beds in less than one hour from one end of the garden to the other. All the cultural directions in this book will recommend sowing or transplanting in rows a certain distance apart, the plants a certain distance apart in the row. Except in the case of corn and winter squash, what I am recommending is a raised bed 3½ to 5 feet wide, with short rows of vegetables across the bed. Cucumbers and melons make a good single row down the center. Summer squash grows well in two long rows down a 4-foot-wide bed.

Many garden "experts" recommend double digging raised beds. This is a laborious procedure, whose purpose it is to maximize production as quickly as possible by pulverizing the soil 24 inches deep and blending in organic matter and rock minerals. However, if a bed is simply not stepped on and vegetation grown continuously while organic matter is applied to the surface, it will gradually soften up to a depth of 18 to 24 inches without double digging. I recommend making up raised beds initially by spreading manure or other organic matter over the garden space with whatever other soil amendments are required to adjust pH or improve mineral nutrition on a long-term basis. Then till the whole plot 6 to 7 inches deep, forming the beds by shoveling out the paths a few inches deep and placing this soil atop the beds. This makes raised beds well fertilized and full of organic matter at least 9 inches deep—a good start. Deep tillage of the beds should never again be necessary if organic matter in moderate amounts is incorporated annually. Double digging might be useful to break up a hardpan, should one exist below the garden.

Rotations

There are numerous rotation schemes in gardening and farming literature and each has been developed for a purpose. Not every scheme fits every soil, crop, or economic situation. I've tried several and no longer attempt a rotation in any specific pattern, because I've found that annual additions of manure or compost and the use of fertilizers eliminate the need to rebuild soil fertility in other ways. However, I do make a firm distinction between my home garden and the three-quarter-acre trial grounds I manage for Territorial Seed Company. These trial grounds do operate on a regular and specific rotation, which deserves explanation.

When I first moved to Lorane, Oregon, in 1978, I was surprised at the lack of planning in my neighbors' gardens. Bare, soggy plots full of weeds couldn't be tilled until Memorial Day; soil was rarely manured; pale, dwarfed corn; bare ground all winter. So, when I started a seed company and began vegetable varietal trials, I decided to test vegetables under conditions similar to those enountered in the average garden around Lorane, figuring if I could discover varieties that would survive and produce something under poor conditions, they would inevitably thrive wonderfully in a rich, well-managed garden.

I had a choice of two sites on my property for the trial grounds. One was a gentle, well-drained, southeast slope; the other a gentle north slope, poorly drained, with a slightly heavier clay soil type. I chose the colder and later north slope. I evolved a rotational system that used manure only one year in three. I did not use raised beds. I did not use insecticides at all unless *every* variety was being ruined, allowing me to discover among other things, varietal resistance to pests like the root maggot in cole crops. I did have to use fertilizer on most crops.

What I found over the years was that despite fertilization, certain types of weakly rooted vegetables would not grow unless the heavy silty clay had been well manured. So I grew these types the year after the plot was manured in fall. Other vegetables would do fine if the manuring was done a year ago, and some would grow excellently from manuring even two years previously. However, when manuring was done, it seemed to require a layer at least 2 inches thick. Now my trial grounds are divided into three plots, each of which is manured in successive years. We are considering a fourth plot, and a fourth year in the rotation, which will be a dry fallow to reduce the population of symphylans.

Note that each year is ended by sowing (when possible) a green manure crop to prevent winter leaching and improve tilth the following year. If the root crops listed in year three are intended for winter harvest, they will be moved to a year

Table 4
Territorial Seed Company Trial Grounds Rotation

Year One	Year Two	Year Three
Potatoes	Cucurbits	Beans
Cole crops	Tomatoes	Peas
Celery	Peppers	Carrots
Onion crops	Eggplants	Parsnips
Mustards	Lettuce	Corn
	Endive	
	Parsley	
Crimson clover or fava beans	Fava beans or ryegrass/field peas	Manuring/Liming/Tilling Crimson clover or fava beans

two section.

I do not encourage the reader to accept this rotation as gospel. It works on one site for one purpose. Farther up the hill, in my personal garden, which has rich raised beds on a slightly less clayey soil type, I rotate at random only for the purpose of preventing disease buildup. What I do is to raise a bed full of one type of crop—for example, early cabbage/broccoli and cauliflower in a massed planting—and then not grow coles there for a year or two (if I can remember). I also manure every year and green manure, too.

Gardening under Cover

There is a thoroughly researched, well-documented book on the market today, whose production was supported by various grants, called *Gardening under Cover*, published by Eugene's Amity Foundation, written from original research done in the maritime Northwest. It contains detailed plans for cold frames and cloches, discusses in depth the problems encountered with producing vegetables under protection, and suggests planting schedules and varieties. If readers find that what follows in the next few pages does not fully prepare them to begin gardening under cover without more information, they should obtain this book.

Greenhouse and Cold Frame Designs for the Northwest

Maritime winters are mild, but dark and rainy. Eastern winters are cold, but sunny. Cold frame and greenhouse design for the East demands insulation and thermal masses. The maritime Northwest demands rain protection and light transmission. So, solar greenhouses and Rodale Press plans have very limited use in the maritime Northwest.

Combine cold soil, slow biological processes from low temperatures, with small input of solar energy from cloudy skies, and unprotected plants cannot grow much at all. Add to this pounding rain day after day, and even frost-hardy plants are weakened, become diseased, and die. Some extremely tough ones, like coles with their waxy "skins" that shed water, and leeks, can take these conditions all winter and even grow a bit when sun shines. Others, like lettuce, endive, radishes, many mustards, and other greens, cannot. However, simply putting a sheet of glass or plastic between an endive plant and the rain is enough to keep it alive all winter, even when outside temperatures drop to seven degrees.

Solar greenhouses are not workable in the maritime Northwest. I've been acquainted with a number of people who enthusiastically built them and found them a good place to store stuff in the winter—not to grow plants. The reason: when the sun shines, most light comes directly from the sun, and so a south-facing glass will allow enough light to enter. However, when skies are overcast, light comes to earth with equal intensity from every direction. In a climate that may grant only a few sunny days a month from November through March, only an all-glass greenhouse will transmit enough light to grow plants during the winter.

Greenhouses, though workable, are expensive to build and do not retain much heat at night. Much more stable temperatures can be had easily by lowering the greenhouse from eight feet to one foot and walking around the outside of it instead of inside it. Having only one foot of air to heat instead of eight, the soil becomes an effective heat sink. A one-foot-high greenhouse that lets light in from all directions is called a cold frame and is very cheap to build.

My garden cold frames are constructed of Cuprinol-treated 2-inch by 10-inch fir planks with 4-inch by 4-inch corner braces and are about 10 feet long by 4 feet wide, covered with recycled window sashes. (Some wood preservatives are

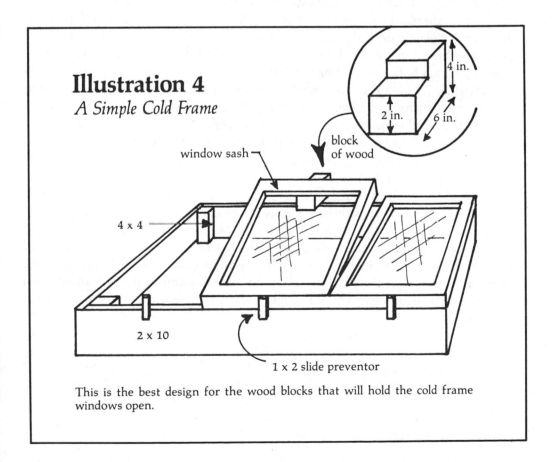

Illustration 4
A Simple Cold Frame

4 in.

2 in.   6 in.

block of wood

window sash

4 x 4

2 x 10

1 x 2 slide preventor

This is the best design for the wood blocks that will hold the cold frame windows open.

toxic to plants and people, so beware.) If I built more frames, I'd construct them out of lighter materials, because it takes two people to move them when such large planks are used. Like all carpenters, I tend to overbuild.

Ten inches is a sufficient height for winter greens. Frames should be sloped to allow rainwater to run off, but I'm a poor carpenter, so instead of sloping the boxes, I slope the bed by raking one side 2 inches lower than the other. The sashes are prevented from sliding off when opened by pieces of 1-inch by 2-inch nailed on one side, sticking up a few inches. The glasses are held open by a block of wood inserted opposite the "slide preventer." There are no felt weather stripping or crosspieces to rest the window on. There are big cracks between the sashes. But it works, permitting maximum light entry while raising the temperature a few degrees at night and keeping off the rain. Almost anyone could design better frames.

I sow these frames in September and October with assorted salad greens. The September-sown frame is harvested December/January, and the October frame is harvested February/March. When the September frame is empty, it is resown with more greens during February, which are ready to harvest in late April/May. By April, when the October frame is through, greens may be sown outside without protection. It's that simple! Salads all winter, and not from cabbage either.

In spring, the gardener can figure that inside a crude frame or cloche the season has been advanced about six weeks, so what would go out in June may be sown or transplanted under a cloche four to six weeks sooner; early April plantings may be started in early March. This extra bit of effort makes much earlier harvests and is well worth it—especially in those unfortunate years when the winter garden is frozen out. Because of our short tomato season, I've taken to setting tomato plants out in a somewhat taller frame about May 1 and growing them under plastic until they are bursting out of the frame in mid-June. Compared to normal plantings, I get ripe fruit in mid-July instead of early to mid-August, which is the usual here in Lorane, where the last anticipated frost is Memorial Day. However, I've found that peppers and eggplants transplanted in May become stunted in a frame because night temperatures drop too low. Even though protected from frost, these sensitive tropicals must not experience lows below forty-five degrees. A frame is also useful for setting over the last bed of mature lettuce in the garden about mid-October, to keep off the rain and permit harvest into early winter.

It's easy to grow in frames. Prepare soil as normal, fertilize as normal, and if the soil gets too dry (not likely in my leaky frames), take the glass or plastic off one drizzly day. Frames may be constructed of glass or plastic, and the easiest is a 10-foot-wide length of clear plastic stretched over 4-foot-wide hoops made of 10-foot sections of half-inch galvanized thin-wall conduit, stuck in the ground like giant croquet hoops, the plastic anchored with soil along the edges and draped over the ends, held down there by clods. Many more sophisticated designs are possible.

Watering the Garden

I've never read a garden book that contained much information about scientific irrigation. Watering the garden is usually ignored on the assumption that "everyone knows that you get the ground good and soaked so the plants have lots of water." Occasionally the reader is advised to use some water-saving tricks during dry spells, like putting a large tin can with a few holes in the bottom next to a tomato plant, filling the can, and *viola!*; or spreading mulch. But mulching is not a very workable practice when the soil needs to get as hot as possible and needs every help to stay that way most summers, and where surface layers of undecomposed organic matter are usually a breeding ground for slugs.

When irrigation is done by the eastern gardener, it is often little more than a short-term expedient to help out the vegetables until the next rain. Most maritime gardeners face a drought every summer, all summer. At Lorane, we usually do not receive useful quantities of rain from mid-May through mid-September and sometimes even later in the season. The same is true through most of the maritime Northwest. I have to start watering my garden and trials from planting time until late summer, not just occasionally. So irrigation is as critical to the maritime gardener as soil improvement and, surprisingly to most people, almost more important than fertilization.

Done incorrectly, watering can harm, not help plant growth in several ways. I know many gardeners work against themselves when they water. I've come to feel that something is needed which is not available in any garden literature—a short, but complete textbook of sprinkler irrigation. I hope my reader's patience is not unduly tested by what follows. But I think having the same kind of information that professional irrigators use is important to gardeners who must depend on irrigation.

Underwatering

Bred from hardy grasses, grain crops will grow under far less than optimum conditions and still be reasonably productive. Should the soil be somewhat nutrient deficient or too hard or somewhat too dry, cereals still mature and yield. Most other field crops have well-developed root systems and are adapted to growing in relatively unenhanced soil. But modern vegetables originated from wild plants much less hardy than grasses and have been bred for centuries to grow in manured and irrigated soils. Even short periods of water stress can greatly lower vegetable quality.

The most apparent consequence of underwatering is soil so dry that plants wilt and die. Slightly less damaging is temporary wilting caused when hot sun evaporates more moisture (transpiration) than the dryish soil will yield to the plants. Although the plants recover in the evening and may look healthy by the next morning, experiencing this stress is a severe shock to vegetables—a shock they won't fully recover from for many days or weeks, if at all. Severely shocked vegetables usually never grow properly again. (Squash may droop its leaves under hot sun, no matter how much water it receives. This is a prosurvival trait of the cucurbit family to reduce transpiration by reducing the leaf area exposed to the sun.)

Underwatered root crops may not show water stress or wilting, but upon harvest the roots may be poorly developed or woody. The stress in this case is not observable because the leaves can draw on the reserves held in the root. Sprouting seeds are rapidly and often fatally affected by dry soil, so getting slow-to-germinate, shallowly sown, small-sized seeds to sprout requires frequent irrigation.

Experienced gardeners understand these principles and have hoses, sprinklers, and nozzles of some sort handy. However, few have carefully designed irrigation systems, nor do they water systematically. When watering is done frequently but insufficiently, the surface five to eight inches of soil can become quite wet, while deeper, soil may be bone-dry. Under these conditions, vegetables do not wilt or show signs of stress, though they frequently become stunted and grow poorly from lack of root development. Vegetables that form a deep taproot and that naturally feed from the subsoil, such as most root crops, are particularly affected by dry subsoil.

Watering by hand with hoses and nozzles especially invites this type of situation, as does watering frequently for a short time with sprinklers. Understanding how

Table 5
Feeder Root Depth of Various Crops

Crop	Depth of Feeder Roots
Alfalfa	6 feet
Beans	2 feet
Beets	3 to 4 feet
Cabbage	2 feet
Carrots	3 to 4 feet
Corn	2½ feet
Cucumbers	2 feet
Lettuce	1 foot
Melons	3 feet
Onions	1½ feet
Peas	2½ feet
Potatoes	2 feet
Tomatoes	2 feet

Table 6
A Wet-to-Dry Scale

Totally Dry	0%
Permanent Wilting Point	20 to 33%
Temporary Wilting Point	50%
Minimum Moisture for Good Vegetable Growth	75%
Field Capacity	100%

water flows into soil prevents this mistake.

When soil is irrigated, each soil particle attracts to itself all the water it can hold against the force of gravity before any water can flow deeper into the ground. The term used to describe a state in which a layer of soil has absorbed all the water it can hold is *field capacity*. The opposite of a soil at field capacity would be totally dry soil. As they dry, soil particles cling harder and harder to moisture, until the point at which these particles cling harder than the roots can extract water. The name for that point on a wet-to-dry scale is the *permanent wilting point*. Before the permanent wilting point is reached, plants are usually experiencing temporary wilting when the sun increases their need for water.

To maximize yields and quality, modern plant breeding has sculpted most vegetables into something that produces large edible portions quickly at the expense of vigorous root system development. Consequently, vegetables can become badly moisture-stressed long before the permanent wilting point has been reached. So, to avoid stress and encourage maximum growth, hold soil as close to field capacity as possible to a depth of about two feet. Practically, when garden soil has dried down to about 70 percent of capacity, it should be watered up to capacity again. Irrigation system designers recommend allowing soils growing lower-valued crops such as cereals to drop to 50 percent of capacity before irrigating.

Leaching

Consider the effect on fertility when soil is overwatered. Nutrients are either available or potentially available. Available nutrients are dissolved in the soil solution. (Potentially available nutrients are in an insoluble state, but can dissolve.) The gardener goes to much expense and trouble increasing the level of available nutrients. Overwatering ruins this effort, and most gardeners don't realize this.

As water flows into soil, it transports dissolved nutrients with it, carrying them deeper. This action of water is called *leaching*. Leached soil is lowered in nutrients; deeper soil is enriched. When water penetration exceeds the depth of plant feeder roots, it has carried available plant nutrients beyond the reach of the plants. If chemical fertilizers were used, the root zone remains leached of nutrients until more fertilizer is applied. If organic fertilizers were used, the root zone is leached until the nutrient level builds back up from further breakdown of

Table 7
Amount of Water Needed to Bring Two Feet of Soil from 70 Percent to Capacity

Soil Type	Irrigation in Inches
Sandy	1/2 to 3/4
Improved sandy (much humus added)	1
Medium (loam)	1
Clayey	1½

potentially available nutrients. Either way, plant growth slows or stops. I suspect most gardeners overwater following the recommendations I've read in garden books and magazines and because of the equipment most gardeners use to irrigate with.

Lawn and garden sprinklers are primarily intended for lawn watering, not vegetable gardening. Although lawn sprinklers don't come with the kind of performance data supplied with agricultural crop sprinklers, it is possible to make estimates of how fast a sprinkler puts down water. It seems that most lawn and garden impact sprinklers produce precipitation rates of 1 to 2 inches per hour. Oscillating sprinklers, which water in rectangular patterns, put down 2 to 4 inches per hour, depending on which setting they are operating at. Soaker hoses and small area coverage sprinklers put out water in a very concentrated manner, resulting in precipitation rates well above 2 inches per hour. How long does the average gardener run one of these sprinklers? (Please refer back to Table 7.)

If you've been using a sprinkler such as this, you can easily test for precipitation rate. Set some empty tin cans or other cylinders in the sprinkler's pattern. Put one near the sprinkler, one near the outer limit of its throw, and a few in between. Run the sprinkler for one hour, average the level of water in the cans, and there's your precipitation rate per hour.

I remember reading with horror an article in *Organic Gardening* by a woman from California's Salinas Valley, who was so pleased with her new high-output irrigation system because if she ran it long enough on her *sandy* ground (six hours or so) she could get puddles to form on the surface. All her previous sprinklers allowed the water to soak in as fast as she put it on. I can imagine that down in the subsoil 6 to 8 feet, there may have been a clay hardpan or some other less permeable layer of soil that blocked the rapid flow of water. After enough hours of watering, she filled the pore space of her sand, all the way from this layer to the surface. What an accomplishment! I'm sure all her available nutrients were well on their way to the Pacific Ocean.

How to Water a Garden

Any sprinkler that wets the ground fairly uniformly can water a garden effectively without leaching if its rate of precipitation is known and allowed for. Once evaporation has dropped the soil moisture from capacity to about 70

Table 8
Peak Soil Moisture Loss in Various Climates

Type of Climate	Inches per Day
Cool climate	0.2
Moderate climate	0.25
Hot climate	0.3
High Desert	0.35
Low Desert	0.45

July and August moisture loss in the warmer areas of the maritime Northwest runs from 0.2 to 0.3 inches per sunny day.

percent of capacity, no more than the amount of water recommended in Table 7 is applied. Understanding the moisture cycle of our maritime Northwest soils enables the gardener to know approximately how fast water is being evaporated from the soil and when to replace it.

West of the Cascades, soils are kept wet to capacity and, worse, leached heavily by winter rains. Usually, they begin to dry down during April and are at about 60 percent of capacity (right to till for most types) sometime in May. Irrigation has to occur from the sowing of small seeds in May until sometime in late summer when rains have again begun, and/or cooler temperatures have slowed water losses greatly. The rate at which sun, wind, and heat dry out soil varies with the season, but not with the type of soil. In June, usually about 1 inch of water per week is removed from maritime Northwest soils. During the intense light and heat of July and early August, water losses can be 1½ inches per week, and during spells of really high heat, it can increase to 2 or slightly more than 2 inches per week. By September, losses are back down to about an inch per week.

In areas practicing extensive commercial irrigation, farmers are guided by timely, governmentally issued data concerning soil moisture losses in their district. Gardeners can go by estimates, adjusting for cloudy days whenever less evaporation occurs, and for any rain received. Remember that sandy soils should not be given more than 3/4 inch of water at one time to avoid leaching and so may have to be watered oftener than clayey ones, which can easily accept 1½ inches of water. More frequent light irrigations may be needed when sprouting seed, nursing small seedlings, or growing lettuce, radishes, and celery.

Sprinklers

It is optimal to water slowly, using small droplets. High-application-rate sprinklers usually put out large droplets from big nozzles, which cause soil compaction, making cultivation and weeding more difficult, and which reduce pore space and plant root development. Some soils tend to puddle and crust more, as large droplets cause a separation of the finer silt/clay fraction from the sands and leave a fine, cementlike layer of silt/clay on the surface, with the sand particles slightly below them. These effects are of no consequence when watering sod. Most lawn sprinklers produce precipitation rates in excess of 2 inches per

Table 9
Holding Capacity of Various Soils

Soil Type	Total Holding Capacity	Amount Held at Permanent Wilting Point
Sandy	1.25 inches per foot	.25 inch per foot
Medium	2.25 inches per foot	.60 inch per foot
Clayey	3.75 inches per foot	1.3 inches per foot

hour, a time-saving convenience to busy homeowners. Usually the droplet size is medium to large. Think what can happen if one of these monsters is forgotten for a few hours.

Agricultural crop sprinklers are available with application rates starting at 1/10 inch per hour, on up. There is one liability with using sprinklers having application rates below 1/2 inch per hour. During midday, hot sun, wind, and high air temperatures can cause almost as much evaporation as a small sprinkler is putting out, especially to an airborne stream of fine droplets. This is not a serious liability, because at rates below 2/10 inch per hour, it is possible to water all night, from bed to breakfast, without overwatering. For rural homesteaders with limited water supplies, this is also the time when there is no competition for the supply from showers, dishwashing, etc. Sprinkler systems with application rates from 1/4 to 1 inch per hour are best used during the morning before 11:00 A.M. to reduce evaporation loss.

Contrary to much commonly held opinion, nighttime watering is not harmful to plants. It may be, in fact, the best time to water. Plants are naturally dampened by dew and do not necessarily come down with assorted diseases. What can harm plants is being watered in early evening and then left damp all night, creating ideal conditions for multiplication of disease organisms. Watering continuously all night washes bacteria and fungus spores off the plants. Then, when the sun comes up, irrigation stops and the plants dry off quickly. This principle is well understood by nurseries that propagate plants by making rooted cuttings under a continuous fine mist.

Sprinkler Patterns

Designing a sprinkler seems to be an attempt at the impossible—to water a circle or a square (in the case of the oscillating sprinkler) uniformly from the center. Uniform water application from a single sprinkler is not economically practical to achieve, as anyone can easily prove to themselves by doing an irrigation rate test on any sprinkler—lawn, garden, agricultural, or commercial. Not only can no sprinkler I know accomplish this, but most fail miserably. The reason is this: there is much more area to be covered in the outer part of the sprinkler's pattern than there is in the center, and a single nozzle cannot gradually and precisely vary from putting ten times the amount of water on the perimeter than it does in the center.

How do you design a nozzle that throws virtually no water in the center,

Table 10
Comparison of High versus Low Application Rate Sprinklers

Nozzle Size	Operating Pressure	Discharge GPM	Radius in Feet	Spacing in Feet	Precipitation Rate in Inches per Hour
.0039	15	0.15	13	13 x 13	0.10
.0039	45	0.28	18	13 x 13	0.16
1/16	30	.45	33	20 x 20	0.11
1/16	60	.79	36	20 x 20	0.19
7/64	30	1.94	33	20 x 20	0.47
7/64	60	2.66	36	20 x 20	0.64
13/64	30	6.78	40	25 x 25	1.05
13/64	60	9.53	45	25 x 25	1.46
5/16	40	17.7	59	40 x 60	0.71
5/16	80	25.7	75	40 x 60	1.03

One-sixteenth-inch nozzles are about the smallest effective low application rate nozzles available. They also permit covering the maximum amount of ground at one time with the least amount of water. With application rates in the vicinity of .15 inch per hour, a ten-hour overnight watering will add 1.5 inches—perfect for bringing a heavy soil from 75 percent to capacity. Smaller nozzles can't spray far enough to achieve low application rates. Larger nozzles increasingly incur the liability of large droplet sizes. Nozzles emitting over about 5 gallons per minute (GPM) are too massive for the vegetable garden, though they might be excellent for pastures, golf courses, or corn fields.

most at the fringe, with every gradation in between? Many design tricks are used to approach this ideal of water distribution, but the best only approximate it. The worst of these is the oscillating sprinkler, which would seem by design to cover uniformly. Unfortunately, the cam arrangement that moves the spray arm holds too long at the turn-around point, so this sprinkler errs in putting too much water at the ends of the rectangle and too little near where the sprinkler sits. The impact sprinkler has the opposite trouble. It puts too much water near the sprinkler, left there by the spraying action of the rocker arm, and too little at the extremes of the pattern. Most garden store impact sprinklers come with a diffuser arm or needle of some sort to shorten the radius, while diffusing the spray. More than the slightest amount of diffusion increases the tendency to overwater the center while leaving the fringes too dry. The more the radius is shortened, the worse this becomes. Agricultural crop sprinklers do not use diffusers, but instead have scientifically designed nozzles that, if used at the correct pressure, diffuse or "spray" properly all by themselves and give fairly uniform coverage, putting only two or so times as much water near the center as they do on the fringes.

The only way I know of to have a fairly uniformly watered garden with a single, fixed-position sprinkler, is to make the garden circular, with a high-quality impact agricultural sprinkler in the center, and with the radius of the sprinkler at least one-third bigger than the radius of the garden, allowing the dry fringe to grow grass or other vegetation. However, circular patterns are hard to rototill or lay out, and most gardens are done sensibly in squares or rectangles. To compensate for this limitation of sprinkler design, farmers set out sprinklers in over-

Illustration 5
Ideal Sprinkler to Garden Radius Ratio

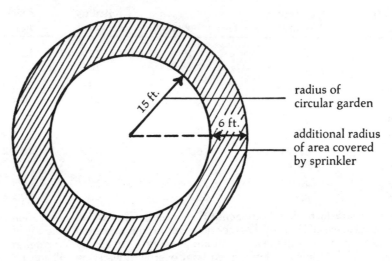

radius of
circular garden

additional radius
of area covered
by sprinkler

The area of the outer, shaded part of the sprinkler pattern is 670 square feet. The area of the inner part of the sprinkler pattern is 710 square feet. How do you design a nozzle that will uniformly throw as much water on the outer part of the pattern as the inner part?

lapping patterns, so that one sprinkler's heavily covered area is another's deficiently covered one, and the differences cancel out. This still leaves a dryish fringe area where fewer overlaps occur. On the farm, these fringes are of no consequence. In a backyard situation, it may be essential to keep overspray out of neighbors' yards or off windows.

Sometimes the patterns of sprinklers are laid out in squares, sometimes in triangles. The triangular pattern covers slightly more uniformly within the pattern, but the square pattern may lend itself better to backyard situations. Agricultural crop sprinklers are designed for spacings of from 13 to 100 feet. The closer the spacing and the shorter the designed radius of the sprinkler, the smaller the fringe area will be, making short-radius sprinklers best for backyard gardens.

Some people use impact sprinklers with part-circle attachments to eliminate fringe areas, putting the sprinklers at the edge of the area to be watered and reducing the sprinkler's arc to 180 or 90 degrees. Doing this can have harmful consequences. Impact sprinklers set on half-circles put out double the amount of water on the space being wetted; set in quarter circles, the precipitation rate quadruples. This should be considered if mixing full- and part-circle sprinklers in the same system. Most part-circle sprinklers need a large nozzle to have sufficient force to actuate the mechanism. Set on quarter-circles, these sorts of sprinklers can have application rates in excess of 4 inches per hour. A simple way to prevent full-circle sprinklers from spraying where they will cause trouble is to make a shield from a cut-out tin can attached directly behind the sprinkler. This is effective, though it does waste water by dumping the blocked spray at the sprinkler's base.

Illustration 6
Sprinkler Patterns

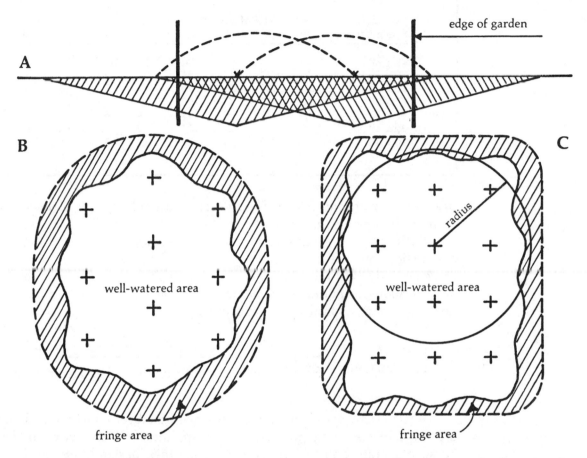

Using several sprinklers permits an overlap in watering patterns that will create an evenly watered garden area. The optimal spacing of these sprinklers is at about 60 percent of the sprinkling radius. (A) A side view of correct sprinkler overlap. The shaded area shows the relative amount of water applied to different parts of the covered radius by an average impact sprinkler; (B) sprinklers laid out in triangular pattern; and (C) sprinklers laid out in square pattern.

Nozzles are designed with different angles of throw. Using high-angle nozzles allows the stream to go its maximum distance, covering the maximum amount of ground with the fewest number of sprinkler heads and the smallest overall use of water. However, high-angle sprinklers are badly affected by wind, which can disperse the stream, blowing it off course and causing high evaporation rates, especially if the sun is shining at the same time. Low-gallonage, high-angle sprinklers can be a wonderful solution for the homesteader with a large garden and a very limited water supply, if one waters at night when the wind is weak and the sun not shining. Low-angle sprinklers are for windy situations. Throwing water at about 6 degrees, their radius is shortened up and the stream is close to the ground. More of these sprinklers are needed to cover a given area, resulting in somewhat higher precipitation rates and a higher water

Table 11
Precipitation Rate in Inches per Hour

Rectangular Spacing (feet)	GPM from Each Full-Circle Sprinkler							
	1	2	3	4	5	6	8	10
20 x 20	.24	.48	.72	.96	1.2	1.4	1.9	
20 x 30	.16	.32	.48	.64	.80	.96	1.3	1.6
20 x 40		.24	.36	.48	.60	.72	.96	1.3
25 x 25	.15	.30	.45	.60	.75	.90	1.2	1.5
30 x 30		.21	.32	.43	.54	.64	.86	1.0
30 x 40			.24	.32	.40	.48	.64	.80
40 x 40			.18	.24	.30	.36	.48	.60

use rate to cover a given area. The shorter radius of low-angle sprinklers may be better in backyard situations.

With sprinkler spacing and emission rate known, the precipitation rate is easy to determine. Table 11 is a handy reference guide. Since few sprinklers are spaced exactly to fit the table above and since nozzles usually do not emit water in one-gallon-per-minute increments, a formula is used to determine precipitation rates for any sprinkler size and spacing:

$$R\text{(ate of precipitation)} = \frac{\text{GPM (nozzle gallons per minute)} \times 96.3}{\text{Sprinkler row spacing} \times \text{sprinkler between-row spacing}}$$

Agricultural sprinklers come with manufacturer's recommendations for spacing and operating pressure. These specifications should be understood, because operating sprinklers too far outside their design limits results in poor performance. Nozzle size, operating pressure, and angle of the nozzle are all interrelated.

In crop sprinkler nozzles, the shape and smoothness of the bore are especially important. If the water stream that jets from the nozzle is run at too low a pressure, the stream doesn't break up and spray properly, and a "doughnut" pattern results, with much too much water being deposited near the sprinkler, some at the fringes, and little in the middle. Run at too high a pressure, the stream mists and breaks up too much, shortening the radius and greatly increasing the rate of application near the sprinkler, making the fringes too dry. Different nozzles are designed to operate from 10 to 100 pounds per square inch.

Sprinkler radii run from 13 to 100 feet. High-angle sprinklers should not be spaced more than about 60 percent of their radius. This allows for overlaps in the pattern and for wind to blow the sprays a small amount without leaving areas dry. Often, sprinkler catalogs only specify pressure and radius without defining proper spacing, assuming the user has sufficient understanding to lay out a proper system.

The best place to obtain agricultural crop sprinklers is either from a farm irrigation company or a large plumbing supply store. They will be a special-order item from the plumbing supply, but most have a Toro and a Rainbird catalog available, and these catalogs are textbooks in themselves for the prospective irrigator. Also available from such a source are tables showing pipe sizes required for amount of water being carried and, probably, lots of good advice on how to assemble such a system.

If a complete, permanently installed system that turns on from a single valve is beyond a gardener's interest or budget, correct irrigation can still be accomplished with a single good sprinkler that has permanent positions set up for it in the garden. For several years, I watered my 1/2-acre trial ground with an ordinary garden hose connected to a single 2½-gallon-per-minute sprinkler (which was all the water my well could produce on a continuous basis in midsummer) that I moved from spot to spot in a portion of the area, six nights a week from 8:00 P.M. to 2:00 A.M., and then reset in a different location from 2:00 A.M. until 8:00 A.M. If I'd had sufficient water to run twelve such spots simultaneously, I could have watered the entire half acre much more easily.

We now use a drip system in the trials and have been able to enlarge the trials somewhat beyond 1/2 acre because of this system. However, I do not recommend drip irrigation to the gardener. We use it simply because drip is the only way to water extensive plots during daylight hours with small gallonages, and because we have little economic stake in the yields we get from the trials. I do not care if every cabbage we grow costs $3.00, because I'm growing information in the trials, not food. Drip systems are costly, impermanent, and troublesome. The tubes are easily cut with a sharp hoe and, despite filters, tend to be plugged up at times. This means they have to be carefully inspected every time they're turned on. Drip lines also move around a lot from expansion and contraction, so they won't stay spot-on a transplant and won't keep a row of seeds wet without a lot of fiddling. Given a choice between drip and overhead sprinklers, I'd always choose sprinklers.

Raising Transplants

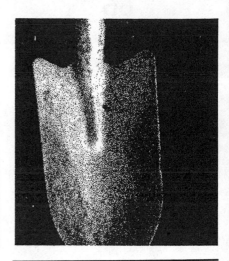

In May, transplants are available almost everywhere—supermarkets, drugstores, bookstores, garden centers; all have displays of bright flowers and eager-looking vegetable seedlings. These store-bought bedding plants can be almost as good as the very best homegrown ones. But only some are. Some are weak specimens, hardly able to endure the shocks of transplanting.

For many gardeners, commercially grown seedlings are more than sufficient, especially if the purchaser knows how to differentiate good bedding plants from poor ones. A good transplant looks sturdy, thick-stemmed, and stocky. The seedlings should have at least three completely developed true leaves, be dark green in color (unless the variety is naturally purple or some other color), and be well rooted without being pot-bound.

It is easy to see if a transplant is stocky and strong, but to inspect the root system, the buyer must carefully invert the pot and shake out the soil ball. This can be done safely. Support the soil in the pot by carefully inserting the fingers of one hand into the space above the pot, fingertips facing the soil, and while not quite supporting the soil mass on the palm of one's hand, tap the inverted pot until seedling, roots, and soil slide out of the pot and into the waiting hand. If roots have not yet filled the pot, the soil will tend to crumble and fall apart and few roots will be seen. If the pot is fully rooted, many root tips will be emerging from the soil ball and a few roots will have begun to wrap around the pot. If the pot is overly rooted, the wrap-around roots will have completely covered the root ball in a thick mass. This is a *pot-bound* plant.

Rooting: The Critical Factor

The rooting of transplants is the most important single factor in smooth and successful transplanting. Weakly rooted seedlings usually experience much root damage when transplanted because the soil ball tends to break apart when handled, moved, or compacted. These often wilt easily. Pot-bound seedlings usually have large tops, because although the roots ran out of area to expand into, the plant still got sufficient nutrients (generally supplied in the water in commercial greenhouses) and grew fairly rapidly. However, this large top is not easily supported by a restricted root mass. When transplanted, it may have to be watered daily for a week or more until the plant manages to force some root tips into the new soil out of its fibrous root ball and develops a root system more in line with the size of its top. Usually growth stops for a time until the seedling is better rooted.

Properly rooted transplants hold their soil ball together while being handled, experience little or no root damage, and begin rooting into the new soil immediately. Usually they'll survive without much special watering if the root ball is buried fairly deeply, below where the soil's surface dries out rapidly. This is why transplanting instructions specify setting the transplant in deeper than it had been, up to the first true leaves, putting the root ball several inches below the surface.

With some types of seedlings, especially coles and particularly cauliflowers, becoming pot-bound can be a disaster. Cabbages, broccoli, and cauliflower may become irreversibly stunted in the pot and never develop to full size before heading out or flowering. The result is a very small plant and little harvest, despite high levels of soil fertility and watering. A transplant can grow from being insufficiently rooted to being pot-bound in a week to ten days. Nurseries often move seedlings from their greenhouse to the point of retail sale several days before they are fully rooted, and may not discard them after a week or more on the shelf. The grower is better off to buy transplants that are not quite fully rooted, hold them in the pot for a few days while hardening the seedlings off, and then transplant them when the root development is just right.

Hard versus Soft Growth

Though it is not easy to see how hard a seedling is, this idea of hardness is a very real thing that greatly affects how a seedling is likely to perform. Plants perform according to their growing conditions. If conditions are very much to their liking, the plants wax happy and grow very rapidly. Their leaves become larger and broader, the stems longer and fatter. This rapid increase is not simply a result of more growth processes taking place. Under warm and fertile conditions without stresses, many plants respond by making larger cells with thinner cell walls that contain more water. This is referred to as "soft" growth. If, on the other hand, conditions are not fully to the plant's liking, it grows smaller leaves and shorter, stockier stems. This type of growth creates harder and tougher plant material, less likely to be damaged in handling or from winds or insects.

A soft plant is also much more likely to be shocked by exposure to stresses it has not yet experienced. These shocks can so weaken a seedling that it becomes diseased or ceases growing for a period, while making repairs internally. For example, a soft-grown pepper plant exposed to a single nighttime low temperature below 50 degrees will be shocked sufficiently to stop growth for a week. Exposed repeatedly to below 45-degree conditions, it may be so severely shocked as to not grow properly again. However, a hard-grown pepper would not be shocked until the lows were about 45 degrees. To a greenhouse-grown plant, the battering of wind can also be a severe shock, especially if the cellular structure is weak and soft. So, too, can cold rains with heavy, large droplets. Frost, even to a potentially frost-hardy seedling, can be shocking if that seedling never experienced temperatures below 45 or 50 before. Loss of roots, which is almost inevitable when handling transplants, is a shock. Combine this with wind, rain, never-before-experienced low temperatures, and the presence of soil diseases and insects, and transplanting can be a fatal experience to a soft seedling.

Greenhouse space is valuable, so there is a natural inclination on the part of some commercial growers to move transplants from seed to sellable seedling as fast as possible. The way to do this is to raise them under warm, fertile conditions. This way, a tomato seedling can be ready to sell in about four weeks. More responsible companies transfer some kinds of seedlings from a hothouse to an unheated greenhouse after two to three weeks in the hothouse, where their growth rate slows and they become harder. Doing this can add a week or more to the total production time, but then, unheated space is not nearly so costly to maintain.

The less protection offered by the cold house, the harder the transplant will be, the slower it grows, and the more costly it becomes to produce. The buyer of commercially raised garden seedlings has no way of knowing how hard a seedling is at the time of purchase, so it is wise to harden off the seedlings at home for a week before transplanting. This hardening-off process consists of gradually introducing the seedlings to environmental shocks. Generally, one brings home new seedlings and leaves them outside in bright shade to become accustomed to wind and light that is unfiltered by glass or plastic. They are brought indoors before sunset. The next morning the seedlings are introduced to morning and/or late afternoon sun and brought in at night. And the next, they encounter full sun all day, and are brought in at night. Then, it's all night outside, unless nighttime lows will be shockingly low, in which case they are brought in again. After a few nights outdoors, they'll be tough enough to transfer to the garden, with a much higher likelihood of surviving the shocks that delay growth and retard maturity.

Direct-Seeding instead of Transplanting

Compared to the environmental menaces it faces, a newly emerged seedling is small and weak. Should the seedling survive its first two weeks and begin to grow rapidly, it will become much stronger and, compared to the insects it is eaten by, much larger, and, compared to many of the diseases surrounding it, much more resistant. Its deeper and more extensive root system is better able to find water and so enable the seedling to survive a spell of hot sunny days that may completely dry out the surface inch to two inches of soil and which would be life-threatening to a sprout.

Many gardeners do not know how to help the more delicate types of small-seeded vegetables go from seed to thriving seedling a few inches tall, or do not feel they have the time, and so set out transplants as a quick solution to establishment of plants under field conditions. But raising transplants or buying transplants may not be necessary. In some cases, direct-seeding is as easy as transplanting itself, if a few tricks are used.

Anyone already raising transplants spends a considerable amount of time and pays close attention to the seedlings for four to six weeks before setting them out. I feel that it takes less time and energy to create conditions outdoors sufficiently welcoming to many kinds of seeds that they'll establish with a fair degree of certainty. Large-scale vegetable farmers almost always direct-seed their crops by creating field conditions that are very good for the types of seed being planted. Farmers know that some types of vegetables can only be successfully grown in certain kinds of soils or in certain climatic areas. Other types of vegetables grow so vigorously that they are widely adapted to many soil and climate situations. Thus, the main commercial tomato and pepper crops are direct-seeded in the South and in California, while northern plantings, done through transplantings, are of limited scope and only for local market. Onions are direct-seeded in sandy loams or peat soils. Celery is direct-seeded along the cool, moist southern California coast, possibly the best celery-growing environment in the world.

Unfortunately, most gardeners do not have an ideal soil type for vegetable crops, nor are they located in the ideal climate to direct-seed many kinds of vegetables. But, garden soils may be improved far beyond the scope a farmer could economically consider, and garden microenvironments may be created that enhance the germination of seeds with only a few simple techniques. Direct-seeding cabbage, broccoli, cauliflower, brussels sprouts, celery, onions, cucumbers, leeks, lettuce, parsley, and squash is very possible in the maritime Northwest and is fully explained in "How to Grow Them: General Recommendations." This chapter outlines procedures to start transplants of those same vegetables and for those types which must have an early start and be transplanted to make any production at all in our cool summers.

Raising Successful Transplants

Raising transplants takes much closer attention than direct-seeding, no matter how difficult it may be to direct-seed. Unfortunately, some vegetables have to be started indoors and transplanted when outdoor conditions will permit growth or they fail to mature in our cool summers. The gardener can often get a head start on the season by setting out good-sized seedlings about the same time that direct-seeding becomes possible. And, too, raising transplants and transplanting may be less work than doing the soil improvement to make a field sufficiently friable to direct-seed. A further possible advantage is that six-week-old transplants will survive insect predators that sprouting seeds would succumb to. And often, very desirable varieties are not available from commercial nurseries.

For these and many other reasons, gardeners get the itch to raise their own transplants. The transplant grower must usually create indoor conditions that match the needs of the seedlings being grown. This means taking responsibility for all the factors of plant growth which, when growing outside, are left to nature. These include light, temperature, moisture, soil quality, and fertility. Success will be in direct proportion to the degree that each of these factors is understood and controlled.

Occasionally, transplants may be grown completely outdoors with no equipment but some flats and a bench to put them on; but ordinarily transplants are grown at a time when outdoor conditions are too hostile to permit this. As a grower becomes more expert at raising transplants indoors, he or she also improves as an outdoor grower.

Temperature Requirements

Most vegetable seeds germinate best at about 75 to 80 degrees Fahrenheit. Some tropical varieties like melons, peppers, and eggplants will not germinate at all below 70, while cool-weather types like the cabbage family will germinate from 50 on up, but do so much faster and make stronger seedlings if the temperature is at least 65 to 70.

Seedlings of tropical vegetables, which only grow outside during the warmest parts of the maritime Northwest summer, thrive at temperatures ranging from 75 to 80 daytime to 60 at night. For melons, cukes, peppers, and eggplants, anything below 65 daytime will produce little or no growth and anything below 50 will shock the seedling and prevent further growth for a while. Cool-weather transplants, the coles, celery, parsley, and lettuce, become very spindly and weak when grown at temperatures suitable for peppers. These types do best with daytime temperatures of 60 to 70 and nighttime lows above 40. Their ideal conditions would be 65 day and 45 to 55 night. Tomatoes do best at 70 day and 55 to 60 night, but are able to tolerate nighttime lows down to 45 without shock. Tomatoes become very spindly and soft if grown at temperatures best suited to peppers.

If the raiser were only producing one type of seedling, it would be feasible to set up and maintain one range of temperatures ideal for the type being grown; but when many types of seedlings are being produced in the same place, a compromise is needed. Probably the best single temperature range that will permit any type of vegetable to thrive and grow fairly close to its best is 68 to 70 day, 52 to 60 night. These temperatures are easiest to achieve in a house.

Table 12
Ideal Growing Temperatures

	Tropical Vegetables	Tomatoes	Cool Weather Vegetables	Best All-Type Compromise Temperature Range
Day	75 to 80	65 to 70	60 to 70	68 to 70
Night	60 to 65	50 to 60	45 to 56	52 to 60

The Proper Soil

Transplants often have delicate root systems, particularly in the seedling stage. For rapid growth and good overall development, their soil should be light and loose and stay that way during the time the seedling is in the pot, usually a four- to eight-week period. If good root system development is prevented by compacted soil, the weakened seedlings may not transplant successfully.

Commercial greenhouses raise seedlings in artificial soil mixes, which are usually sterilized. The basic ingredients are not soil at all, but consist of moss, vermiculite, perlite, and compost. These mixes are sometimes purchased premixed and prefertilized; sometimes the nursery makes its own. The gardener should understand that commercial mixes, even if chemically fertilized, have only sufficient nutrients to grow plants for a few weeks at most. Here are a few sample commercial mix formulations:

#1 U.C. Mix
75 percent coarse sand
25 percent sphagnum peat moss
Then add to each cubic yard of mix:

    7½ pounds dolomite lime
    2½ pounds agricultural lime
    3   pounds 10-20-10

#2 Cornell "Peat-Lite" Mix
11 bushels sphagnum peat moss
11 bushels horticultural grade vermiculite (No. 2 or No. 4) or perlite
 5 pounds dolomite lime
 1 pound superphosphate
12 pounds 5-10-5

Sphagnum moss is the dried remains of acid-bog plants. It is usually sterile and has the capacity to absorb ten to twenty times its own weight in water. Sphagnum moss provides almost no nutrients itself and has a pH of about 3.5. It also contains some natural fungistatic substances that tend to inhibit damping-off diseases. Sphagnum moss usually comes finely ground and completely dehydrated. Slow to take up water when completely dry, it should be thoroughly moistened before use.

Vermiculite is a naturally occurring rock that expands greatly when heated until it pops like popcorn. When expanded, it weighs six to ten pounds per cubic foot, has a pH of about 7.0, and is able to absorb three to five times its own weight in water. Like clays, vermiculite has the ability to attract and hold onto mineral nutrient molecules like potassium and nitrogen (cation exchange capacity). But unlike clays, vermiculite remains loose and light when wet and dried again and again unless compressed when wet (destroying its porous structure). This ability to attract nutrient molecules tends to reduce the amount of fertilizer lost when water passes through the pot. Vermiculite is graded into four horticultural sizes. No. 1 is a bit too coarse for bedding plant soils; No. 2 is the regular horticultural grade; very fine No's. 3 and 4 are usually used for seed-germinating media in commercial greenhouses. Vermiculite is usually sterile.

Perlite is a gray-white pumicelike material, mined from lava flows. The rock is crushed and heated so it pops like vermiculite, expanding the particles to small, spongelike bits that are very light, weighing five to eight pounds per cubic foot. Perlite will hold three to four times its weight in water. It has no ability to hold nutrients as does vermiculite, has a pH of about 7.0, and is usually used to lighten and aerate a soil mix.

Compost is a highly variable material available from many garden centers by the sack and often made at home by individuals. It consists of well-rotted organic matter and may have pH's ranging from 4.0 to 7.0. Sometimes it is quite nutrient-rich, sometimes not. Compost has the ability to hold onto many times its weight in water and loosens soils. Using composts in soil mixes is no assurance that no further fertilization will be needed. Composts are not usually sterile.

Though premixed potting/bedding plant soils can be purchased at most nurseries and garden stores, much money can be saved by mixing potting soil at home. Here is a formula we use at Territorial Seed Company when growing seedlings for our variety trials. It is not sterilized.

#3 Territorial Seed Company Mix
2 parts by volume garden soil (ours is a well-manured, heavy, silty clay)
1 part by volume sphagnum moss
Add to each cubic foot of mix:
    1 cup agricultural lime or dolomite
    ½ to 1 cup cottonseed meal or other seed meal or fish meal
    1 pint soft rock phosphate *or* 1 cup steamed bone meal
    1 cup kelp meal

This soil mix will be adequate for all gardeners except those who have very heavy clay soils. Clays tend to compact and limit root development and though sphagnum moss will improve them, it is often better to further lighten up clays with compost or larger quantities of sphagnum moss.

Because of the natural tendency to water bedding plants so that water runs out the bottom of the pot, any soluble fertilizer in the pot tends to be quickly washed away. Chemically fertilized soil mixes can become completely devoid of nutrients with only a few good waterings. Soil mixes fertilized with organic fertilizers like cottonseed meal have the capacity to rebuild their fertility levels after watering, from the further breakdown of nutrient-rich organic matter. The Territorial Seed Company mix will grow many types of bedding plants without additional fertilization if the basis is rich garden soil. Often, small amounts of liquid fertilizer can significantly boost seedling growth.

Watering

Being shallow, bedding plant pots and trays have to be watered frequently. Daily watering is usually required, and when grown outdoors in full sun, watering late morning and midafternoon may be needed. This need for frequent watering makes it essential to grow seedlings in soil that will repeatedly absorb water and dry out without compacting or crusting over. Compacted and/or crusted soils may not absorb water well. If the soil shrinks away from the sides of the pot, water may quickly run down the sides of the pot and out the bottom without really wetting the soil. If the surface crusts over, absorption may slow so much that the grower thinks the pot is saturated with water when it actually is very dry. This is why bedding plant soil mixes use sphagnum moss, perlite, and vermiculite. These materials can take on and release water without becoming compacted. However, a strange anomaly occurs with using sphagnum moss. When allowed to dry out fully, sphagnum moss is very difficult to remoisten and may inhibit water uptake in bedding trays. Thirty-three percent concentration is near the maximum safe level.

Tiny seedlings growing in light soil can be disturbed easily, their root systems exposed or damaged if not watered gently. No one system or device is ideal for this purpose. On a garden-sized scale, the gentlest and easiest system to use is the siphon. Made from a gallon container and a small diameter plastic tube, the siphon gently pours water into the plant pot. Water pressure may be adjusted easily by changing the height of the water supply above the seedling trays. Usually one or two feet of drop is more than enough. Allowed to stand for several hours or a day before using, a water jug can reach room temperature. This avoids giving many kinds of seedlings the mild shock that comes from putting cold water on their roots. Because 1/4- or 3/8-inch-diameter plastic tubing is very flexible and light, the water supply may be conveniently located several feet away from the growing seedlings.

Because soil takes time to absorb water, it is very helpful not to overfill seedling trays with soil. If 1/4 to 1/2 inch of empty space remains on the top of the tray, water may be added fairly quickly and allowed to percolate slowly.

Containers

Growing seedlings require increasing amounts of root room. When deprived of space, the seedlings do not stop making roots, but instead increase the density of their root systems and wrap new roots around the outside of whatever soil is available to them, becoming what is called "pot-bound."

The simplest way to raise most kinds of bedding plants is in a container large enough to accommodate them from sprouting to transplanting size without becoming pot-bound. This method is not used commercially because growing bedding plants for profit demands the most efficient use of greenhouse space, so seedlings grown for money are started in one soil, "pricked out" when they are about one week old, and transplanted into the tray they will be sold from. This time-consuming practice is more efficient than starting one seedling per pot because it allows for nongerminating seeds and seedlings that die shortly after sprouting. By the time the week-old seedlings are transplanted, most damping-off losses will have occurred. Pricking out seedlings is also more economical on the commercial scale than sowing several seeds per pot and thinning.

It is not possible to specify exactly which pot size to use for each type of vegetable. Many factors can influence the growth rate and root-size-to-top ratio such that a single type of vegetable may behave differently under different soil, light, and fertility conditions. However, two square inches of soil about two inches deep provides ample room for a fast-growing seedling until it is large enough to transplant; and for many kinds of vegetables, it's best to transplant them small. However, in the case of certain tropical plants like peppers, eggplant, tomatoes, melons, and cukes, and for starting very large and fast-growing vegetables like squashes, large individual pots are useful. This way, very large plants can be grown before conditions in the garden are good enough for them, giving the plant a big head start. In any case, do not permit seedlings to become pot-bound. Careful transplanting from a six-pack tray or small pot to a larger container will cause little or no growth check.

Drainage is a very important consideration when selecting a growing pot. Home transplant raisers are often very innovative about adapting ordinary household items into bedding plant pots. Styrofoam cups, egg cartons, and milk carton bottoms have all been used, as have aluminum disposable cake tins. None of these containers has drainage holes. If water is allowed to stand in the bottom of the pot, many kinds of seedlings will become sickly or die, so large drainage holes should be made in the bottom of each pot to allow excess water to run out. Sometimes when using liquid fertilizers to promote seedling growth, it is necessary to wash out the soil by running enough water through the pot to dissolve and remove all leftover fertilizer before adding more.

Light Requirements

Light quality and intensity are essential elements of plant growth. For example, many kinds of plants only flower well under reddish light, such as naturally occurs in late summer and early autumn. In greenhouse experiments with several different kinds of intense light sources, such as halide, sodium, and mercury lamps, great distortions in plant growth could be induced by using lamp combinations that differed from natural sunlight spectral composition. Also, under low light intensity, many kinds of fruiting plants will make only vegetative growth, or if fruit is set, will not develop or ripen. And, under very low light intensities, many plants become spindly and long stemmed. The name for this phenomenon is *etoliation*. Etoliation can be demonstrated easily by putting a potted plant in a dark closet for a few weeks. In extremes, the vinelike stems become ten or more times as long as usual, the leaves barely developed.

East of the Cascades, the sun shines brightly more days than it is cloudy, so it is a common home garden practice to grow bedding plants in a sunny, south-facing window. However, in the maritime Northwest, window sill-grown plants do not receive enough light during the months of February, March, and April (and some years, even May is frequently overcast) to make proper growth, and consequently become spindly and weak. This inescapable fact means that the maritime Northwest gardener must make more serious provisions and invest a bit more money and effort when deciding to raise healthy, strong bedding plants.

There are two common solutions to our low light levels: indoor grow-lights and protected outdoor spaces such as cold frames, hot frames, and greenhouses. By far, the most inexpensive and easily manageable solution is the indoor fluorescent grow-light. Naturally adapted to unfiltered direct sunlight, vegetable seedling growth suffers to the degree that the light source differs from natural sunlight. Experiments conducted to grow plants under high-intensity artificial light have demonstrated that no one source of artificial light matches the sun, and for plants to perform optimally, a mixture of different kinds of light is required. This is quite impractical in the home, especially since some light sources such as mercury, halide, and sodium lights can cost upwards of $200 per lamp and are capable of illuminating more than fifty square feet each with an intensity equal to noon at the equator. Fortunately, one common and fairly inexpensive light source, the cool-white fluorescent, produces a light quality that promotes very good vegetative plant growth, though fluorescents don't prompt good flowering or fruit formation. Sylvania Gro-Lux tubes may be slightly better.

Fluorescent lights are of fairly low intensity and are impractical if large plants are to be grown under them. However, they are quite sufficient to produce smaller size vegetable seedlings such as are sold in sixes and twelves. Commonly available in four- and eight-foot lengths, the four-foot fluorescent is the usual at-home choice. Two to six cool-white or Gro-Lux tubes suspended over the growing area can produce healthy, stocky seedlings indoors at low cost. For best growth, the tubes should be placed as close together as possible. The distance between the lamps and the leaves must be increased as the seedlings grow, so either the lamps have to be suspended in such a way as to be movable, or the shelf holding the growing containers must be movable, or the containers themselves must be on platforms, which are gradually lowered as the seedlings grow.

Almost all kinds of plants need a period of darkness to conduct certain kinds of growth activities. However, this period need not be longer than four hours in many cases. So if maximum growth rate is desired, lights can be run for twenty hours per day as a general rule. A minimum duration of fourteen hours is suggested. However, some kinds of vegetables are photoperiodic, meaning that they respond to the length of dark versus light by altering their growth from vegetative to flowering or bulbing. Included in this group are onions, mustards,

Table 13
Using Grow-Lights

Number of Tubes	Maximum Height above Top of Seedlings	Width of Strongly Illuminated Area	Period of Growth with Sufficient Light
2	2 inches	6 inches	4 weeks
4	3 inches	9 inches	6 weeks
6	4 inches	12 inches	8 weeks

and spinach. Details on how to handle these types of seedlings under artificial lights are in the "How to Grow Them" section.

Plants also seem to alter their growth unfavorably when the light/dark periods are irregular. Inexpensive timers are available that can be set to turn lights on and off at preset times every day. I highly recommend them.

Fertilizer

Liquid fertilizer is almost absolutely necessary when growing bedding plants. Never yet have I used a premade or homemade soil mix which would produce maximally vigorous plant growth for the duration. Really strong mixes made with lots of organic fertilizers tend to burn seedlings or even reduce germination because of nutrient buildup in a small volume of soil. On the other hand, if the pots are watered to the extent that water runs out the bottom, this will wash out (leach) all the nutrients in the soil, greatly slowing growth. After many years of trying, I came to the conclusion that the most *reliable* system was to make the soil a medium for root development, providing only background nutrition while regulating growth through feedings of liquid fertilizer.

Unfortunately, liquid organic fertilizers tend to be unbalanced and expensive. Liquid fish is usually 7-2-2 or thereabouts, while seaweed or kelp concentrations are usually ½-1-1 more or less. The best organic combination would be four or five parts liquid seaweed and one part liquid fish, diluted to half the recommended strength. Chemical fertilizers intended to coax bedding plants are generally about 20-20-20, with trace elements added, and composed of many different types of compounds so that no aspect of needed plant nutrition might be overlooked. The best of these is Rapid Gro. When used to fertilize bedding plants, dilute to half the recommended strength.

Fertilizer is recommended for use half-strength because the home grower can add enough slow-release organic fertilizer to the soil mix to produce a slow and steady growth rate without danger of burning the seedlings. This is supplemented with liquid feedings, resulting in controlled growth without overfeeding. Too much fertilizer, particularly too much nitrogen fertilizer, tends to result in lush, soft growth and tall, spindly stems, particularly when combined with higher growing temperatures. If one feeding of half-strength fertilizer does not result in rapid enough growth, a second feeding a few days later can be done to see if the plant will respond to higher concentrations of available nutrients without danger of burning the plant or triggering wildly uncontrolled growth. Feed plants every ten days to two weeks, or when growth slows.

Cold and Hot Frames

A cold frame is an inexpensive and crude greenhouse. Often put together of recycled planks and window sashes or covered with plastic, fiber glass, or polyethylene sheeting, cold frames create an improved growing environment helpful to the transplant raiser. A poorly constructed frame that is not well sealed at night is still capable of holding nighttime temperatures 7 to 10 degrees warmer, especially if a blanket is thrown over the frame when frosts are predicted. A well-built frame with insulated walls and well-fitted windows, caulked and sealed, can hold nighttime temperatures 12 to 15 degrees warmer at night.

Having a cold frame is advantageous. By April, the light levels in the frame are much higher than can be produced by fluorescents indoors. Daytime temperatures, regulated by opening one of the windows, can be kept cooler than indoors. This makes a frame an excellent place to put one- to two-week-old cabbage family transplants, where they'll grow slowly and hard, stocky and strong. About two to three weeks before tomatoes are usually transplanted, a cold frame creates conditions suitable for their growth. If six-week-old seedlings are transferred to larger pots and grown for two to three weeks in the frame, they'll be well hardened off and quite large, usually yielding more and much earlier. About the time no more frosts are expected, the frame becomes a suitable home for peppers and eggplants, melons and cucumbers. Started indoors, these can be repotted and hardened off in the frame before setting them out a few weeks later when outdoor conditions are really summery.

A hot frame is nothing but a cold frame with heat below. In the old days, frames were heated by building them over a pit filled with fresh, strong manure. Now most people heat the frame with an electric cable, thermostatically controlled. Hot frames are an interesting luxury that will permit one to grow tropical plants like peppers outside after March 1 if so desired and to germinate seeds outside, eliminating the need for fluorescent lights inside and removing all gardening clutter from the house. Hot frames are not necessary for successful gardening. However, any serious transplant raiser is going to want a cold frame eventually.

Sowing Seeds

In commercial greenhouse operations, seeds are germinated in flats. Rows of fungicide-treated seeds are sown 1½ inches apart such that the sprouts stand 1/4 to 1/2 inch apart in the row, in a shallow tray filled with extremely fine, sterile soil made almost entirely of vermiculite and sphagnum moss. The trays are placed atop electrically heated tabletops and held at from 70 to 80 degrees until the seeds sprout. After about one week of growth, just as the first true leaf is beginning to develop, the seedlings are delicately lifted out of the tray and transplanted into individual pots or small trays containing four, six, or more and kept in bright shade for a few days until well rooted. This convenient system is commercially profitable and efficient. Usually, sterilized soil and fungicide-treated seeds prevent damping-off disease from eliminating any of the newly sprouted seedlings.

If garden soil and untreated seed were to be used instead, germination might drop from over 90 percent to somewhere around 50 to 60 percent at best. Unprotected by fungicide, even more of these seedlings die from damping-off diseases during their first week. Perhaps only two-thirds of those that do sprout will survive to mature beyond that dangerous period, and if the variety is open-pollinated, many of these will not be particularly vigorous specimens. The home gardener is best off to recognize the truth of the nature of seed—that most batches of seed contain some individuals of higher vigor than others and these may be chosen by the grower over the weaker specimens, resulting in better growth for the balance of the plant's life. The home gardener can plant at least ten seeds for every plant desired and cull out the weak ones. With this approach, damping-off diseases are an easy way to allow nature to do some thinning of more disease-susceptible specimens.

When sowing seeds, I recommend punching a small hole to the proper depth into the soil with the blunt end of a pencil and placing a pinch of ten or so seeds in the hole, covering them, and letting them sprout. Then, thin down to about three plants per spot within the first week and continue to thin as the pot or tray becomes crowded, not permitting plants to shade each other or compete. Thinning is best done with a small, sharp scissors, snipping off the stem at the soil line.

Because almost any kind of seed sprouts much faster when held from 70 to 80 degrees, newly seeded trays and pots are best located on a shelf above the fluorescent light bank, where the heat generated by the lamps and ballasts creates ideal germination conditions. The moisture level of soil has a strong effect on the amount of damping-off and the rapidity and effectiveness of germination. Soil should be on the dry side. When squeezed into a ball, it should crumble easily into fine particles. Once the seeds are sown, a proper moisture level may be maintained without watering by covering the tray or pot with a very thin, clear plastic wrap until the seeds emerge. Fiber pots and trays tend to lose moisture through their sides, so when sprouting seeds within these, it is useful to place the pot within a clear polyethylene bag and seal it until emergence.

How to Grow Them

Beans

Sow 1½ inches deep, two seeds per individual 2-inch pot. Sprout at 65 to 75 degrees. Thin promptly to one plant. Grow about two weeks at 65 to 75 degrees until one true leaf is well developed. Transplant at the same time seeds are sown outdoors. Lima beans are the only type that almost must be grown for transplanting in the maritime Northwest. Snap beans will mature early enough if direct-seeded, but may be transplanted if earlier production is desired.

Broccoli

Sow 1/2 inch deep in clumps of five to ten seeds in individual 2-inch pots or six-pack trays. Sprout at 60 to 75 degrees. Grow about five weeks at 60 to 70 degrees day, over 40 night. Thin gradually so seedlings don't compete for light. Transfer to a cold frame, if available, after two weeks. When seedlings have two or three true leaves, they should be fully rooted and ready to set out. Seedlings becoming pot-bound or stunted from poor growing conditions may not head out well in the garden. May to July sowings may be grown on an outdoor bench in full sun or direct-seeded. Simply elevating the growing pots a few feet off the ground virtually eliminates flea beetle damage. Indoor growing temperatures over 70 may cause spindly growth.

Beets

Individual seeds usually produce clusters of seedlings. In March or April sow one or two seeds per individual 2-inch pot, 1/2 inch deep. Sprout at 60 to 75 degrees. Grow three to four weeks at 60 to 70 degrees. (Transfer to cold frame after two to three weeks under fluorescent lights.) Do not thin. Transplant 8 inches apart in rows 18 inches apart. Each cluster of beets produces four to six nice roots at maturity. Transplants are raised commercially for earliest harvest in England. Use a slow-to-bolt variety like Early Wonder for this purpose.

Brussels Sprouts

Like broccoli.

Cabbage

Like broccoli.

Cauliflower

Like broccoli. Especially sensitive to being pot-bound or stunting, causing later growth without head formation.

Celery

Sow 1/4 inch deep in clumps of five to ten seeds in individual 2- to 3-inch pots or six-pack trays. Sprout at 60 to 75 degrees. Thin gradually without permitting light competition. Grow at 65 to 75 degrees day, 50 to 60 degrees night. Slow growing, celery requires high moisture and fertility levels, and eight to ten weeks to attain transplanting size. Better started on the late side and transferred to the cold frame after three to four weeks under lights, once frame conditions hold above 50 at night (nights outside generally over 40). Though frost hardy, exposure to too much below-50-degree temperatures may induce premature flowering (bolting).

Sweet Corn

Like beans if earliest production is desired. Sow four to six seeds per pot. Do not thin. Transplant clumps of seedlings 30 inches apart in rows 30 inches apart.

Cucumbers

Sprouting cucumber seed (and other members of the squash family) requires warm, slightly damp conditions if mildews are to be avoided. Test potting soil carefully. It should barely form a soil ball when squeezed hard and break up easily afterward. If too damp, allow to dry out before using. About the time tomato seedlings are set outside, sow clumps of four to six seeds 1 inch deep in individual 3- to 4-inch pots. Place pot inside an airtight, lightweight polyethylene bag—such as those you find in the supermarket produce department—to hold moisture content stable until germination. Hold pots over 70 degrees until germination. Best temperature is closer to 80 degrees. When seedlings emerge, remove polyethylene bags. Grow under lights or in a hot frame for about two weeks at 70 to 80 day, over 55 night, and thin to best two plants by the time they have developed one true leaf. Transfer to cold frame if available for the final week of growth. Early vine growth of squash family plants is prevented by cool or damp conditions, so this family is better started late and set outside only after nighttime lows and weather have moderated.

Eggplants

Like peppers, but even more sensitive to below-50 temperatures when seedlings. See peppers.

Kale

Like broccoli, but so vigorously sprouting and growing that direct-seeding is much preferable to raising transplants.

Kohlrabi

Like broccoli. Though there may be some reasons to transplant spring crops, those sown for fall harvest are easiest direct-seeded.

Leeks

If early fall harvest is desired, start transplants in early spring. If harvest after October is acceptable, direct-seed in late spring. Raise transplants like onions, but bury the stems to the depth of the first leaf joint when transplanting.

Lettuce

Raise transplants for earliest harvest; otherwise direct-seed. Grow like broccoli. Seed is usually uniform, so two to three seeds sown per plant ultimately desired is enough.

Melons

Like cucumbers, but even more sensitive to low temperatures and damp conditions in the seedling stages.

Onions

For the largest bulb onions or earliest scallions, raise transplants. In February or early March, sow seeds 1/2 inch deep, four to eight seeds per inch, in two furrows across a six-pack tray. Sprout at 60 to 75 degrees. Grow at 50 to 70 day, 40 to 50 night. Very cold, hardy onions may be transferred to the cold frame after mid-March, where higher light levels make stockier plants. Do not thin. With sharp scissors, cut the tops back to 3 inches long every few weeks to promote thicker stems and better developed root systems. Transplant after May 1 when well rooted and stocky. Onions transplant very easily, even bare rooted, so the individual seedlings may be separated by shaking them apart. Indoors, grow onions under fourteen hours of daylight or longer to prevent premature bulbing.

Parsley

Slow germinating, parsley is often transplanted, though it is easily direct-seeded if sown before May 1, when conditions stay damp outside. Otherwise, grow like broccoli. Germination can take fourteen to seventeen days at 70 degrees.

Peppers

Peppers are tropical plants. If grown soft, they are shocked by below-50-degree temperatures. If grown as hard as a pepper can be grown without becoming stunted, they will continue growing after exposure to a 45-degree low.

Most people make the mistake of setting out peppers at the same time as tomatoes—right after there is no further frost danger. But this will almost certainly expose the sensitive seedlings to lows below 45 degrees. It is better by far to wait two or three weeks more before setting out peppers. Because their growth stops when September becomes cool and rainy, and because any surprisingly cool night during June can shock peppers sufficiently to stop their growth for a time, it is a wise practice to set out the largest-sized transplants possible. Start slow-growing seeds about six to eight weeks before the last expected frost date. (If a hot frame or greenhouse is available, they may be sown even earlier.) In 2- to 4-inch individual pots or six-pack trays, sow a pinch of five to eight seeds 1/2 inch deep. Sprout this heat-demanding seed *over* 70 degrees and better about 75. Grow at 65 to 80 day, over 50 night. (A 4-inch pot will hold the seedling for eight to ten weeks.) By the time no further danger of frost exists, the seedlings will be outgrowing fluorescent lighting and may be transferred to the cold frame and repotted in 4- to 6-inch pots. Make sure the frame stays over 50 at night. Grow in the frame until summer is really on. Pepper plants will make more growth in the frame if given ample room to root than they will unprotected or in a cloche, which offers less nighttime heat gain. If a hot frame is used, remove the bottom heat two weeks before transplanting to harden off the plants.

Squashes (Pumpkins)

Generally grow like cucumbers, but since squash seedlings are so large and make such rapid growth, very large pots are needed if a seedling of any size is to be produced. At Territorial Seed Company trials, we germinate squash seed much like that of cucumbers in individual 2-inch pots, avoiding the danger of chilly and damp spring soils ruining the germination process. Then, once they are up, we grow them only two to four days in the pots until sufficiently rooted to hold the root ball together, and then transplant.

Tomatoes

For the earliest possible production, grow the largest possible plants. We start our home garden tomatoes about March 1 at Lorane, move them to the hot frame about April 1, to the cold frame about April 20, and to the garden when they are 18 to 24 inches tall in one-gallon pots about May 15. Then we grow them in a large cloche until they are ripening tomatoes or bursting out the sides or need to be trained up strings, having outgrown the 24-inch stakes inside the cloche. These tomatoes begin ripening by mid-July in a bad summer. More commonly (and this is what we do in our trial plots), start tomatoes six weeks before the last expected frost date in six-pack trays or individual 2- to 3-inch pots. Sow a clump of four to six seeds, 1/2 inch deep. Sprout at 70 to 75 degrees. Grow at 65 to 75 day, 50 to 60 night. Thin gradually. Transplant after danger of frost is past. If a cold frame is available, harden them off there for their last two weeks before transplanting.

Diseases and Pests in the Maritime Northwest

Oh, if only more gardeners truly understood Sir Albert Howard's maxim about the cause of disease and insect damage. Howard's belief is that a plant in trouble usually already was an unhealthy plant in some respect, and that a vigorous and healthy plant can outgrow insect damage and not succumb to disease. Insect populations do, however, get unbalanced—usually from human interference with nature—and can sometimes reach plague levels that require further intervention. An example of out-of-balance pest levels can be found in Washington's Skagit Valley. There, many acres are devoted to insecticide-sprayed cole family crops. Consequently, the cabbage fly is so numerous and without natural predators that controls must be used or cole crops cannot be grown.

We have little trouble with carrot rust fly larvae at Lorane. A few carrots will have maggots in them, but far less than 1 percent. This is especially true at the end of the valley where my trial grounds/garden are located. In other parts of the valley where soils are better, gardeners report more maggot damage. I think the difference is the quality of the pastures surrounding the gardens. In my less-fertile end of the valley, wild carrot is a dominant weed in poorly managed pastures. Farther down the valley are better pastures with less wild carrot. Large, stable populations of wild carrot mean stable populations of carrot fly *and* predators of the fly. In areas where there are few wild carrots, the fly breeds unchecked by predation whenever it discovers garden carrots and becomes a serious plague. In the same way, we have lots of wild cabbage and less difficulty with the cabbage fly than gardeners in most areas. Only those coles with weaker root development succumb, even if no protective measures are used at all. When the literature blames the existence of wild carrot for difficulties with the carrot fly, it is, as usual, an inversion of the truth. The blame should be on the lack of sufficient wild carrot.

Before You Spray

The best approach to handling insect difficulties in the garden is first to wonder if the plant may not be growing well enough to outgrow the predation. This is the usual "cause" of most problems. Sometimes infertile soil is the culprit; sometimes bad weather or sowing too early will retard growth and lower the health of the plant. Often, the first action to be taken is a feeding of liquid fertilizer. Many, many times this one action will cure up a plant within a day or two, producing a vigorous growth response and a healthy plant. And, if slow-growing seedlings are being chewed down by slugs, flea beetles, or some other insect, and if fertilization doesn't solve it, most likely the seeds were sown too early or too thinly. Sowing many more seeds than the final number of plants desired permits one to have a benign attitude about insects that are helping to thin the stand out, and sowing later when soils are warmer and more active and the sun stronger allows seedlings to grow much faster from the start.

Many kinds of vegetables will thrive in a soil type not particularly suited to vegetable culture, if only they get a bit of fertilizer and/or lime. These are considered the "easy-to-grow" vegetables like sweet corn, snap beans, lettuce, carrots, radishes, and members of the squash (cucurbit) family. Other types of vegetables are weak-rooted and will only grow in heavier soils if they have been recently and well amended with organic matter. On our clay soil trial grounds, members of the cabbage family, beets, and onions will not grow unless they follow a moderate manuring. If manuring was done a year ago, these vegetables barely grow, despite fertilization, and after two years without manure, they succumb inevitably to insects of one sort or another, or refuse to develop, no matter how well fertilized.

Spraying is not always the solution after fertilization is tried. When bad weather causes no-growth conditions at the beginning of the season, sprays can retard damage while plants wait for weather to moderate and for growth to resume. But, bad weather or lowering light levels at the season's end can also prompt troubles with insects and diseases. Spraying at this time is relatively pointless, as the plants cannot grow anyway, and their life cycle is through.

Peaceful Coexistence

Not having to battle insects that might be threatening my food supply allows me to see the pests as potential allies, and I often use the pests to help me grow a better garden. By following the lead of the pests, I discover paths to more natural gardening. One important step along this road is to abandon austerity and begin to produce an abundance of food—so much that pests and diseases could take one-third of the garden without threatening one's food supply. Nature's tithe is rarely more than 10 percent. Then, even if one-third of the cauliflowers are taken by maggots, so what! And, even if *all* the tomatoes succumb to late blight because poor, cloudy weather weakened the vines too much, there are still peppers and cucumbers and squash and corn and beans and cabbages. Some years *are* cabbage years in the maritime Northwest.

Some people fight insects because of what I call the "American Sanitary Model." You know that in a supermarket, should a leaf have a hole in it, no one would buy it, and should a consumer find a cooked cabbage worm in his or her steamed broccoli, the store might well be threatened with a lawsuit or an investigation by the government. Food is supposed to be *clean*, isn't it? Proponents of spraying vegetables are absolutely right when they argue with organic growers: without sprays, one cannot raise most commercial vegetables absolutely free of insects. Many commercial growers would go broke if they tried, and the public would not buy unsprayed vegetables with a consciousness that demands produce that is absolutely unblemished.

Why not coexist with insects? Remove as many of them as possible when the food is being prepared and overlook the one that may occasionally escape the cook's scrutiny. There is a big difference between a plant showing the effects of a few insects and one that has been severely damaged by them. As long as the plant is still growing vigorously, pinholes in the leaves don't matter. Leave cosmetic spraying to the commercial farmer and their unrealistic clientele.

Meeting Pests Head-On

As nice as all this high-minded talk seems, still there are occasions when insects are so widespread that they must be fought or the crop lost. What follows is a summary of what little I've learned about the common garden pests of the maritime Northwest. Unfortunately, I am the wrong person to write an authoritative statement about insects and insect control. In my garden, only the most ubiquitous and prolific pests make their presence felt at all, though I'm sure there are others lurking unnoticed. So I do not know the whys and wherefores of the brown-spotted cucumber flower nibbler, the hybrid sweet corn borer, the purple-poppy plucker, or the sneaky weed nabber. I am intimately acquainted with only a few types of bugs and, of course, slugs and some other critters that burrow under my garden beds.

However, if what follows does not describe your persistent plague nor indicate how to lessen its effect or control it without poisons, let me suggest asking your friendly garden center owner or extension agent. They have a battery of high-powered sprays and poisons that can kill almost anything living in or around the soil.

Symphylans

Most gardeners are unaware that symphylans live in almost all maritime Northwest soils. When their natural humusy forest habitat is changed by the plow, symphylans probably alter their diet slightly to include more root tips and less humus. They do this in proportion to the amount the soil organic matter is lowered. Irrigation increases symphylan population manyfold. In some farm fields where cultural practice results in very low organic matter, symphylans become so hungry that large, circular bare spots are created by them where nothing will grow.

It's a common belief that first there were no symphylans in a field, then the grower manured, then the symphylans became worse and worse. "The symphylans came to this spot in the manure," is a common lament. Actually, symphylans were already there in small numbers. Manure, along with irrigation, permitted a population increase. Relatively slow-breeding critters for insects, symphylans take several years to increase and match the humus content in the soil.

The first year after manuring, crops grow wonderfully because manure increases fertility and the ability of the crops to develop root systems. From this point, the story can go two ways. If sufficient manure is worked in to further increase soil friability, fertility, and tilth, crops further increase their ability to grow rapidly, making more roots than the symphylans will want to eat. And, as the symphylans increase, so do certain predator beetles. Eventually, a stasis is reached in the symphylan population. At this point, crops still grow excellently. If organic matter additions are insufficient after the initial manuring, soil humus begins to decline rapidly, while symphylan population has increased. Harder, less friable soil also limits the predator beetle's ability to move through the soil, and limits the crop's ability to develop good root systems. Within two or three years, the soil organic matter returns to its native level—or possibly lower if fertilizers are used without green manuring or other soil-building practices.

In the garden, the first thing is to recognize that symphylans may be the problem. Small, stunted plants that wilt easily and that don't grow despite fertilization or watering are a warning signal. Sometimes seeds won't germinate because symphylans eat off the root tip of the seedling before the leaves even emerge from the soil. This happens especially to members of the cabbage family. Symphylans are about one-quarter-inch long, skinny, yellowish or cream-colored, with many legs. They live in soil and if exposed to light will scurry rapidly back into the soil. They can be discovered around the poorly rooted stems of stunted plants.

If symphylan damage is occurring, increase the humus content of the soil by annual manuring. Chicken manure has too low an organic matter content for this purpose, but one or two inches of horse, cow, goat, or rabbit manure, or an inch of compost tilled in annually will coax the symphylans away from roots, while improving root development in general, and allow you to coexist better. Sowing more seed than usual may permit symphylans to eat some, while leaving enough to establish a stand. Another strategy is to set out transplants instead of direct-seeding if damage is so severe that tiny seedlings don't grow or won't even sprout. At the Territorial Seed Company trial grounds, we have to grow broccoli, cabbage, and cauliflower trials this way, though in my personal garden, which is manured annually, symphylans are not a problem at all.

Another treatment similar to manuring is to feed the symphylans rootlets of a ground cover that the symphylans like to nibble on, then set vegetables into this ground cover and hoe away the trap crop as the vegetables grow. We sow our cabbage family trials thickly with buckwheat about two weeks before the transplants are ready to go out, then set the transplants into a well-fertilized bare spot made with a hoe in the living buckwheat mulch. As the seedlings grow, the buckwheat is hoed back and away. Buckwheat is used because (1) symphylans like to eat it; (2) it is easily killed by hoeing and grows lushly in even fairly infertile soil, and (3) the seed is cheap and easily available at feed dealers and from health food stores. If buckwheat were not sown and the ground tilled bare, which is the usual practice before transplants are set out, every symphylan there would eat the small transplants. When the ground is covered with alternative good food, the symphylans have no reason to concentrate on vegetables.

Flea Beetles

Flea beetles are tiny, black, hopping insects that bore holes in the leaves of members of the cabbage family and potatoes, but that occasionally can feed off many other vegetables. They particularly like sucking on the cotyledons (the first two leaves that emerge) of seedling cabbage family members. In heavy numbers they can stunt and even kill seedlings. However, fast-growing, healthy plants will not be seriously stunted, though their leaves may be highly perforated.

Overwintering adult beetles migrate to the garden in spring from surrounding fields where they naturally feed on wild plants, and begin to feed on vegetables as soon as they have sprouted or been transplanted. Later in spring, the adults lay eggs, which quickly hatch out in the soil. These larvae feed on various roots and potato tubers until they pupate. After maturing, the beetles then continue to feed

Chart 8

*The Effect of Single Manuring on Symphylan
Population and Plant Growth*

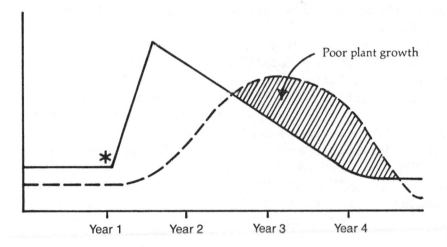

Poor plant growth

Year 1   Year 2   Year 3   Year 4

*The Effect of Repeated Manuring on Symphylan
Population and Plant Growth*

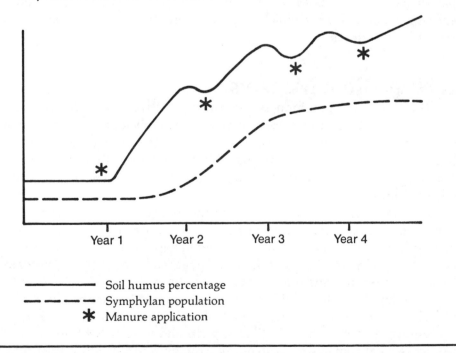

Year 1   Year 2   Year 3   Year 4

——————— Soil humus percentage
— — — — — Symphylan population
✻ Manure application

on the garden until they hibernate in fall.

With cabbage family vegetables, flea beetles can usually be handled by raising transplants or overseeding. Simply moving the growing transplants to a tabletop three feet off the ground prevents the beetles from hopping up on the leaves.

Once the transplants are in the two-leaf stage and growing fast, and *if* they continue rapid growth once set out, little flea beetle damage will occur. To overseed, plant ten to fifteen seeds for every mature plant wanted, allowing nature to do a bit of thinning via the flea beetle and then completing the job yourself after the seedlings are well up and growing fast.

Severe infestations can be handled with several types of pesticides, the safest being rotenone, an organic spray made from ground plant root and available as a dust or as a powder to mix with water. Rotenone is very effective, though short-lasting, and should be sprayed every few days until the seedlings are growing well.

If well-developed plants are being too heavily damaged, it is likely that the best strategy is to improve the soil tilth by additions of manure or compost and/or to increase the level of fertilizer.

In England, there is a seed treatment commonly used called gamma beta toxin—essentially a virus culture—that is used to coat seeds in the cole family. The virus is fatal to flea beetles. Seed treated with this substance is unbothered by flea beetles for about six weeks after emergence. This is long enough, because after six weeks, coles have developed several true leaves and cannot be much harmed by flea beetles unless their growth is almost entirely checked. I know gamma beta toxin works because I've received trial samples from English seed companies. The treatment costs about fifty cents per pound of seed, or about fifty cents per acre!

I cannot sell seed treated with this substance, nor import it for commercial sale, because it has not been approved by the Environmental Protection Agency. To obtain such approval would cost over two million dollars, and no one I've approached about it has shown the interest or seen the commercial potential of replacing chemical sprays, which cost a lot more than fifty cents per acre, with a safe, organic material.

Cabbage Root Maggots

The cabbage fly, an innocent-appearing relative of the common housefly, usually waits until the root system of a cabbage family member is large enough to support a brood of larvae before laying its eggs on the soil's surface near the plant. After hatching, the larvae (or maggots) burrow down and begin to feed on the root system of the host plant. Heavy infestations on small plants can wilt, stunt, or kill the host.

The gardener discovers the work of the maggot when his cabbage, broccoli, cauliflower, and brussels sprout plants wilt and collapse or become stunted and barely grow. The maggots are also discovered happily tunneling into turnips and radishes—though they tend to leave rutabagas alone. Usually, the damage is already done by the time the maggots are noticed.

Growing the more weakly rooted cabbage family members without pesticides can require persistent attention. Making soil more fertile so that it contains an abundance of nutrients (fertilizing well) and is very light and airy (adding manure) so that root systems can develop rapidly and strongly is the first step. In very fertile garden soil around Lorane, the root maggots do not do noticeable damage to better-rooted varieties of cabbage, broccoli, or brussels sprouts, though the delicately rooted cauliflower is often destroyed. Radishes and turnips do become riddled with larvae and their brown tunnels. Severity of maggots depends on location and on the year's weather.

To protect root crops and other cabbage family members additionally, fine sawdust is a good control. A collar of sawdust around the plant 1 to 1½ inches thick and 4 to 6 inches in diameter, if carefully maintained, will prevent the fly from laying its eggs on the soil's surface. Sowing radish and turnip seeds on the soil's surface instead of in a furrow, and covering them with a 4-inch-wide, 1-inch-deep band of sawdust, does the same thing.

The late Blair Adams, research horticulturist for Washington State University Extension Service, did extensive trials with the traditional root maggot remedies and found this sawdust collar to be the most effective. He also found that treatments with wood ashes increased maggot numbers, though they might also increase the growth ability of cabbage family plants in acid soils enough to compensate for that.

Root maggots have a population cycle and the gardener can avoid much trouble by planting around their population curve. There are usually high levels of maggots during May to early June and again in late summer. Usually mature plants are not ruined by maggots, so if a cole plant is sown in early June after the spring population peak, it will be full sized before the maggots again reach plague level.

The Cabbage Worm

Larvae of a small, white butterfly often seen fluttering about the garden, the cabbage worm quickly hatches from clusters of small, round, greenish eggs laid on leaves of cole plants during the summer. The larvae grow rapidly as they consume leaves of the host plant and can do a great deal of damage in the few days it takes them to reach their full length of one inch.

In a small garden, handpicking the larvae and tossing them away from any cabbage family plant is sufficient control. An extremely effective, nontoxic pesticide called *Bacillus thuringiensis*, is available, and marketed as BT, Dipel, or Thuricide, available in many garden centers. BT can be sprayed the day of harvest because it is a bacterial culture lethal only to the cabbage worm and a few close relatives.

Illustration 7

Using a Sawdust Collar to Protect against Cabbage Root Maggots

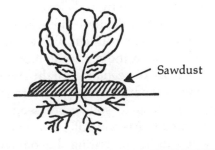

Sawdust

Mexican Bean Beetles

Similar in appearance to the beneficial ladybug, the bean beetle adult is yellow, with sixteen black spots arranged in rows on its back. The beetles and their larvae attack pods, stems, and leaves of bean plants primarily, but also eat beet seedlings and other garden vegetables on occasion. The adult beetles hibernate during the winter in weeds and begin feeding in spring. After a few weeks of feeding, small, yellowish eggs are laid on the underside of leaves, which then hatch into small, yellow, many-legged larvae that feed on and skeletonize leaves and bean pods. The larvae pupate on the leaves and in ten days hatch as adults. Two to three generations are produced each summer.

Damage to plants is usually minimal, though in cool weather, slow-growing bean seedlings can be chewed down as fast as they grow and many pods can be damaged when the plants are in full production. To combat an infestation, rotenone is very effective sprayed or dusted. Because the beetles overwinter on garden debris, carefully composting all bean plant waste and other vegetation preferred by the adult beetles possibly will reduce their number.

Aphids

Aphids (or plant lice) are small, soft-bodied insects that cluster on leaves and stems, sucking sap from the plant. Their presence causes leaves to curl and cup. In large numbers, they can weaken or stunt a plant, reducing yields. Aphids can multiply with amazing rapidity. They also carry plant diseases such as pea enation.

Aphids often have a close relationship with ants. The ants breed aphids, place them on leaves, and then harvest a sweet secretion produced by the aphids. Controlling aphids often entails elimination of ant colonies.

Aphids can be sprayed off leaves with a hose and, once removed, will not find their way back to the host plant. Safer's Soap or a tobacco spray (nicotine sulfate) will effectively end aphid infestations. If ants are colonizing aphids in the garden, they may be eliminated safely by setting out ant poison stakes. These contain sugar poisoned with arsenic; the ants carry the sugar into their nest and feed it to their larvae and queen, thus wiping out the nest.

We have noticed in our trial grounds that aphids prefer certain varieties and usually attack only the more poorly growing ones; so good soil and healthy plants eliminate many problems.

Slugs

More garden damage is done by the small gray slug than by its larger and more noticeable relatives. Slugs eat seedlings, can ruin new plantings in a few nights, and nestle inside lettuce and cabbage heads. They'll also damage fruit, preferring ripening tomatoes.

Slugs hide and breed under garden debris, so keeping soil clean, removing garden trash carefully to a compost pile, and eliminating daytime hiding places will reduce population levels. Slugs are one reason that year-round mulch gardening, so popular in the East, is an unworkable technique in the maritime Northwest. Gardeners who find slugs totally consuming rows of seedlings might switch to later sowings when weather conditions are warmer and seedling growth faster. Another technique to improve seedling survival is to sow more seeds than actually wanted so the slugs will have something to eat and still leave a stand of plants. Banding fertilizer below seedlings also aids in preventing slug damage by acceleration of seedling growth rates.

Large populations of slugs may be reduced by trapping. The easiest method is to lay 1-inch by 6-inch boards on the garden paths. Each morning at sunrise, the slugs will hide under these boards. The gardener can then turn the boards over during the day, handpick the slugs, and drop them into a jar of detergent solution, salt water, or gasoline, or sprinkle a bit of salt on them. Though I am generally opposed to using chemical insecticides, slug baits made only with methaldehyde are acceptable to me, but not to really "religious" organic gardeners! Methaldehyde is a simple organic substance similar to wood alcohol that the slugs love to intoxicate themselves to death with. It need not be used in the garden to control garden slugs, but instead may be sprinkled in a 12-inch-wide band outside the entire garden like a fence or barrier. Since slugs do not know where they are located and travel at random, a barrier of slug bait will prevent slugs outside the garden from entering for several weeks, while the slugs in the garden tend to leave it, also dying on the barrier. Reactivated every few weeks, a slug bait barrier can quickly reduce the garden population to less than 10 percent of what it was.

Leaf Miners

Leaf miners are the larvae of a small fly, similar to the cabbage or carrot fly. However, these larvae enjoy tunneling through the leaves of beets, chard, and spinach, as well as occasionally enjoying other plants, too. I have not had any trouble with leaf miners, fortunately.

Lately, a new product came on the market called Reemay, which is a spun-polyester fabric somewhat like very light mosquito netting, used both for insect control and as a growth-enhancing cloche. A section of this material was sent to a Washington gardener who complained of leaf miners completely ruining every beet crop he grew. The gardener carefully covered most of a beet bed with Reemay after the seeds were large enough to thin and weed and kept it there until harvest. The unprotected beets nearby were totally ruined—not one plant survived to make a beet. Under the Reemay, there was a fine harvest, though the fabric did drop light levels by about 15 percent, and the beets were a bit toppy, with smaller roots than he would have liked. The solution is probably to thin them a bit further than usual. I know of no organic insecticide that will control leaf miners effectively, and only this screening-out approach seems workable. Reemay is also a good control for the cabbage root maggot and carrot maggot.

Carrot Maggots

This is a pest with which I have had little experience. I know from literature that the fly begins breeding rapidly in late summer and will go through a generation every month, often increasing in numbers through midwinter if the weather isn't too severe. Carrots started in late May after the spring hatch is through may well finish their cycle relatively unharmed and be harvested by late summer. However, carrots left in the ground become increasingly infested as the winter progresses.

By covering the carrot bed with Reemay when the tops are three inches tall, and thinning the carrots to about 150 percent of their normal spacing to allow for the slight loss of light, a gardener can expect a crop of maggot-free carrots. Gardeners have used solutions similar to Reemay for years, building screened cages for their carrots to prevent the fly from gaining access to the roots.

Storing the carrots during winter by carefully laying a few inches of straw over them for insulation and covering that with a piece of plastic that has its edges well buried might prevent fly access to the stored roots, though it will make a wonderful haven for field mice.

Know Your "Attacker"

When something has been attacking your garden, be sure you know what is actually causing the trouble before you spray or take other action. Go out and observe the plants carefully until you *see* the culprit. If necessary, go out at night with a flashlight. Are the "cutworms" really rabbits? One grower I know had wilting tomato plants. He was told that nematodes (little worms that infest roots) were at fault and that a soil poison was called for. He investigated himself and found to his chagrin that the soil under the tomatoes was bone-dry, starting at about eight inches. He had been underwatering.

It is early September as I write these paragraphs. Back in July, I planted some cabbage plants for my winter harvest. A few weeks after I sowed the nursery bed, I worked up a rich growing area for the cabbages. When the transplants were about four inches tall, I set them out into their growing bed, but I had eight transplants left over. Not wanting to destroy them, I searched the garden and finally found a spot in the corner where I had not done any soil improvement. The area had never been manured and had no rock phosphate. I had not needed that space before, but it was inside the deer fence. "What the hell," I said to myself. "I'll set those plants in that spot and fertilize them well."

Now it is September. The cabbages set out in prepared soil are all about two feet in diameter, healthy, vigorous, and heading up. The ones in the unimproved soil are about eight inches in diameter, and they have been severely attacked by both cabbage worms (for which I sprayed with Dipel) and slugs (which I hand-picked every few days), and now aphids are settling on them in droves. The healthy plants were never bothered by anything. Needless to say, I have finally abandoned the little ones and am letting the bugs have them.

Some organicists believe that insects actually are like the wolves that trail a caribou herd. They fulfill the beneficial function of letting the strong ones reproduce. If you grow a strong seed in weak soil, it becomes a weak plant subject to insect attack.

Once I had a row of brussels sprouts. Only one of the twelve plants was attacked by aphids, and it was repeatedly reinfested after I washed them off. Out of curiosity, instead of spraying, I eventually dug the plant out and found that the root system had been damaged when I had transplanted it months ago. There was a sort of a J in the root that crimped it and reduced the flow of nutrients to the leaves.

I could relate many similar anecdotes. If the gardener will simply make fertile soil, tithe to nature, learn to accept bugs without being squeamish, and abandon efforts to get something for nothing, gardening can become a source of almost unparalleled pleasure.

How to Grow Them: General Recommendations

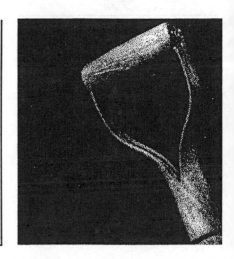

Like most garden writers, I tend to generalize from my own experience. It is not my intention, however, for the reader to take my recommendations as gospel. All my maritime Northwest gardening has been done on one soil series, on one Coast Range hillside in Lorane, Oregon. The soil is fairly poor from the perspective of growing vegetables, though the fir trees increase two feet a year on it. Lorane's climate is more severe than in the Willamette Valley. Since I left California, I have not had the pleasure of growing things on any Class-One, or even Class-Two agricultural ground. Every time I visit the variety trials at Oregon State University's Corvallis Vegetable Crops Research Farm, I am reminded how vegetables are supposed to perform when expertly grown on first-class soil.

In some ways, it is fortunate I did not get good soil and a benevolent microclimate to work with. If I can grow something at Lorane, then almost anyone in the maritime Northwest should be able to. For example, at my trial grounds, most onion varieties do not bulb well, and those that do bulb make only medium-small-sized onions. At the Oregon State University trials, every variety we've ever failed with grows big, beautiful onions of the largest sizes. So, I've learned to coax a bulb out of an onion on soil that is not suited to this crop, as well as finding varieties that require the minimum of coaxing.

It may be much easier to grow some types of vegetables than I suggest it is—in certain soils and in certain locations. But everything I suggest works for me and derives from my experience—and that experience includes six years of conducting cultural and varietal trials for a regional seed company, growing hundreds of varieties each year on three-quarters acre of handworked plots. Following my advice should work for almost anyone anywhere in the maritime Northwest.

Vegetable Varieties

Maritime Northwest gardeners are well advised to get smart about vegetable varieties. In some cases, like carrots, any variety will perform as long as the soil is not too heavy or shallow. But other types of vegetables demand critical choices. For example, with our 120- to 175-day frost-free growing season, sweet corn varieties that take more than 85 days to mature usually do not ripen before the weather falls apart in October. Early tomatoes ripen midsummer at best; "mid-season" varieties ripen in September many years; while "main-season" varieties never ripen at all. And only the warmest parts of the maritime Northwest will permit melons to make good vine growth or ripen fruit at all—and at that, only a few varieties will grow well.

Yes, hot-weather crops grow much more slowly in the cool summers of the maritime Northwest than they do at the home office of midwestern or eastern seed companies. But cool-weather crops grow just about as fast here as they do back east, so varieties that are bred for the East, to mature and be harvested by sometime in October, do not give the gardener a chance at long-standing winter harvesting west of the Cascades. This book makes specific recommendations about vegetable varieties, based on carefully conducted varietal trials and research. However, if your favorite variety is not mentioned, this does not mean I disapprove or disagree. My trials have not included every popular variety on the market, nor have they studied everything offered by every United States seed company. But what I recommend *will* work, and it will taste good and grow well in a home garden environment.

I wish I could wholeheartedly recommend the offerings found on local seed racks, but I cannot. First of all, most seed rack jobbers serve more territory than the maritime Northwest. They apparently feel that to make a profit, a single assortment must be set out in their entire service area, while at the same time, their growing instructions must be so vague as to apply universally. (The pictures on seed packets are often not even pictures of the enclosed varieties, but are what is called in the trade, "representative photos.") When I see a Willamette Valley rack selling okra or Hale's Best Jumbo melons, I get very sad. Both may do very well *east* of the Cascades.

Rack companies also feel they are in a severely competitive business. After paying the store 50 percent on sales and deducting overhead and distribution costs, there is not much left to cover the large number of unsold and dated packets that must be discarded each year. So the packets are usually filled with the most inexpensive seed obtainable, or with very small quantities of more expensive items. To make the packeting process more efficient, their automatic seed packeting machines run all summer and fall, filling shiny packets with year-old seed, stamped "packed for next year." This year-old seed is not warehoused under climate-controlled conditions, and though it certainly will germinate above minimum levels prescribed under the state and federal seed laws, it often does not retain sufficient vigor to please the buyer.

Buying garden seed by mail is not necessarily a sure way to get top-quality seed at better prices. Even more than rack jobbers, mail-order garden seed companies are trying to serve as large a region as possible. They cannot tell the reader which variety is best adapted to their location, but instead must describe how the vegetable grows either at the home office trial grounds, or in that district of the country where the variety is grown commercially.

Some mail-order companies are also selling cheap seed that may not be fresh or vigorous. They purchase seed from the same low-priced seed wholesalers used by the rack jobbers, presenting mediocre items in glowing terms with beautiful color pictures. Fortunately, many seed sellers are not this unethical, and there are a few sellers of quality seed whose selections also largely suit our region that I can recommend without qualification. There are other excellent companies, like Park, for example, which I do not list in this book because most of their effort and descriptive information is oriented to the South. Not being recommended in this book is no condemnation. Generally, if one buys seed from a mail-order supplier that has a large commercial trade, the same high-quality seed sold to the farmer will be available.

I can broadly recommend two companies, since almost everything in their catalogs will grow well in the maritime Northwest. One is Johnny's Selected Seeds, Albion, Maine 04910. The other is my own company, Territorial Seed Company, P.O. Box 27, Lorane, Oregon 97451. Located in a cool area of Maine and selling only varieties that do well at their trial grounds, Johnny's services gardeners and growers across the northernmost tier of the United States and southern Canada. Johnny's is a small, privately owned company. Maine is similar climatically to the maritime Northwest *in the summertime,* so Johnny's summer vegetables do well in our cool region. However, their fall crops are better adapted to short seasons and mature too quickly in many cases. They all grow well here, but shorten fall harvests by the speed of their maturity. Johnny's sells only top-quality seeds and has in-house germination standards that are much higher than those the Federal Seed Act prescribes. Their seeds usually have good vigor.

My own company, Territorial Seed Company, serves only western Oregon and western Washington, with a few customers in coastal northern California and the Lower Mainland of British Columbia. All varietal descriptions and cultural suggestions apply to performance at Lorane, Oregon. Territorial offers almost every type of vegetable that can be grown in a maritime region and obtains these seeds from England, Holland, Denmark, and Japan, as well as from quality United States primary seed producing companies. Because ambient conditions at Lorane are very humid most of the year, the seed is stored under climate control to reduce deterioration and enhance vigor. Territorial has its own in-house germination standards, designed to eliminate seed lacking in vigor. All work of this company is done on a five-acre homestead.

Stokes Seeds, 737 Main Street, Buffalo, New York 14240 is a medium-sized private company that sells primarily to commercial growers in the northern United States and southern Canada. Its commercial offerings are of the highest quality. Stokes also sells some home-garden varieties of lower quality, though still with acceptable germination and vigor. Stokes obtains seed from major suppliers throughout the world, as well as growing a few dozen varieties of their own. The Stokes catalog is an amazingly complete and overwhelming experience. Before I went into the seed business, I bought from this company almost exclusively because I was delighted at such a large and interesting selection.

The Joseph Harris Company, Moreton Farm, Rochester, New York 14624, is a large corporation and one of the finest commercial seed suppliers in the world. Harris has an active and vigorous breeding program, producing their own hybrid varieties. Harris does not sell much "home garden quality" seed. Were I a commercial grower, I'd be their customer. Harris tends to serve the North, so much of their stuff grows well in the maritime Northwest, though some of it demands more heat than we get. I'd avoid all but their very earliest hot-weather varieties.

Saving on Seed Purchases

Most gardeners are fearful of using leftover seed and so purchase small packets each year. This usually is false economy because most of the cost of a small packet of inexpensive seed is not the seed itself, but handling. Usually the envelope costs more than the seed when low-priced, small packets are bought. For example, a half-gram packet of open-pollinated cabbage seed may sell for 70¢, while four grams sells for 90¢ and one ounce (twenty-eight grams) sells for $1.50. On a unit cost basis, the seed in a small packet costs twelve times as much per gram as an ounce packet.

Most seed has a useful life of over one year—in fact, most seed will germinate vigorously for three or more years after harvest. If reasonably fresh seed is purchased (which it will likely be if obtained from a reputable source), the gardener can expect to use it for several seasons and often longer. For example, I once bought an ounce of rutabaga seed from the Harris Company in 1973, which still sprouted excellently in 1979 when I went into the seed business myself. That ounce had grown all my rutabaga patches from 1973 until 1979 for hardly twice the price of a small-sized packet. The only types of seed I'd hesitate to stock up on would be very expensive hybrids and leek, onion, scallion, parsnip, spinach, and hybrid corn, all of which tend to be very short-lived.

Storing Seed

The way to overcome the fear of using old seed is to adopt the practice of discarding any packet immediately after germination if it no longer sprouts strongly and grows rapidly after emergence (if the weather is favorable). Slow, weak germination is a reliable indication of loss of vigor; and very likely, a slightly weak lot will be much too weak a year later. However, if the lot came up well one year, it can be reasonably expected to do so the next. The gardener can also greatly retard the aging of seed by careful storage, easily making seed last four times as long as it would under normal household conditions.

There is a rule of thumb about seed storage that states: for every drop in temperature of 10 degrees Fahrenheit, combined with a corresponding reduction of seed moisture content of 1 percent, the life of the seed doubles. So, if normal room conditions are 70 degrees and 70 percent relative humidity, dropping the temperature to 50 degrees and lowering the humidity of the air by 20 to 30 percent will drop the seed moisture 3 to 4 percent, quadrupling the storage life. This is very easily accomplished at home. Simply putting used packets in a sealed mason jar in the refrigerator *with* an effective desiccant in the jar drops the temperature to nearly 40 degrees and greatly reduces the seed moisture content. An inch of fresh, dry, powdered milk on the bottom of the storage jar makes a reasonably good desiccant. Even better is a rechargeable silica gel packet such as expensive electronic equipment comes packed with. These can sometimes be obtained from chemical supply companies and from home food preservation stores. It would not be unreasonable to expect a bag of fresh brassica or carrot seed to last ten years under climate-controlled storage.

Hybrid versus Open-Pollinated Seeds

The issue of hybrid versus open-pollinated seeds was raised by scientists and politicians associated with third-world projects and the United Nations agricultural development effort. They pointed out that as modern agriculture penetrated the underdeveloped nations, farmers were switching to new varieties provided by their governments and the international seed companies. These improved crops were grown with chemical fertilizers and sprays obtained from multinational corporations, and many of these international conglomerates included the very same seed companies producing the seeds. When the farmers grew new varieties, they allowed their traditional open-pollinated varieties to disappear and, consequently, a huge genetic resource for plant breeders was fast disappearing. Where a district might have used hundreds of traditional varieties, now only one might be grown, and that one was often a hybrid. Since the disappearing varieties had previously provided genetic material to western plant breeders that enabled them to develop disease- or insect-resistant new types, the loss of this genetic resource could well mean that the next new crop disease might reign unopposed.

Some overzealous proponents of this concern point to the links between the multinationals and their effect on the planet and infer a plot to dominate the earth by controlling food production through seed and chemical monopoly. Technological advances of these companies are often viewed by their critics as nefarious schemes. It is true that the growth and power of the multinational seed companies are aided by plant variety patenting laws, and supposedly only large seed companies have the resources to develop hybrid seeds with qualities much superior to the older open-pollinated types, so their opponents attack hybrid seeds as a trap for the small farmer and poor nations both, and organize anti-plant variety protection actions when such laws are being made.

It is also said that hybrids do not make viable seeds themselves, so the user of hybrids is totally dependent on his or her supplier for new seed each year. This may lead, it is feared, to control of world food supplies by multinationals. In truth, hybrids *do* make viable seeds that can be saved by the gardener. However, the seed produced will not grow uniform plants exactly like the parents. Instead, the progeny of a hybrid will consist of many variable types, some productive, some relatively useless. Within a season or two, a decent open-pollinated strain could be refined out of this assortment by an amateur plant breeder. This means that should suppliers of hybrid seeds become arrogant or overly greedy, and should this greed not be checked by competition between multinationals, and should open-pollinated varieties *totally* disappear from the market, seed consumers still have the choice of developing their own varieties and of growing seeds themselves.

Rapidly increasing populations demand more food production, and modern varieties seem more productive if grown with sufficient petro-chemical inputs. So farmers and planners in undeveloped nations are virtually forced by population pressures to increase production by any means possible, even if this means the extinction of traditional varieties. When the American gardener says, as many have, "I will avoid hybrid vegetable seeds because I wish to prevent the loss of open-pollinated varieties," he or she is attempting to resist a very powerful trend.

Actually, the situation hardly concerns vegetable seeds at all. Crops such as wheat, rice, corn, sorghum, barley, oats, millet, and sesame are the world's major food sources. Should genetic impoverishment result in massive cabbage failures or a complete loss of tomatoes, some growers might be bankrupted and the public inconvenienced. But, should there be a wheat disaster, the planet might well experience widespread starvation and the accompanying social unrest. Additionally, the companies producing vegetable seed are usually not the same as those in the field seed business.

So it behooves gardeners to consider carefully if there are any advantages to hybrid vegetable varieties, before discarding their use out of hand. During the past six years, I have been doing exactly that myself, on a scale far beyond that of the home gardener, and rather scientifically. Reluctantly, I have come to believe that hybrid seeds are a lot better for the home garden than many of the existing open-pollinated types still available. I did not wish to discover this and, in fact, it took me several years of trials for the condition of open-pollinated vegetable varieties and their contemporary deterioration to dawn on me. My initial bias was toward open-pollinated types, so my first years of trials compared these varieties, intentionally avoiding hybrids. But, an occasional hybrid variety did get into our trials and inevitably outperformed all the open-pollinated seeds. Eventually, our trial grounds included both types freely.

In many cases, today's open-pollinated vegetable varieties are not what they once were. Commercial demand today is for hybrids. This means the open-pollinated varieties get short shrift from breeding/quality control sections of the major seed-producing companies and, consequently, their uniformity is deteriorating rapidly. Lack of commercial interest in open-pollinated varieties also means that when they are produced, it is mainly for the garden seed trade. Gardeners, not understanding fully the nature of seed quality, are what is commonly (and privately) referred to in the seed trade as "not a critical trade." In other words, gardeners do not have the experience with seed to know if what they are getting is of good quality or not. So open-pollinated varieties are allowed to become very ragged because roguing fields and stock seed maintenance are expensive. Seed for open-pollinated varieties is not produced as frequently as it used to be when they were commercial items. This means that when a gardener buys an old standard, he or she is most likely receiving seed with less vigor that has been in the warehouse for many years before being sold. Top commercial varieties, on the other hand, have a huge market demand, and are grown frequently by the primary producers of seed. So, if hybrids are available, they have taken over the commercial market and will almost inevitably be the best, strongest, and freshest seed, as well as being highly uniform.

Hybridization produces seed with additional vigor. This phenomenon of "hybrid vigor" is well known to breeders. We have experienced it ourselves in our trials. Hybrid seeds sprout a little quicker and stronger. Hybrid seedlings grow a little faster and, in general, resist insects and diseases a little better. Their edible portions are a little larger, appear a bit sooner, and sometimes taste a little better. Many commercial hybrids are bred more for appearance and strong growth than for superior flavor and table qualities, but many hybrids are truly superior vegetables that have excellent eating qualities and have a place in even the most gourmet vegetable garden.

Hybrids are particularly useful in the small garden, where every plant counts. Not only is every plant more likely to grow and yield, but the uniformity of hybrids can be especially important in this situation. If the gardener is only growing three cabbages, all three are vital. If one should fail to head properly, it is a minor disaster. Hybrid varieties are much less likely to grow improperly. Poorly rogued, variable open-pollinated varieties often contain plants that do not make properly formed food. It is common, for example, in our cabbage trials to inspect open-pollinated varieties that have a 60 percent round heading rate—40 percent of the plants are so atypical that they don't make decent heads. Sown commercially, ragged varieties like this would probably result in a lawsuit. Sown in the garden by a "noncritical" individual, they usually result in a confusion as to why those individual plants failed to head out—was it weather? Fertility?

Many types of good open-pollinated varieties still exist, primarily because hybridization of these species is not commercially feasible at this time. So, there are no hybrid lettuces on the market yet, nor hybrid beans or peas. High-quality open-pollinated stocks of these sorts are still sold. However, hybrid cabbages, broccoli, and brussels sprouts have virtually replaced the open-pollinated varieties on the commercial market, leaving few open-pollinated selections of any quality at this time. Hybrid cucumbers and melons are becoming dominant rapidly. Hybrid summer squashes are already the industry standards. Hybrid carrots are soon to replace the open-pollinated types. Hybrid corn took over the market twenty-five years ago, and today open-pollinated corn varieties yield at best half of that derived from hybrids.

New Propagation Technology

Recently, a combination of new technologies has promised to eliminate the use of seeds altogether on crops that can be raised from transplants. The first is modular transplanting. Not too well known in the United States, transplanting can be accelerated and made more efficient by the use of small, modular growing trays that contain individual seedlings in tiny cells. Field survival rates of modularized seedlings are very high, *and* transplanting itself can be done mechanically. In Europe, many farmers no longer seed their crops nor grow their own transplants, but instead buy transplants from professional growers. In some cases, the transplant grower also possesses automated transplanting machines and contracts to set them out for a very low fixed cost per acre.

The European seed industry has responded to this development by producing seed of amazingly high uniformity and germination ability, so the modular trays can be direct-seeded and will contain over ninety-five plants per hundred spaces.

Another recent advance is called micropropagation or tissue culture. In a laboratory, plants may be divided up into microscopic slices containing only a few cells each. Each cutting is propagated under controlled conditions in special nutrient baths in tiny test tubes. Within a short time, tiny new seedlings can be produced ready to transplant into modular growing trays. Literally hundreds of thousands of seedling-sized plants can be developed from a single parent. This means that it may soon be commercially feasible to produce transplants from "mother plants" by the million without ever using seed.

The ramifications of this are mind-boggling! Though it is possible to hybridize cabbage inexpensively and grow extraordinarily uniform and vigorous plants from hybrid seed, it is not possible to do so with lettuce, for example. I once saw twenty-five row feet of hybrid lettuce growing at the Oregon State University trial grounds. Every seed had to have been made by careful "surgery" of lettuce flowers, and if produced for sale would have cost several dollars a seed. (Plant breeders do this frequently to produce new open-pollinated varieties.) Compared to some well-grown standard varieties in adjoining rows, this hybrid was twice the size. Imagine fast-growing head lettuces the size of *large* cabbages!

Plant breeders frequently can produce amazing individual plants. The trick is then to get a true-breeding seed stock similar to this amazing individual. But with micropropagation and modular transplanting systems, it would be possible to take any unique plant and make a commercial variety of it, keeping the mother plants alive in a greenhouse and selling seedlings. Doing so would avoid the years of refinement needed by standard plant breeding technologies.

I do not know how the seed industry could deal with a situation in which seed were no longer needed and in which any lucky cross could become a variety and in which micropropagation laboratories would be relatively inexpensive to set up. The future is very interesting and in no way certain to go one way or another.

Saving Seed at Home

In the first edition of this book, a fair amount of space was devoted to information about saving seeds at home. Had I been more aware of the factors going into making good seed, I would not have recommended the practice so glibly. Producing vegetable seeds of high vigor and purity is a specialist's art, though a few types of vegetables do readily lend themselves to home seed production.

Every gardener is capable of producing good bean and pea seed by simply allowing a few choice plants to mature seeds without harvesting any of the pods, drying them on the vine, and storing them in a paper sack in the back of a closet until the next year. These are also the types of seed my customers spend the most money on. Beans do not cross-pollinate and require no isolation. Peas rarely cross and for garden purposes this slight tendency may be ignored. Tomato and pepper seed from open-pollinated varieties is also easily kept.

In the cultural information that follows, I have retained information from the previous edition about how to grow and harvest seed of most garden vegetables. To obtain really vigorous seed of many species, weather conditions during the period of seed formation and timely harvest when seed is at the proper moisture level are critical. That is why commercial seed crops are concentrated in certain districts where the climate is as perfect as possible for the type being grown. So virtually all the world's cabbage, beet, and spinach seed is grown in the Skagit Valley; most of the carrot seed in the United States and for many European companies is produced in the Columbia Basin; onion seed comes from eastern Oregon/western Idaho; bean, pea, and sweet corn seed from southern Idaho; lettuce seed from California; squash seed from the high plains of Colorado and in the Sacramento Valley; broccoli seed from the Imperial Valley.

The home gardener cannot produce seed for every vegetable with the same vigor and quality as is done under optimal weather conditions, yet seed of acceptable vigor and quality can be grown at home most years. However, it may not retain high vigor as long. And, of course, some years home-grown seed can be better if weather conditions were not favorable in the commercial seed growing districts. Seed growing is a dicey business, and it is common to discover that a seed harvest has failed to germinate well enough to sell.

The home seed grower should take great care to allow seed time to dry down fully before harvest (if weather permits), or to dry it under cover before thrashing if necessary, and to store seed under very dry, cool conditions. Seed should not be dried at temperatures in excess of 85 degrees as a general rule. Additionally, seed should be harvested as soon as it dries down. Allowing seed to be repeatedly dampened by dews and to dry out weakens the seed greatly.

Planting Dates

Throughout this section, specific planting dates are given for each type of vegetable. These dates reflect average performance at Lorane, Oregon. To make this information more useful to others in the maritime Northwest, a table is included that shows how Lorane's climate relates to other microclimates in our region. It may also be helpful for the reader to know what the climate of Lorane is like.

Lorane, Oregon, is a small community located in the foothills of the Coast Range due west of Cottage Grove. The Lorane Valley is a mile wide at best, following the Siuslaw River for about ten miles and starting near the river's headwaters. Elevation of the valley floor is about 900 feet. Compared to Eugene, located twenty miles north of us (400 feet elevation), our temperatures are consistently 3 to 4 degrees cooler; Lorane's frost-free growing season is usually two weeks shorter on either end; and, our winter lows make conditions as severe as folks experience in western Washington.

Generally, this book's planting dates are quite workable anywhere in the maritime Northwest, though Willamette Valley, coastal, and southern Oregon gardeners might want to start hot-weather vegetables a few weeks earlier than I recommend and start crops for fall/winter harvest a week or so later than I suggest to avoid the earlier maturity that results from faster summer growth in warmer locales. Washington gardeners might want to plant fall/winter vegetables a week or so earlier than I suggest, so they attain sufficient size before winter sets in.

Every year there are differences in planting dates and growing times due to seasonal variation of weather. Though the dates given in this book do not reflect those variations, they are all what I consider to be "safe" dates. I've tried to be very conservative about not planting too early, nor suggesting that late sowings will

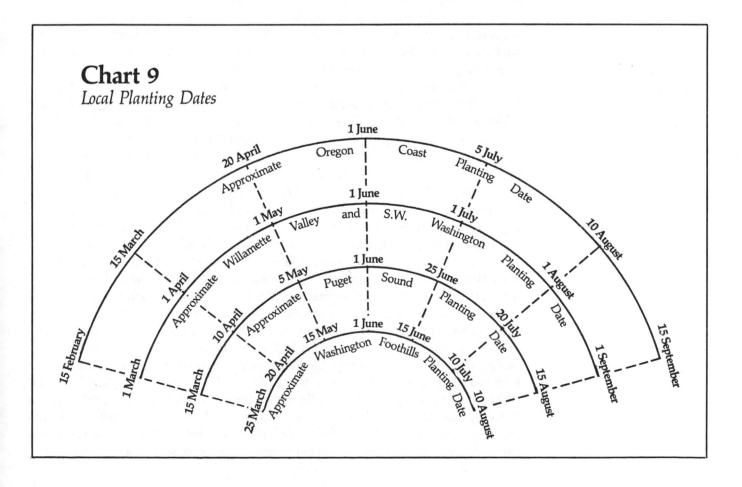

Chart 9
Local Planting Dates

have time to mature. But some years, sowing later than I recommend will work because the weather in late summer is warm and sunny with correspondingly rapid growth rates. Other years, spring is warm, sunny, and settled as early as March, allowing much earlier planting of most vegetables.

The smart gardener will begin to take these variations into account, getting a feel for weather conditions and soil temperatures. Guessing wrong can be financially catastrophic to a farmer, but the gardener will be out only some seed and work if sowing is done too soon, though sowing too late can mean no crop and a much higher food bill at the supermarket.

There is an aid one can use to anticipate the weather—observing growing plants. Much lore about planting dates exists and all of it involves observing the behavior of other plants as indicators of what to do. For example, when the crocus comes up, I know that overwintered alliums can now begin their spring growth rush and should be fertilized. When the apple trees begin to bloom, I know lettuce will grow; when the bloom is over, carrots will grow. I've found that a reliable indicator of a safe time to plant frost-sensitive things like tomatoes is when the cow parsnips bloom along the creek near my house.

Fertilizer Recommendations

Throughout the growing directions that follow, I recommend only organic fertilizers. Most frequently, the complete organic fertilizer blend I suggested in the beginning of this book is more than adequate. Sometimes variations on the blend are suggested to raise or lower the amount of and speed of nitrogen release compared to the other nutrients. All fertilizer is best banded below the seeds or seedlings, though occasionally side-dressing (sprinkling fertilizer on the soil's surface directly above the plant's root system) is required. For example, overwintered plants are side-dressed in early spring to hasten regrowth.

It is hard to make precise recommendations for quantities needed. Some soils have a high level of natural nutrient release, others are extremely poor. Regular additions of mineralized rocks and manures or composts will gradually build up even poor soils to the point that they may begin to release good levels of nutrients. So, fertilizer recommendations are given in ranges. The low range is what is suggested for fertile soils, where the soil itself might almost grow the plant adequately and only a bit of extra "vitamin" is needed. The higher amount is intended for new gardens in poor soils that haven't been much improved, especially in heavier soil types where as yet highly acid clays may attract and hold fertilizer-released nutrients almost as fast as they break down.

Many university-trained extension agents scoff at organic fertilizers and state firmly that they cannot release enough nutrients to grow a plant well. Let me state from my own experience that plants are capable of being overfertilized or "burned" by too heavy doses of seed meals and blood meal, to the point where seeds fail to sprout, seedlings stunt themselves, and plants fail to make much growth at all. One year I grew a bed of early coles, broccoli, cabbage, and cauliflower, transplanted early April with nearly a cup of organic fertilizer under each seedling. The previous year, this bed would have needed all this fertilizer. That year, the bed grew those coles rather poorly, even though I fertilized a bit more by side-dressing them, and even though the bed had been well composted the previous fall. Slightly puzzled, after harvesting the smallish plants, I resowed the bed to beets, and none would germinate or grow, despite a second sowing of several ounces of seed on the 100-square-foot bed. Next spring, after the bed would not grow fall-sown green manure either, I had the spot soil tested and it showed more than adequate nutritional levels for any crop, *after being leached heavily all winter.* The recommendation from the soil tester was no more fertilizer for several years, unless slow growth prompted a very light side-dressing on the most demanding of vegetables.

Plant Spacing

As discussed previously, there is no fixed rule for correct spacing of vegetables. Suggested spacings in the following section are what I use. In my garden and in the trials, these plant densities grow well-developed vegetables in moderately well-built-up soil with sufficient irrigation. Someone in the Willamette or more so in southern Oregon might want to space peppers farther apart than I suggest because, having a longer growing season, each plant will yield more. Lovers of giant beets might wish to increase my recommended spacing; lovers of baby beets might wish to decrease them. The same is true of cabbages, which will often vary considerably in size according to nutrition and spacing.

However, there are limits. Increasing plant spacing very much beyond what this book recommends will only create gaps in the row that serve no purpose unless irrigation is in short supply. That is because I like my vegetables well developed and large. Decreasing spacings below what I suggest may be all right for some crops and not for others. Lettuce, for example, especially heading varieties, will not form right if crowded. Carrots that compete with each other for light do not make good roots. Bush beans, on the other hand, will make larger yields of slightly smaller pods when grown on high densities. This may be desirable in a small, crowded backyard garden *if* the gardener doesn't mind spending a lot more time harvesting.

How to Grow Them: The Vegetable Families

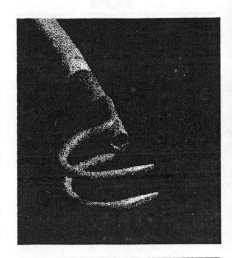

This, the largest section of my book, gives detailed cultural information by cultural group. Those scientifically trained might be slightly amused because I have not followed the strict rules of botanical classification, but instead have grouped vegetables as I think of them myself. But understanding vegetables as members of larger families that all are grown similarly helps a gardener handle new and unfamiliar species. I believe that thinking this way will also encourage you to experiment. These are the groups I use:

Solanaceae: eggplants, peppers, tomatoes

Legumes: beans, peas, green manures

Greens: celery, celeriac, corn salad, endive, lettuce, mustard, parsley, spinach, Swiss chard

Brassicas: broccoli, brussels sprouts, cabbage, Chinese cabbage, cauliflower, collards, kale, kohlrabi, rutabagas, turnips

Roots: beets, carrots, chicory, parsley, parsnips, potatoes, radishes

Cucurbits: cucumbers, melons, pumpkins, squashes

Alliums: garlic and shallots, leeks, onions

Miscellaneous: asparagus, sweet corn, dill

Solanaceae

Solanaceae are semitropical or tropical plants that we in the Northwest grow as frost-sensitive annuals that must be coddled and rushed into maturity before summer's end. In the tropics, some solanaceae may be perennials, making a continuous yield until they have exhausted their soil and lost vigor.

Very intolerant of cool conditions, especially in the seedling stages, solanaceae must be raised under climate-controlled conditions when small. Were seeds to be sown outdoors, germination might not be possible until mid-June when soils are approaching 70 degrees, and though growth might be rapid from such a sowing, the first ripe fruits would not appear until the end of summer at best. Instead, solanaceae are given a six- to eight-week head start by raising transplants in the house or hot/cold frame. This head start allows two and sometimes slightly more than two months of harvest.

It is not absolutely true that solanaceae must be started in a nursery as transplants. Professor Baggett always direct-seeds a considerable portion of his tomato trials at Oregon State University, Corvallis. Not interested in the absolute earliest yield and desiring to inspect many, many varieties and experimental crosses, he finds that if seeds are sown thickly about two weeks before transplants would normally be set out, the seeds germinate just when there is no longer any frost danger. The rate of germination is low. The soil at the Oregon State University trial grounds is also light and coarse, warming up much more rapidly in spring than a heavier type would. These direct-seeded tomatoes mature their first ripe fruit about two weeks later than the six-week-old transplants set out at the same time. Yields remain somewhat lower and the plants are always somewhat smaller than transplanted ones.

Unless the weather is really warm and sunny and the nights stay close to 60-degree-minimum temperatures, peppers and eggplants grow slowly. One year I saw an amazing demonstration of how poorly these plants are adapted to maritime conditions. It was the year I first used a superduper hot frame equipped with a variable-temperature heating cable. I quickly discovered that I could grow solanaceous plants at an amazing rate if I turned up the soil temperature to 78 degrees instead of the more usual 70. These soft plants had huge leaves such as I had not seen since I left California. I transplanted them in mid-June when they were over eighteen inches tall and bearing half-sized fruit. Though the summer weather that year was excellent and the plants continued to grow, the rate of growth slowed and the size of the leaves cut in half! What happened was that nighttime lows were dropping into the fifties and some days did not exceed 72 degrees. In the frame, nights had not fallen below 60 and daytime temperatures were between 80 and 85. If the summer had been a cool one, the rate of growth might have virtually ceased, and instead of 24- to 30-inch-tall plants by mid-August, I might have been lucky to be harvesting from 12-inch plants by the end of summer. In a greenhouse in California, peppers can reach 4 feet of height in one season!

Many gardeners do not understand this relationship between temperature and growth, thinking growth to be mostly an effect of soil fertility, and thus treating slow-growing solanaceae by fertilizing them. This can be a destructive decision. Slow-growing plants have little use for fertilizer. Unable to build new leaf tissue with the nutrients, they concentrate them in the plant's vascular system as soluble salts that can reach toxic concentrations, stunting the plant and preventing future growth.

Being tropical plants, solanaceae seedlings can be easily shocked by cold conditions. Minor shocks will stop growth for a day or two until recovery. Severe, repeated shocks will stunt plants and prevent proper growth from ever occurring, even if conditions improve and become virtually ideal. Cold soil is a shock. Nighttime lows below 40 to 50 degrees (depending on type) can be shocking, sometimes severely shocking, especially to peppers and eggplants. However, seedlings may be hardened off somewhat, becoming more tolerant to low temperatures than nonhardened seedlings would be, though still not infinitely more tolerant. Raising quality seedlings means walking a tightrope between hardening off seedlings as fast as possible and not overshocking them in the process. One is much better off to delay transplanting by sowing later or raising larger seedlings in larger pots than to risk early transplanting and the severe shocks that can easily occur during late May/early June, when nighttime temperatures frequently drop into the low forties. Gardeners who buy transplants are well advised to purchase pepper and eggplant transplants in mid-May, construct a cold frame, repot the seedlings in 4- to 6-inch pots and grow them in the frame until mid-June.

Solanaceae prefer somewhat acidic soils—not highly acidic, but somewhere about 6.0 on the pH scale. They will grow fine anywhere from 5.5 to 7.0. All are fairly heavy-feeding plants, but overabundant nitrogen is not helpful to a fruiting plant, tending to prompt too much vegetative growth while reducing fruit-set. One moderate feeding of complete organic fertilizer below the transplants when setting them out will provide about six weeks of high fertility levels, perfect while the seedling is making rapid vegetative growth, and then naturally decreasing by midsummer as the plant begins to set and ripen fruit.

Solanaceae are generally self-fertile. Some occasional crossing may occur in peppers and eggplants, but isolations of twenty feet are sufficient to prevent most unwanted crosses. Hybridization of solanaceae will increase vigor and yield, though open-pollinated tomatoes and peppers will yield excellently. In marginal areas, where the weather barely suits the species, that extra bit of hybrid vigor can make a considerable improvement, particularly in peppers and eggplants.

Eggplants

Eggplants are the most sensitive of the solanaceae when in the seedling stages, requiring the warmest conditions to sprout and make initial vegetative growth. However, once eggplants have four or five true leaves and have hardened off, they will make more vegetative growth under cool conditions than will peppers. But cool nights are very contrary to fruiting, and most areas of the maritime Northwest require warming up nighttime temperatures somewhat to permit good fruit-set and large fruit development. South of Longview, a black plastic mulch is sufficient, but along the coasts and in the rest of Washington State, large cloches or a greenhouse are probably required.

Culture

Raise transplants like peppers (directions in the section on raising transplants). However, be more cautious about hardening off eggplant seedlings. At Lorane, we delay transplanting until mid-June to avoid shockingly cold nights (below 50 degrees). Over the bed, lay a sheet of black plastic 3 to 4 feet wide. Anchor the plastic with soil around the edges, taking care to leave as much plastic exposed to the sun as possible. The plastic soaks up solar energy, raising soil temperatures 2 to 4 degrees overall and radiating heat at night, creating a warmer microclimate. Cut small holes in the plastic about 24 by 24 inches apart, work from 1/4 to 1/2 cup of complete organic fertilizer into the soil below the holes, and set out transplants. The plants should make good vegetative growth until late August. If growth slows while weather conditions are still sunny and warm, feed liquid fertilizer to provoke a renewed growth response.

Garden Planning

A healthy plant will produce five or six large fruits in a season. Japanese types produce fifteen to twenty fruits each. Eggplants follow well in succession behind early peas or overwintered or spring-planted green manure crops.

Insects and Diseases

Eggplants are rarely bothered by anything but low temperatures. Problems after mid-September are but a symptom of cold and low light levels and should be ignored.

Harvest

The fruits are best picked while slightly immature, before much seed development has occurred. This stage can be recognized when the fruit has stopped enlarging rapidly but the skin is still shiny and thin. About mid-September, the plants cease growth due to cooler temperatures and lower light levels. At this time, harvest all well-developed fruit. The smallest ones may as well be left in hopes that sunny, warm temperatures will prevail, allowing some further development.

Saving Seed

If open-pollinated types would grow in our very marginal area, saving seed would be simple. However, with the exception of a few Japanese types, only hybrid vigor will permit decent growth and early enough maturity. Eggplants are almost completely self-pollinated, but an occasional extraordinarily energetic bee does effect crossing. Purity can be insured by a 20-foot separation between varieties. Seeds mature after fruits reach full size and the skin has toughened. Harvest an overmature fruit, crush the fruit into a mass of pulp and seeds, and wash the seeds free of the pulp. Finally, dry the seeds completely on a newspaper at room temperature.

Varieties

In our trials and those at Oregon State University, only a few varieties consistently produce much fruit, the best of them being Dusky Hybrid (TSC, STK, HAR). Early Black Egg (JSS, TSC) is an open-pollinated Japanese type that makes smallish European-shaped fruit that is very early. Short Tom (TSC) is a long-fruited Japanese hybrid, extremely early and productive under cool conditions. Be quite wary of other varieties. Even though old standards like Black Beauty will produce big, healthy-looking bushes in our climate, they won't set fruit in our cool nights.

Peppers

Climatic variations make quite a difference in pepper varietal performance in the maritime Northwest. South of Roseburg, Oregon, almost any variety will do all right. In the Willamette, certain of the more heat-demanding, small-fruited types and some of the standard California bell types do not perform well at all. North of Longview, Washington, and along the coasts, peppers will not grow well outside of cloches or greenhouses. Hot pepper varieties are somewhat earlier and easier to grow in many cases.

Culture

Nighttime lows below 50 degrees will shock seedling pepper plants. Hardening off can improve that only by a degree or two. Though slightly benefited by black plastic mulch, peppers will usually do all right without any forcing if transplanting is delayed until nighttime lows are not below 48 to 50 degrees, which is about mid-June at Lorane. In cool summers, we have had much greater harvests by growing peppers under a cloche. Transplant about 18 by 18 inches with 1/4 to 1/2 cup complete organic fertilizer worked into the soil below the transplants. In warm-summer areas, increase spacing to 24 by 24.

Garden Planning

Bell types usually produce six to ten fruits per plant. Small-fruited types make dozens.

Insects and Diseases

Insects and diseases are rarely a problem.

Harvest

Many bell types ripen and change from green to red or yellow if you let them, acquiring a sweeter taste in the process. This is also true of thick-walled hot peppers, such as Jalapeños and Hungarian Hot Wax. If types of hot peppers used dried, such as Cayenne and Red Chile, have not yet matured by summer's end, harvest the entire plant before frost or excessive rains rot the fruit, and hang the plant upside down in a cool, dim place. All the fruit will ripen and dry simultaneously.

Saving Seed

The procedure for seed saving is similar to that for eggplant, though the seed is much easier to remove. Allow the fruit to ripen fully before harvest to obtain fully mature, high-germination seed. Peppers have a somewhat higher likelihood of crossing than eggplant, and varieties should be given 50 feet of isolation—especially if growing sweet and hot types in the garden at the same time.

Varieties

We have noticed great differences in the ability of different varieties of pepper to grow and make fruit under cool conditions. Small, hot, very tropical types like Serrano will hardly grow in our trials, while standard California market peppers like Cal Wonder, Keystone Resistant Giant, and Yolo Wonder are all very late to mature fruit and yield poorly, though these would likely do fine in southern Oregon. Staddon's Select (TSC, STK, HAR, JSS) is the best adapted open-pollinated bell type, and we've found Golden Bell (TSC, HAR) to be the best-flavored, largest-yielding hybrid bell type. Other hybrid bell types with the earlier maturity dates will probably do fine—they do at the Oregon State University trial grounds. Most small-fruited types, both hot and sweet, grow well enough, though we've noticed that Hungarian Hot Wax and its hybrid variants are the earliest, making more growth under cool conditions than the others, with Cayenne Long Thin and Cubanelle close behind. Early Jalapeño is much better than the standard type. Avoid any variety with later maturity dates.

Tomatoes

Tomato seedlings can make vine growth, achieve good size, and set fruit even under cool conditions or in poor soil (if fertilized). However, getting a large harvest of ripe fruit is not always so certain. Varietal selection and proper handling are vital.

Culture

Tomatoes cannot ripen fruit if they have not yet set it. The earlier fruit-set can occur, the sooner the fruits can mature. That's obvious. The gardener can do several things to encourage early fruit-set. One, choosing the correct variety, is discussed below. The other is to transplant a hardened-off seedling so that no check in growth occurs. At Lorane we do not transplant unprotected tomatoes until June 1, as our valley is subject to late frosts. However, even this late in the season there are still nights that occasionally drop to the high thirties or low forties. If the seedlings have been growing in a cold frame for the past three weeks or so, they are already adapted to chilly nights, and encountering a 40-degree low is no threat to them. However, if tender seedlings are purchased from a nursery the day before transplanting and set out, they'll be severely shocked within a few nights, and stop growing for a week or two. This check is enough to retard greatly the first set of fruit and thus the first maturity date. At Lorane, that can be the difference between August 7 and August 20 in a usual year with early varieties. Those who buy seedlings from nurseries are advised to construct their own cold frame, transplant store-bought seedlings into 3- to 4-inch individual pots, and grow them in the frame for a few weeks before transplanting; or erect a large cloche over the tomato bed sufficient to cover the seedlings for three or more weeks; or cover each seedling with a large hot cap.

I get my earliest and largest harvests by having 6- to 8-inch-tall seedlings coming from the cold frame about three weeks before the last usual frost date, transplanting these under a large tunnel cloche, and growing them in this cloche until the entire bed is a green mass pushing against the sides—which is usually early July. Then the cloche is removed. This way, I harvest ripe fruits starting about mid-July in a good year. Tomato harvests increase geometrically over time; that is, if each week one were to harvest the bed and weigh the harvest, as we've done in yield trials, weekly weights might run one pound the first week, two pounds the second, four pounds the third, eight pounds the fourth, sixteen pounds the fifth week, and so forth. The big harvests come at the end of the season. If one doesn't start harvesting until late August, there are not many weeks left until the vines fall apart from cool nights and fall rains.

Determinate tomato types make compact bushes that do not benefit from trellising or staking up, and they have been bred to hold much of their fruit off the ground. Growing them this easy way does lose a few fruits to slugs and rot, but the losses are offset by large yields and earlier ripening. Most determinate tomato varieties may be set out 12 to 18 inches by 18 to 24 inches, depending on the size of the bush. Indeterminate tomatoes may also be allowed to sprawl on the ground, in which case they should be set out at least 24 inches apart by 36 inches apart. Indeterminate varieties can be grown more tidily and produce larger and slightly earlier-maturing fruit if trained up a stake or string. My favorite system with indeterminate vines is to plant them 18 inches apart in rows 36 inches apart—two rows down a 4-by-25-foot raised bed. Above this, I erect horizontal two-by-fours held up by two-by-two posts about 6 feet above the bed. From the beam above the ground, I drop lengths of twine that are loosely tied to the base of each tomato vine, two strings to each plant. Then the plant is pruned to two leaders, and as each leader grows, it is twisted around the twine. If the vine reaches the top, it is allowed to drape over the two-by-four and return toward the earth, though most seasons, 6 feet of vine growth is all I get before the season ends.

Fertilize tomato vines with 1/4 to 1/2 cup complete organic fertilizer worked into the soil below each transplant.

Garden Planning

We have harvested from two to nine pounds per plant (depending on variety) of sauce tomatoes from determinate types grown 24 by 48 inches, though they could have been grown 18 by 24 just as well. One well-grown 100-square-foot bed will keep our family in fresh tomatoes during the season, and our family of four is a tomato eating family, consuming them by the large soup bowlful, making whole meals of cold tomato soup when the season is on. Tomatoes best follow an overwintered or spring-sown legume green manure crop. I usually start the early bed for the family's fresh use by chopping in a bed of clover or overwintered favas with a hoe, covering the bed with a tunnel cloche, waiting a week or so for the soil to heat up, then transplanting six-week-old, cold frame-raised seedlings in early May.

Insects and Diseases

Flea beetles are notorious for attacking newly transplanted seedlings, though I've found that well-hardened plants that are not shocked by transplanting are never touched. Rotenone, sprayed every two or three days, will protect soft seedlings until they harden off, come out of shock, and begin growth. Tomato horn worms can be handled with Dipel.

Most of the diseases that tomatoes have been bred to resist are found only in commercial tomato-growing areas like Florida or California. Tomato late blight, which took almost all maritime Northwest tomatoes in 1983, comes about when the unhealthy vines are growing under cool, damp conditions that both weaken them and promote the development of the fungus. The disease may be considered to be caused by the weather. Though farmers may spray fungicides to prevent the disease, once the disease strikes, there is no cure. There is no known varietal resistance to the blight, though scattered plants did survive in 1983, mostly located in very favorable microclimates, such as against a whitewashed wall under a roof overhang that kept off most of the rains we had that year in early summer.

Two of the main problems with tomatoes appear to be diseases but are actually the result of fluctuating soil moisture and poor nutrition. If large amounts of water are added to dry soil, tomatoes often respond by curling their leaves, and the blossom ends of the fruits blacken and rot. These problems can be prevented by proper irrigation, which maintains a good, steady moisture content, and by having a soil which makes available sufficient calcium. End rot comes about because moisture fluctuations interfere with calcium uptake. That is only one reason my complete organic fertilizer contains lime.

Harvest

There are at least three cultural practices that will improve the harvest. Thinning, by removing over half the flower clusters from determinate tomato types, lightens the fruit load. This permits the vines to make bigger and better-tasting fruit, similar to the way apple trees are thinned. Otherwise, determinate vines usually have so many fruits that both the size suffers and the flavor drops. Then, complete ripening of the fruit can be encouraged by removing all flowers and newly formed, immature tomatoes beginning about September 1, forcing the vines to ripen the fruit they are already carrying. Another trick is to attempt to kill the vines by withholding water, starting mid- to late August, depending on how water retentive the soil is. If the vines can be put under severe water stress, starting about mid-September, they'll ripen all their fruit as they die. However, nature often defeats this strategy by sending late summer rains, which also cause the vines to fall apart and become diseased.

Green tomatoes, if harvested when fully sized but not ripe and brought in before touched by frost, will ripen in the house. We usually bring in several bucketfuls just before the last frost and they keep us in tomatoes for six to eight weeks. Though there are many involved systems for handling unripe tomatoes, we've found that if the buckets are sorted every few days for ripening fruit, most ripen and few rot.

[handwritten margin note: pick off begining flowers to allow formed tomatoes to ripen]

Saving Seed

Tomatoes are invariably self-fertilized. To save seed on open-pollinated varieties, simply remove the pulp from a few fully ripe fruits (overripe, slug-eaten ones hiding under thick foliage are ideal) and place the pulp in a small glass on the kitchen counter, allowing the pulp to ferment. Stir daily. After three to five days, the seeds settle to the bottom and the pulp rises to the top. Slowly running water into the glass floats off the pulp; the seeds are poured into a strainer, washed, and then dried on a newspaper. The only trick to obtaining high-germination seed is to conduct the fermentation at a temperature of about 70 degrees so the fermentation goes fast. Fermentation that lasts over one week usually results in dead seed.

Varieties

Any variety listed in a seed catalog as over "seventy-two days to maturity" will not likely mature north of Roseburg, Oregon. Beefsteak types do not do well in the maritime Northwest, nor do some others that may be listed as maturing in less than seventy-two days. This is because fruit-set on tomatoes will abort when nighttime lows drop below 50 degrees, more or less, and there is a considerable varietal difference as to when fruit-set begins and how much nighttime heat is needed to enhance ripening. One very interesting variety is Oregon 11 (eleven) (TSC), which will set fruit parthenocarpically (without fertilization) at a much lower temperature than any other variety at the date of this writing (though I'm sure this trait will be bred into other varieties in the near future). Oregon 11 matures several weeks earlier than any known variety at Lorane, though its flavor is only average. I feel the best-flavored slicing tomato is Fantastic Hybrid (TSC, STK). Other excellent table varieties popular today include Early Cascade, Pik Red, Bonny Best, IPB, Kootenai, Willamette, and New Yorker. Generally, varieties listed as early in any seed company catalog will perform. Watch out for those listed as midseason (seventy days or more), as is Fantastic Hybrid for example. While for many types of vegetables varietal adaptation is not that critical, with tomatoes there are amazing differences. The major catalogs present a bewildering assortment, and in the case of large, fruited tomato variety selection, I'd advise the gardener to follow the advice found in the Territorial Seed Company catalog.

Gardeners who make tomato sauce or paste using anything but varieties bred for that purpose may be practicing false economy. Salad or slicing varieties have high water content, and a potful of these will cook down to only a small amount of thick sauce, while varieties bred for sauce-making have little juice and a high percentage of solids. Sauce varieties cook down rapidly and yield lots of sauce. Our trials indicate that standard sauce varieties like Nova, Roma, and San Marzano, which are carried by most major seed companies, don't produce nearly as much as Chico III, Sprinter, Ropreco, and Peto No. 95. However, where summers are warmer, yields might well be different.

Most of the small-fruited types are fairly early, though yellow pear and yellow plum are almost as late as the large-fruited yellow types. Though Golden Jubilee makes the most delicious, rich-flavored yellow tomatoes—if they mature before mid-September's loss of light intensity—many summers we hardly harvest any before the summer is through. Golden Delight is a much better choice for all but those lucky gardeners in southern Oregon with long, hot summers to enjoy.

Legumes and Other Green Manures

Lustily growing legumes are a good source of free nitrogen fertilizer, as well as being excellent producers of organic matter when grown as green manures. To get lush growth, nitrogen fertilizer is not usually needed. In fact, the presence of too much soil nitrogen (nitrate) prevents nitrogen fixation, while the legumes consume what is already available to them in the soil.

Legumes feed heavily on potassium, phosphorus, calcium, and magnesium. There is an old farmer's adage that goes, "Feed your phosphate to your clover, then feed your clover to your corn (plow it in), and you can't go wrong." On our trial grounds, when the soil has been manured within the past two years, we fertilize legumes with equal parts of dolomitic lime, rock phosphate, and kelp meal, banding only a small quantity below the seeds because our trial grounds have been well limed and spread with rock phosphate already. If the trial plot has not been recently manured and the soil become so devoid of organic matter as to retard nitrogen fixation by lowering the supply of soil air, we include some seed meal in the fertilizer. Perhaps the finest single fertilizing substance for legumes would be bone meal, containing small quantities of nitrogen and large quantities of phosphorus and calcium.

Legumes growing in light soil containing a fair amount of organic matter can fix all the nitrogen they need for their own growth. In the case of garden beans and peas, this amounts to sixty to eighty pounds of nitrate nitrogen per acre— enough to feed a following crop of grain, beets, carrots, or other low-demanding crop. Clovers fix more nitrogen. Well-grown Crimson clover may fix nearly one hundred pounds of nitrogen per acre in the root system stubble alone, with perhaps another thirty to fifty pounds more in the vegetation if it is tilled in. In many cases, that is enough to grow medium-demanding crops like sweet corn, lettuce, and squash. The most amazing nitrogen fixer is fava beans. Over-wintered or sown in early spring, favas will create over two hundred pounds of nitrogen, often enough to grow the more demanding brassicas.

Legume vegetation is so rich in nitrogen that when tilled in (before becoming woody) will rot and allow sowing of seed within two weeks, without having stubble tangling up planters, rakes, and hoes. Nonlegume green manures can require an additional week to rot and, if overly mature and woody when tilled in, can retard sowing by a month. Tilling in the tops as well as the root system can tie up soil nutrients a little longer while bacteria do the job of primary decomposition.

Legumes do not actually fix nitrogen themselves, but do so in cooperation with certain specialized types of soil bacteria that colonize their roots. Much money is needlessly spent by gardeners on legume seed inoculants to prime the seed with the correct bacterial strains. If a soil contains a reasonable amount of organic matter, it will also contain balanced and active populations of micro-organisms. Dead soils, chemically farmed for years, have had most of their organic matter burned out by nitrogen fertilizers. Under these conditions, legumes may not encounter the correct bacteria and may well need nitrogen fertilizer like any other vegetable. In cases like this, inoculation may reduce or eliminate the need for nitrogen fertilizer on legume crops. I have found that when peas are sown very early in cold soil, natural bacterial activity is so slow that inoculation may improve growth until the soil warms up. I do not inoculate peas sown after April 1.

Bush Beans

Bush beans were primarily developed for canneries and other commercial purposes to save the cost of erecting trellising and permitting mechanical harvest. Their taste is not the equal of the pole bean, and I doubt that it is possible to breed a high-yielding, really good-tasting bush variety. This is so because the ratio of food manufacturing area (leaf) to pod production determines how much flavor is available to be stored in each pod. In this respect, bush beans are similar to highly determinate early tomato varieties like the subarctic series—all fruit and virtually no leaf—and virtually no flavor. Pole beans, with large leaves well spaced out, can capture the sunlight falling on a much larger area and consequently manufacture much more food to pack into each pod. Some bush varieties do have fairly good flavor, but when I'm doing both bush bean and pole bean variety trials, the family won't harvest or eat the bush types at all.

Culture

Beans like warm soils and most varieties will not germinate if soil temperature is below 60 degrees. We make our first sowing about June 1. Should cloudy or rainy weather follow sowing bean seed, it may likely not germinate, or if it does sprout, the seedlings will be in a shocked condition and won't grow until conditions improve. Standing there with only two puny leaves, waiting for warmth and sun, shocked bean seedlings are defenseless against the Mexican bean beetle. These hungry critters can chew up the leaves rapidly. Under good growing conditions in decent soil, new bean seedlings will outgrow any predators. When making an early sowing, I try to outguess the weather and sow just before a spell of settled, sunny weather. Later sowings usually sprout well despite the weather because soil temperatures have stably increased above 60 degrees. Sow bush bean seed 1½ inches deep, four to six seeds per foot, rows 18 inches apart. After the seedlings are established and growing well, thin to about 6 inches apart in the row.

Garden Planning

Two sowings of bush beans about three to four weeks apart are often desirable, especially if a continuous harvest for the table is desired. Bush beans have been bred for a concentrated harvest, and the first sowing usually stops producing much earlier in September. Able to grow well in soils of lower fertility, beans go well in beds that have not been recently manured, or that did not get a legume green manure over the winter for some reason or other. About 50 row feet of bush beans or a 100-square-foot bed will produce all the beans most families want to eat fresh and preserve. For fresh table use only, I'd grow half that much, and be better off with pole types.

Insects and Diseases

Mexican bean beetles overeating on shocked seedlings can be controlled with rotenone by being sprayed every few days until the weather improves. Once the plants are growing fast, beetle damage becomes minor and can be ignored. There are no other significant garden insect pests of beans that I know of. Beans are sensitive to several types of diseases that are spread by the grower touching damp plants. Wait until the sun has dried off the morning dew before handling bean plants. Most new types of bush beans are disease-resistant.

Harvest

Keeping the plants carefully picked will extend their production period. Bean bushes are delicate and easily damaged from handling, so remove the pods carefully. Small beans about four-fifths sized out have much better and tenderer texture.

Saving Seed

Crosses between varieties of snap beans rarely happen naturally, so isolation is unnecessary. Select a few plants that have the best initial appearance and that produce the most pods the soonest, or that appear to have the best raw flavor, and do not harvest these. Allow the pods to form seed and that seed to mature and dry. Should the pods not be fully dried out by late September's rains and heavy dews, pull the plants and hang them upside down under cover or indoors to permit the pods to fully dry out. Then, thrash out the seed (see the "Saving Seed" portion of the "Dry Beans" section for an improved method).

Varieties

In our trials, every variety of bush bean has yielded well enough, though some better than others. There seems to be little difference in flavor between bush bean varieties, especially after cooking. This is also true of the "wax" varieties. There are much larger differences between flavor of the raw pods, and we like Blue Lake types and a wax variety called Golden Butterwax for raw bush bean flavor. OSU 1604B is the Blue Lake strain preferred by commercial growers in the Willamette, and vigorous seed for this variety is usually available. Its flavor is equal to any Blue Lake type and its yield and adaptation to maritime conditions is superior. Purple-podded beans, which turn green when blanched, are slightly more vigorous sprouters and growers under cool conditions, and they should be considered seriously for the first sowings in coastal and cooler microclimate gardens. I think Royalty Purple Pod is not the equal of a newer purple variety called Royal Burgundy. All bush bean varieties we've grown in our trials mature beans within a week or so of each other. Wax bush beans do not become really waxy in our trials, and I cannot see any reason to use them except for their different color. However, an old pole type, Kentucky Wonder Wax, does develop a unique waxy texture and flavor.

An heirloom variety called variously White Half Runner or Mountaineer is a short-vined pole type which may be grown on the ground without trellising. The short, fat pods have excellent flavor, though they tend to be a bit hard to harvest out of the tangle of vines that result from on-the-ground culture. Growing Half Runners up a 3-foot fence or low trellis is not a bad compromise between the high trellis needed for pole beans and the ease of bush bean culture. Seed formation on Half Runners is rapid (a bad trait for snap beans that is always accompanied by string formation and toughening of the pod), so the pods have to be harvested very promptly. But at the same time, Half Runners make good shelling beans, whose immature white seeds can be eaten like horticultural beans. Blue Lake Bush 1604B, on the other hand, has such slow seed and string development that the pods hold a very long time on the bush without losing good eating quality; however, seed companies have difficulty producing the slow-to-mature seed and have to charge more for it.

Horticultural Beans

These are bush varieties grown not for their tender pods, but because they have rapid seed development. The seeds are harvested when fully formed, but not dried out, and eaten as shell beans. Horticultural beans are usually very early to mature and are sometimes used as snap beans and then later as shell beans and then as dry beans. Horticultural beans are grown just like bush snap beans.

Varieties

Taylor's or French Horticultural are the two standards. There are others popular in Europe. Taylor's is known widely in the maritime Northwest as Speckled Bays or Bayos or any of twenty other names, and are quite good as dry beans.

Pole Snap Beans

Pole beans are larger yielders than bush varieties, and with their larger leaf structures spread out to receive more light, they can fill their pods with more flavor and likely more nutrition. They also begin producing slightly later than bush types.

Culture

Pole varieties must be grown on a trellis. The traditional Willamette Valley commercial trellising method for Blue Lake Poles was to zigzag a string every 8 inches up and down between parallel stout wires, one a few inches above the ground, the other slightly over 6 feet. We've also used 6-foot-tall garden netting in our trials. The pioneers used skinny fir poles with the bark left on, often set up as tripods lashed together at the top, and grew a few vines up each pole. Along a trellis, sow the seeds as usual but thin the seedlings to about 8 inches apart to allow for the more massive leaves. Otherwise grow as bush beans.

Garden Planning

Pole varieties can yield continuously to the end of summer, so only one planting is required. Fifty row feet or a double row up a 4-foot-wide by 25-foot-long raised bed produces more beans than my family can use fresh. Serious bean fanciers might consider a small sowing of bush beans to harvest for a week or so until the pole types come on. (Bush beans may be grown under a cloche for harvest even ten days to two weeks earlier than normal, something not possible with pole types.)

Insects and Diseases

Same as for bush varieties.

Harvest

It is essential to keep pole varieties picked clean. Allowing only a few pods on a vine to form seed will prevent further pod set. If carefully and completely harvested, most pole varieties will produce until the end of September. Like all snap beans, the pods are better flavored and tenderer if picked on the immature side, with the exception of Kentucky Wonder Wax.

Saving Seed

Same as for bush beans.

Varieties

Blue Lake Pole has the slowest seed and string development—its round pods are slightly longer than the bush variety. This is the bean that made the

Willamette Valley canneries famous nationwide. Bush 1604B, though good for a bush variety, is insipid in comparison to the original pole type. Kentucky Wonders have a richer, beanier flavor, especially eaten raw. There are two Kentucky Wonder strains, brown- and white-seeded. The brown-seeded type has rapid seed development and makes a good general-purpose bean for snap beans and shelling beans. The white-seeded type is slightly earlier to mature and has much slower seed and string formation. I prefer it. Kentucky Wonder Wax is a unique variety that I like very much for its tender, waxy texture and bland flavor. We've grown over thirty European and Japanese gourmet bean varieties. We can find great differences in their yield and pod shape and size, but there are only very slight differences in raw flavor and virtually no difference in their taste when cooked. Also, none are better adapted to our conditions than Blue Lake Pole or Kentucky Wonder. None are earlier by more than a few days either, and the early ones tend to quit producing long before the old American standards give up. Another unique bean is the Oregon Giant pole bean, sold on Lilly Miller seed racks throughout the maritime Northwest. Oregon Giant has a large, purple-and-green mottled pod with a very juicy, tender, and mild flavor compared to the other pole types. It, too, is an early bean with very large seeds that form quickly, making a good shelling variety. Oregon Giant does have a tendency to quit producing well before the others do.

Runner Beans

This type of pole bean is popular in Europe, particularly in England. In fact, in that country, people do not think that the snap beans we like to eat have any flavor at all. And compared to runner beans, they're right. Runner beans produce very long, fuzzy pods that have an intense beany flavor—too intense for pleasurable raw consumption—that, when cooked, are as rich as beefsteak. I've come to prefer runner beans myself.

Culture

Grow runner beans exactly like pole beans. They tend to be a bit later to mature, but grow well in cold conditions.

Garden Planning

Same as for pole beans.

Insects and Diseases

Same as for bush beans.

Harvest

The better culinary varieties have very slow seed development, but the long pods are much tenderer if picked about three-quarters grown.

Saving Seed

Runner beans are in a different botanical group than are the snap beans. There is some tendency for the varieties to cross, so seed savers should grow only one. Some have white flowers, some red.

Varieties

Scarlet Runner is the old standard variety most seed companies offer. Prizewinner is another red-flowered type I like better. There are many, many varieties in English seed catalogs and most will probably please anyone who likes this type of bean, though I could see virtually no difference in the several we've observed in our variety trials. One unique runner bean is called the Oregon Lima by loyal seed savers in the maritime Northwest. Oregon Lima is not a true lima at all, but a large-seeded, white-flowered runner bean that has poorly flavored pods but very rapid seed development. Oregon Lima seed can only be obtained from a neighbor, or by being a regional seedman who doesn't sell them—in which case, every year five to ten well-meaning people will send samples, thinking that since they grow so well and aren't in the catalog, the seedman must be unaware of them.

Fava Beans

Large-seeded favas are known to some as "horse beans," to the English as "broad beans" or "winter beans" in the case of their small-seeded varieties intended for overwintering, or as "tick beans" for English small-seeded, spring-sown types. They should be much better known to Americans, particularly those living in the maritime Northwest, because the fava bean is amazingly well adapted to our climate. All the main field crops of the maritime Northwest are grown over the winter, and favas have this potential, too. Winter wheat, barley, and oats are farm staples. Overwintered biennial seed crops have made the Skagit Valley famous worldwide as the finest place on earth to produce cabbage seed. Eighty-five percent of the entire world's cabbage seed production is done there. The Skagit also produces significant amounts of the world's spinach and beet seed, also grown over the winter. Overwintered crops are sown in late summer/early fall after the natural rainfall has softened the soil, grow slowly in our mild, lush winters, and burst into maturity in spring, drying down as our soils dry out in early summer to be harvested by August. Overwintered crops don't usually require irrigation.

In contrast, spring-sown seed crops demand very light soils that dry down rapidly and are tillable before April. There are few maritime Northwest soils like this. A liability of soil this light is that it may dry out too quickly in summer—well before the crop is ready to dry down—and thus demand irrigation. A self-sufficient homesteader trying to produce the family's staples by growing peas or lentils faces this prospect. Though it is possible to mud in a few hundred square feet of peas for early summer harvest, I wouldn't want to face sowing a quarter acre of peas for soup pea seed in spring—not west of the Cascades. Hot-weather seed crops like dry beans (and millet, sunflowers, amaranth, or other late spring-sown grains) have two liabilities: they must be irrigated through their long growing season, demanding a good water supply, and they must be harvested at summer's end when the rains have begun. This makes drying down difficult or impossible, which is why little commercial seed of this type is produced in the maritime Northwest.

So, for self-sufficient maritime Northwest food supplies, it is winter wheat, barley, and oats for grain; favas for legumes; and poppy seed for vegetable oil. Annual poppies are widely overwintered in other mild-winter climates as an oilseed crop and should be recognized by the self-sufficiency-minded gardener as the most likely source of vegetable oil for the maritime Northwest homestead. All other oilseed crops demand heat, irrigation, and late-September harvest. Well-adapted to nonmechanized agriculture and fairly infertile soils, these relatives of the thistle produce about sixteen hundred pounds of oilseed per acre, yielding over 50 percent oil that can be simply pressed out without chemical extraction and which is equal in quality to olive oil. Unfortunately, growing large tracts of these types of colorful flowers is an invitation to the Feds for a visit and possibly a jail term, though in Europe, opium poppies are a common garden flower and the seed for them is commonly found in English and Danish home garden seed catalogs.

Fava beans taste pretty good. They can be consumed in the green stage as are peas, and at the same time of the year. At that time of year, however, I prefer the sweeter peas. When dried down, favas make bean soups and stews as good as any, and some varieties are very superior eating. Favas also make the best of green manures.

Culture

Favas need soil similar in qualities to those needed by other beans. Sow favas in late October or in early spring, depending on the hardiness of the variety being grown and the location. Favas freeze out from 10 to 18 degrees, depending on variety. Areas where winter lows generally exceed 10 degrees should not consider overwintering favas. Sow one seed every 3 inches, 1½ inches deep, in rows 18 to 30 inches apart, depending on the method of cultivation. Keeping the weeds down in winter and spring takes persistence, and if row space can be wide enough to permit mechanical cultivation with a rototiller, much work can be saved.

Garden Planning

Dry seed yields run two tons per acre on most varieties, which amounts to about one hundred pounds per thousand square feet. If growing for seed, plan to follow with midsummer-sown, overwintered brassica crops like Purple Sprouting broccoli or overwintered cauliflower, fast-growing, coarse brassicas like kale, or with beds of lettuce/endive for fall harvest. Very likely, no fertilizer will be needed for crops following favas. If grown for shell beans, the harvest will likely end before July 1, and fall/winter brassica transplants may be set into the beds when the favas are done.

Insects and Diseases

I have been growing favas, both spring-sown and overwintered, since 1979 in the maritime Northwest and have not noted any difficulties with insects or disease. There is virtually no information about favas in the United States.

Harvest

Pods form in May at Lorane, with shell beans beginning to be ready by early June, and the pods dried down by July. The taller varieties have a tendency to fall over (lodge) from the weight of the forming seed pods, and it has proven helpful to pinch the growing tip of tall varieties one time when it gets about 16 inches tall, causing the plant to bush out and produce a number of shorter stalks that have less tendency to lodge. The seeds are held tightly within the pod and the stalks are gathered up when dried down, windrowed on a tarp in the sun for a few days, and covered at night to keep off dew. When dried crisp, the pods are thrashed with a flail or by walking on them, and then the chaff may be cleaned out with a fan. If the stalks have lodged and the weather has been wet, a portion of the seed may become discolored.

Saving Seed

Similar to dry beans, but favas do have some tendency to cross, and different varieties should be separated by a hundred feet or more.

Varieties

All United States seed companies offer an old, dark-colored, large-seeded variety called Windsor, not hardy enough to overwinter except in the most mild locations, such as along the southern Oregon coast. Seeds of the big-seeded types can be as large as a 25¢-piece in diameter. Aquadulce Claudia is a light-colored, large-seeded type which came originally from Spain, where it is grown over the winter. Territorial Seed Company has a strain of Aquadulce Claudia hardy to about 12 degrees that will overwinter nicely and that has flavor as good as the finest dry bean I know. It also makes a very high-quality green shell bean. Banner is a new type imported from England by Territorial that has a seed similar in size to a red kidney bean, though squarish in shape. Banner is hardy to at least 10 degrees, and during the December 1983 freeze, it had about 75 percent survival with about an inch of snow cover for insulation, at temperatures of 7 degrees. Banner has what the British call "stiff straw," meaning that it has a very stocky stem, so Banner has very little tendency to lodge. Banner is a good-tasting dry bean and acceptable fare as a shell bean.

Field Beans (Dry)

Growing dry beans is possible in the maritime Northwest, but good harvesting conditions do not usually exist in late September. People south of Roseburg, Oregon, have a much easier time with dry beans. Gardeners seeking to produce their own supply of legumes should seriously consider growing overwintered fava beans instead.

Culture

Grow like bush beans. However, the varieties tend to be less tidy and compact, and many do better with a 24-inch row spacing. Stop irrigation in late August and hope they dry down and mature before the rains come.

Garden Planning

Bean seed yields run from one to two tons per acre, which is about fifty to one hundred pounds per thousand square feet.

Insects and Diseases

Same as for bush beans.

Harvest

When 90 percent of the leaves have yellowed and the pods have dried in the field, but before the pods begin to shatter, it is time to harvest. At that time, the plants are pulled from the dry earth and windrowed in the field for a few days to finish drying. Then the seeds are thrashed. That's how one grows dry beans in Idaho or other areas where intense summer heat matures the beans by September and where there are usually few rains in late summer. However, in the maritime Northwest, few varieties even approach this stage of maturity before conditions deteriorate in late summer. Usually the plants have to be dried indoors, either bunched and hung or loosely stacked on a porch and carefully turned daily. (Again, consider growing favas.) Thrashing can be done with a flail or by banging plants held by the roots against the side of a fifty-five-gallon oil drum, causing the seeds to fall to the bottom. Then, fully clean the seed and make sure it is really dry before storage. To prevent bean weevils from ruining the seed, freeze it for a week or two to kill the eggs or larvae, and then put it into storage.

Saving Seed

A certain amount of variation and mutation develops in all beans. Quality seed stocks are maintained by selecting a few perfect plants and flagging them in the field, harvesting these separately, and then increasing their seed for seed stock. For the highest quality, grow out the progeny of each selected plant in a separate row and then only save seed from those rows that appear perfectly uniform with all the desirable traits selected for. This good seed may be "bulked" together and increased for stock seed. This type of purification is done each year by the highest quality bean seed growers. In the home garden, it might be done once in four or five years, if at all.

Varieties

As mentioned before, Taylor's Horticultural is widely grown in the maritime Northwest as a dry bean because it is one of the earliest. Lorane, Oregon, is a poor spot to mature dry beans, and very few of the varieties included in our trials actually drop most of their leaves and mature seeds in dried-down pods before October 1, which is the standard for acceptable varieties in my garden. Soldier beans do, but most of the varieties sent me by Willamette Valley gardeners do not. Soldiers are interesting in another respect: they'll form deep, extensive root systems and in clayey soils may mature beans without irrigation if well spaced out and carefully hoed. Grown this way, yields are not anywhere near two thousand pounds per acre. There is a lot of difference in flavor among dry beans, and someone who likes to eat them would do well to grow many home garden types, as the commercial types are selected mainly for highest yield and good commercial potential rather than superior flavor. Johnny's sells several good home garden varieties.

Lima Beans

I have not yet succeeded with limas, though I've been told by some that King of the Garden pole will mature in the Willamette Valley and more certainly south of Roseburg *if* started as transplants and set out about the time that peppers will grow outdoors. Limas are a very heat-loving type.

Soybeans

Soybeans are heat lovers, though somewhat more tolerant to cool nights than limas. A few varieties will mature most years, though not likely much north of Longview, Washington, or along the cool coasts.

Culture

Grow like beans, in general, sowing a little later than snap beans because soybeans germinate poorly below about 65-degree soil temperature. Sow about 1 inch deep, one seed per inch, in rows about 12 inches apart. Thin to about 2 inches apart in the row. Soybeans aren't vigorous sprouters and won't push through heavily crusted soil.

Garden Planning

Soybeans mature all at once, so 10 to 20 row feet will probably be plenty.

Insects and Diseases
We've had no difficulties at Lorane.

Harvest
Obtaining dry beans is not very certain most years, but harvest as immature shell beans is very likely. The Japanese people love immature soybeans, steamed in the shell for a short time and eaten by sliding the hot, salted pods between the teeth and shelling the seeds into one's mouth.

Saving Seed
Same as for bush beans.

Varieties
We've had good luck maturing Envy and Fiskeby (JSS). Beware of other varieties, no matter how early the catalog lists them. Soybeans mature according to photoperiod, and beans bred for more southerly latitudes may well not mature in the North, no matter how quickly they may go from sowing to harvest even a few hundred miles south of the forty-fifth parallel.

Peas
Any pea variety makes great maritime Northwest garden food from late May through June. However, when weather turns hot and sunny, a disease called pea enation wipes out traditional home garden types. There are now resistant varieties. These may be sown later and harvested through summer, but I've found pea flavor decreases as light intensity drops off, and so I don't grow peas to mature after mid-July.

Culture
Peas are subject to various root diseases, especially when soils are wet and cold. February sowings of peas are usually successful only on coarse-textured soils, which warm quickly and drain fast. Heavier soils should not be sown until March or even April. With enation-resistant varieties, sowings made as late as mid-May will do well and taste good. If sowing in rows, plant the seed thickly, several seeds per inch, about 1½ inches deep, and do not thin. The best fertilizer for early sowings of peas is five or so pounds of bone meal per 50 to 100 row feet, providing abundant phosphorus and a little nitrogen at a time when cold soils don't release much of these vital nutrients and when microbial activities are slow, preventing much nitrogen fixation. Inoculating early pea sowings may also improve early growth. On raised beds, broadcast about a pound of seed per hundred square feet and chop it in with a hoe.

Older varieties of peas were trellised to enhance harvest and pod development, but most modern dwarf varieties will not even climb a trellis if one is available.

Garden Planning
A 100-square-foot bed of dwarf peas supplies our family's fresh table needs for one to two weeks of intense harvesting. I like to sow several beds in succession *and* grow some climbing snow peas, too. Climbing varieties are usually indeterminate and will keep on producing until their soil is exhausted or disease takes the

vines. Any bed that ends up bare of green manure in spring is a good candidate for peas. If you don't eat them, the vines can be rototilled as green manure.

Insects and Diseases

There are a lot of pea diseases—wilts, yellows, streaks, and enation, to name a few. Wet, damp, cloudy weather encourages disease, but usually the main trouble in the maritime Northwest is from enation. Spread by the green peach aphid, which begins to move about when the weather turns warm, enation causes a mottled, warty appearance to the pod, ends flowering and pod set, and then kills the vine. Many gardeners think the vine died from hot weather. None of the old home garden standards are enation-resistant, though these may still be grown if sown early to mature before June's heat. Some of the later varieties do not ever seem to mature in time at Lorane. Of course, my cold, heavy soil is not conducive to rapid early spring growth, and gardeners on lighter soils may well be more fortunate with them.

Harvest

Pods are best picked before the seeds have begun to get tough, so harvest on the small side. Keeping the vines picked clean encourages somewhat more production. Freezer types are bred to form lots of pods and then fill them all out at once, making a concentrated harvest.

Saving Seed

Let some vines mature seed, harvest the dried pods, thrash, and fully dry before storage. Very simple!

Varieties

The earlier old standards like Little Marvel, Lincoln, Dark Skinned Perfection, Early Frosty, and the like need no trellising and will mature if sown early. Alderman, or Tall Telephone, requires a trellis and fast growth to mature in time. We have not succeeded with Alderman at our trials. The enation-resistant types like Maestro, Corvallis, Knight, Olympia, Grenadier, and Mayfair are much better adapted to our maritime conditions. All these are dwarf. Oregon Sugar Pod is a highly disease-resistant snow pea. Developed to create a new Willamette Valley farming business, Oregon Sugar Pod has successfully allowed small growers to supply the national snow pea market during summer. Two other non-enation-resistant varieties have finer home garden qualities and produce prolifically if sown early. They are Dwarf White Sugar and Rembrandt (TSC). The old Dwarf Gray Sugar has very poor quality pods—at least in our trials—and Mammoth Melting Sugar is another old variety that is indeterminate and too late most years, though its pods are superb. (Mammoth Melting Sugar is the variety grown on poles along the California coast that sells for outrageous amounts out of season.) Snap peas are the new thing and we like them very much, though as yet none are enation-resistant. Sugar Snap, an indeterminate trellised type, is often a bit on the late side for much production. Sugar Rae, Sugar Mel, and Sugar Bon, touted as being equally good, dwarves, and earlier than Sugar Snap, are not of the same quality, but the new Sugar Ann is excellent and about three weeks earlier than Sugar Snap. I think there will be a lot of new snap peas in and out of the marketplace during the next few years, and we can hope that one of the new types will resist pea enation.

Green Manures

Green manure crops have useful places in rotational schemes. Legume green manures have the advantage of creating soil nitrogen in addition to organic matter, but there are other nonleguminous plants which are also very useful. Some of them are not only good green manures, but are also edible. Anything edible that grows over the winter—even if not absolutely choice fare—is a very interesting crop to many maritime Northwest gardeners.

Green manures lend themselves naturally to raised bed gardening, especially when the entire bed was planted to a single type of plant or a single crop. This permits easy planting of green manures. On raised beds, most green manures are easily sown by broadcasting the seed rather thickly and chopping it in shallowly with a hoe. When late September/early October is rainy, it is often sufficient to allow the seed to sprout lying on the soil's surface. If a good thick stand is established, grasses and weeds will be shaded and crowded out, greatly reducing the amount of weed seed that is formed next spring.

The roots of well-grown green manure crops will densely penetrate the soil of an uncompacted raised bed 18 to 24 inches. When the green manure crop is removed, its roots rot rapidly and naturally fracture the soil. No tillage system, short of double digging, could break up ground that deeply. Other types of green manures than those mentioned in this chapter are possible, but care should be taken before using an unknown green manure. Some types of vegetation are tough and hard to handle without heavy equipment. All green manures I recommend are tender and succulent, easily adapted to hand tools or small tillers.

Crimson Clover

This is the most broadly usable cover crop for the maritime Northwest. Though it grows poorly in badly drained soils and will be very disappointing on very acid or infertile ones, Crimson clover is easy to sow, hardy, and easily worked in spring. It also makes over one hundred pounds of nitrogen per acre and prepares soil sufficiently well to grow good low-to-medium-demanding crops without further fertilizer. One pound of seed covers 200 to 400 square feet of bed. Sow late September to mid-October, broadcasting the seed and chopping it in about 1/2 inch deep if possible. At one pound per 200 square feet, Crimson clover may be scattered in beds of brussels sprouts or other winter crops and allowed to sprout on the soil's surface. Low growing and noncompetitive until spring, it will take over the beds in March, swallowing the stumps and remains of winter crops. Crimson clover flowers late in April to early May, depending on the weather and location. Once in full bloom, it should be turned in as soon as possible. When seed formation starts, the stems become tougher and woodier, taking longer to break down. On raised beds or small plots, clover may be scythed down or mowed, the vegetation raked up and composted, while the root stubble is hoed in. Doing this accelerates breakdown and sowing of seeds can be done within days. Roto-tilled in, tops and all, it can take slightly over a week before planting is possible. Early in spring, beds of Crimson clover may be shallowly and gently hoed in, tops and all. The very succulent small greens are rotted within days, permitting easy sowings of spring mustards and spinaches without rototillage, even on pretty wet raised beds.

Beware of other types of clover. Crimson clover is an *annual* and succulent—easily killed with a hoe or tiller. Perennial clovers like Red clover form strong clumps that resist tillage and reroot. Perennial clovers also propagate through underground runners and can become one of the worst of weeds to eliminate. I know, because years ago, an ignorant or unscrupulous merchant sold me some "Crimson clover" that was really Red clover. There was quite a difference, believe me. I still have clumps of it coming up in my trials after all these years.

Austrian Field Peas

This green manure is a very small-seeded pea variety, much more winter hardy than garden peas. Austrian Field peas may be grown alone or in combination with grain, such as wheat or barley. Interplanted with grain, the nitrogen fixed by the peas improves the growth of the grain, while the grain supports the pea vines. The combination produces an enormous amount of biomass. Peas and grain are hard to handle with light equipment, and it takes a tractor-drawn tiller or plow to turn them in. It also takes over two weeks for grains to break down enough to allow easy planting. Field peas may be grown alone and are especially good on raised beds. Field peas tend to tangle small tillers when the vines have become long, but instead of tilling them in, the vines are *easily* pulled out of raised beds by hand, leaving a fine-tilthed seedbed. Any stubble is hoed in and the bed is ready to rake out and plant.

Field peas will grow well in soils not quite well enough drained or fertile enough for clovers and have the advantage of maturing somewhat later than clover, giving heavier, poorer draining soils more time to dry out before the maturing vegetation demands tillage. Field peas are sown at the same time as clover at rates of 100 to 200 square feet per pound of seed, whether alone or mixed with grain. They, too, are rather insignificant during winter, but grow rapidly in spring. Field peas produce sixty to eighty pounds of nitrogen per acre, plus an abundance of biomass. They also leave a beautiful, fine-tilthed seedbed.

Fava Beans

Small-seeded favas make the most excellent overwintered green manures for locations where they won't freeze out. Seed for them is not widely available currently, but it probably will become so in a few years as more maritime Northwest gardeners discover favas. Favas produce nearly two hundred pounds of nitrogen per acre, a huge quantity of organic matter, and grow in soils of only average fertility, even if not excellently drained. One variety, Friedrichs, is hardy to about 15 degrees, and when overwintered grows 6 to 8 feet tall in stands so dense they'll completely crowd out all competing weeds. Another fall variety is Banner, described earlier as a "winter bean." Banner is hardy to at least 10 degrees. Seed for both is available only from Territorial Seed Company at this time.

As a green manure, sow favas in late October to early November. Sow slightly earlier in colder areas, slightly later in warmer winter sites. Sow seeds about 1 inch deep. Friedrichs is grown as silage in the Skagit Valley, and there it is sown from a grain drill in rows 7 inches apart at about one hundred fifty pounds per acre. The gardener should broadcast the seed at about one pound to 100 to 200 square feet of bed. Favas also make an excellent spring-sown green manure, sprouting well in early March sowings, as do peas. Spring sown, they will only be 3 to 4 feet tall before planting time.

When the stalks are in full bloom and pods are forming, it is time to turn in favas. This usually happens by mid-May at Lorane. Handle favas like clover. Cut off the vegetation at ground level and chop in the stubble, or till in—favas are brittle and do not tangle walk-behind rear-end tillers. Fava vegetation rots incredibly rapidly and leaves the soil in beautiful condition. I've come to feel so strongly in favor of favas that I'd chance their freeze-out and plan to resow them in spring if this should happen.

Tyfon

Tyfon is a brassica—a cross between stubble turnips and Chinese cabbage. It is hardy to about 10 degrees, forms deep taproots which break up soil, and has mild, edible greens similar to mustard spinach. The vegetation can be cut and will regrow several times in a year. Tyfon may be sown from May through September at rates of one ounce per 100 to 200 square feet or ten pounds per acre, broadcasting the seed and chopping it in shallowly. It grows amazingly rapidly and flowers only in late March after overwintering. The unopened flowers aren't a bad sort of "broccoli." I like Tyfon on beds I'm going to plant early in spring, because the long taproots pull out easily from my raised beds, leaving no stubble and a ready-to-plant rough seedbed; I try to sow it for this purpose early in September. Earlier sowings may be cut and the vegetation raked up and composted several times before winter checks growth. Commercially, the very palatable leaves are used as animal feed, producing more biomass per unit of time than virtually any known crop.

Corn Salad

Discussed later on as a salad green, this very hardy vegetation may also be densely sown on raised beds, harvested through the winter for salads, and then allowed to go through a rapid growth period in early spring to flower by late April, when it should be chopped in. Corn salad produces a fair amount of biomass and creates a very finely tilthed seedbed. As a green manure, sow about one ounce of seed per 100 square feet of bed. I like to grow one bed of it each winter.

Grains

Any winter grain—wheat, barley, oats, or rye—may be used as a green manure. They'll grow on fairly wet, poor soils, but have several liabilities—being tough (requiring large equipment) and slow to rot and making a late garden if the spring is a wet one. The one that "yields to the disc" most easily is winter wheat, and soft white varieties can be obtained anywhere in the Willamette at feed and grain stores or health food stores. One pound of seed covers 100 to 200 square feet, sown mid-September through mid-October. Be sure to till in before the seed heads form completely and the stalks get woody.

Buckwheat

Buckwheat is the unexcelled summertime green manure! It grows on soil of even low fertility without much irrigation and rapidly forms such a dense cover that it shades out grasses and weeds, retarding their growth and seed formation. Buckwheat is not frost hardy and will only make rapid growth from May through July. By August, decreasing day lengths force buckwheat into bloom almost as soon as it sprouts, making it useless as a green manure. Buckwheat is also one of the best "weeds" you could have in the garden, being very easily hoed out or tilled in. I've even tilled in hip-high stands of brittle buckwheat stalks with a front-end tiller without tangling (a supposed impossibility according to the companies touting rear-end tillers).

Buckwheat goes from sprout to full bloom in five to six weeks. Once in full bloom, vegetative growth stops and the stalks get woody. I'd suggest buckwheat as a short-term green manure on spots where something will be going in a month or so, or as a way of developing a new field by suppressing weed growth and improving tilth. For this latter purpose, sow in early May. Then, about mid- to late June, it will be ready to till in or pull out. If tilled in, broadcast more buckwheat seed among the standing vegetation, till shallowly, and water. The new seedlings emerge as the old vegetation rots. This second crop is through in August, and the plot may be sown to Tyfon or planted to winter greens.

One pound of seed covers 300 to 600 square feet and should be broadcast and hoed in about 1 inch deep.

Greens

There is no botanical classification called "greens." The vegetables I classify in this group actually are members of many different families of plants. Greens are plants that have been bred to rush into their vegetative growth stage immediately after germination and are harvested before they begin to flower. They are grown in fertile soils and produce thick, succulent, and usually sweet leaves, and sometimes juicy stalks.

Nutrient requirements of plants change somewhat as they go through their growth stages, which I consider to be "seedling," "vegetative," and "seed formation." During the seedling stage, plants do best with little nitrogen, but abundant phosphorus and potassium. Once established and into their vegetative stage, most benefit from much more nitrogen relative to other nutrients. Then, when flowering, fruiting, and seed formation occur, vegetative growth usually stops or slows, though there are a few vegetables that grow vegetatively and make fruit on a continuous basis as long as the weather permits. When forming fruit and seeds, plants do not need much nitrogen and often transport nitrogen from leaf cells to the fruit or seed instead of absorbing any. Too much soil nitrogen at this stage can interfere with making fruit.

Greens uniformly require high levels of soil moisture, moderate amounts of phosphorus and potassium, and fairly high amounts of nitrogen. I suspect that breeders have selected greens for limited root development in favor of more abundant greens, so maintaining soil moisture and close placement of fertilizer is essential. Rich garden soil will generally supply enough nitrogen and other nutrients for most types of greens after it has warmed up well, but in early spring fertilizer is very helpful. Unless the soil is extremely rich, small amounts of fertilizer will also produce faster growth during late spring and summer, and consequently the greens will be more succulent and sweeter. However, greens grown for fall harvest will be more resistant to cold if they grow slightly less lushly, and fertilizer should be withheld or greatly reduced on crops sown after mid-July.

Celery

Celery is the most demanding crop I know of, requiring twice the fertilization of corn and amazing amounts of water. It also grows best under cool conditions with intense sunlight, so commercial crops are grown along the southern California coast, close to the sea where the maritime influence is strong, yet light intense. Slow growing at all stages, celery transplants can take ten to twelve weeks to size up enough to set out. Though celery can be transplanted in mid-April and consequently may be started as early as mid-January, this is a lot of effort and a task fraught with some peril, for celery has a tendency to bolt prematurely if given too much exposure to below-50-degree temperatures. I've found it much more satisfying to be harvesting celery as a fall salad green that stands a chance to overwinter some mild years.

Culture

Celery has a very small lateral root system. If direct-seeded, a taproot will extend down 3 feet or more, drawing on subsoil moisture. Lateral roots are very few and close to the plant. Transplanted celery has its taproot broken and forms a more fibrous and shallow root system that extends out a little farther laterally. Transplanted celery requires even higher moisture levels in the surface foot of soil. The root system is not strong and celery does much better in coarser soils, or peat or bog soils. Its natural habitat is swampland with subirrigation. Clayey soils should be well amended with organic matter at least a foot deep.

From mid-April through the first of June, form a 3- to 4-inch-deep furrow with a garden hoe, sprinkle 1/4 to 1/2 cup complete organic fertilizer per 5 row feet in the shallow trench, and cover. Atop the band of fertilizer, sow celery seed. The seed is tiny and if sprinkled thinly in a 1/4-inch-deep furrow, it will come up in a good stand. Celery seed germinates slowly, taking two weeks or so, depending on the temperature. April and early May sowings are usually kept moist by natural conditions, but it is helpful to cover the shallowly sown seed with a mixture of peat moss and soil or sifted compost to retain moisture. (This is a useful trick for germinating any small seed in sunny weather.) In sunny weather, water the seeds daily until they germinate. Then, gradually thin the seedlings. Final spacing of celery should be about 12 inches between plants in rows about 24 inches apart. *Keep the plants well watered* during summer's heat. If growth slows, water with liquid fertilizer every two to three weeks, or side-dress with seed meal or blood meal. My favorite side-dressing material at this time is a mixture of half blood meal, half kelp meal. I think the kelp meal mostly stretches out the blood meal and makes it easier to apply thinly, though it, too, will slowly break down on the soil's surface, adding potassium and trace mineral nutrition. I sprinkle about a teaspoonful per half-grown plant close to the stalks, *spread thinly*. One side-dressing like this lasts a month. If celery does not grow rapidly, it becomes tough, stringy, and bitter. Stop fertilizing about August 15 to harden off the plants somewhat.

Garden Planning

A dozen plants will spruce up your salads without being picked bare.

Insects and Diseases

We've had no problems at Lorane.

Harvest

Stalks will be of harvestable size by late summer from direct-seeded plants, and early-sown transplants can be ready by midsummer. Do not harvest entire plants, but instead cut off large outer stalks as wanted. If the winter is not too hard, celery will stand until spring, allowing light pickings. When the plants bolt and begin seed formation in spring, the unopened flowers and the tender stalks below them are delicious salad greens. Mature celery plants might be a good candidate for protection by a tall cloche over the winter, where they'll make more winter growth and be more likely to survive.

Saving Seed

Celery is a biennial, flowering its second year unless it freezes out. Too much cold weather in the seedling stages can make celery "think" that it has over-wintered and it can then bolt the first season before fully grown, which makes early spring planting somewhat hazardous. This is also a bad trait, and early bolters should be culled out by the seed saver, though plants that bolt in summer are not likely to mature seed in any case. Celery crosses easily with other varieties and with celeriac, so to prevent most crossing, isolate varieties by at least 200 feet. Probably it would be a poor idea to grow both celery seed and celeriac seed the same year. Celery seed will last seven to ten years if it forms under decent conditions and is properly stored and dried, making it possible to grow one's own seed in the maritime Northwest. Even at frosty Lorane, Oregon, celery survives about one winter in three or four. Celery flowers are small, white umbels, similar to wild carrot. The seed detaches from the drying flowers easily, so use care in harvesting. Dry the seed heads indoors on newspaper to catch shattering seeds.

Varieties

All seed companies offer Utah 52-70 in one variant or another. Avoid the "Florida" selections. Harris calls their Utah celery Clean-Cut, and it is as good as the best. Pascal types are more resistant to early bolting and so are better for an early transplanted crop. Golden or Golden Self Blanching celeries have shorter stalks and usually less vigorous growth. Generally I've had poor luck with them. At this time, I have also discovered something called Pink celery, which is grown in England and which is under trial on our trial grounds at the time this is being written.

Celeriac

Celeriac is a type of celery grown for its bulbous root that is peeled and then steamed, fried, or ground into soup stocks. Its flavor is much like that of celery and it is a very nonstarchy root. We like it a lot slowly fried to a crispy golden brown atop the woodstove in early winter. Celeriac root has almost no tendency to absorb butter or other fats when fried! It is cultured exactly like celery and should be spaced and fertilized identically and should definitely be considered a fall crop. Well-grown roots can be 8 inches in diameter. All mail-order seed companies sell some sort of celeriac. All of it comes from Europe, where the crop is a commercial item; but much of the seed sold in the United States is only of home garden quality because there is virtually no commercial market here for celeriac roots. Good quality selections are fairly free of lateral roots and are smooth, avoiding much waste. The best variety we've examined is Arvi (TSC), which is the commercial market standard in Europe at this time, and which costs eight times as much as cheap selections.

Chicory

See Roots.

Corn Salad

In Europe, small grains like wheat, barley, and oats are called "corn," and what we call corn in America, they call maize. Corn salad was a small weed that came up in the stubble of harvested grain fields late in summer and was winter hardy. The weeds made good salad greens, so they were bred to increase leaf size and flavor. If allowed to go to seed in the garden, corn salad will naturalize as an edible weed.

Culture

Because of its recent adaptation by man as a vegetable, its native ability to grow well in soils of only moderate fertility has not been lost. Ordinary garden soil is usually rich enough to allow this vegetable to grow lustily without fertilization. The seed will not germinate until soil temperatures drop from their August peak. Sow the seed thickly 1/2 inch deep in rows at least 12 inches apart. Do not thin. (Corn salad may also be grown as a green manure crop by broadcasting the seed thickly.) Early September sowings are sized up for use by midwinter. Sowings made later are cut in early to midspring. Do not sow after early October. Corn salad goes to seed in April, and the flowering stalks are a bit spicy compared to the leaves, but still edible.

Garden Planning

Fifty row feet is enough to create a winter-long supply.

Insects and Diseases

We've had no problems at Lorane.

Harvest

The small leaves are cut off with a sharp knife in clumps, allowing the plants to regrow.

Saving Seed

The light, irregular seeds form in late spring and begin dropping to earth or blowing good distances in strong winds. Spread a sheet of cardboard under the plants and catch the falling seed, collecting it daily. Corn salad seed has a short life of only a year or two, so be sure to dry seed carefully before storage. Corn salad tends to naturalize in the garden as an edible weed.

Varieties

Several strains are available, some with larger leaves than others and with slightly earlier or later bolting dates, but the differences are mostly insignificant. All varieties are more than hardy enough for our maritime Northwest winters.

Endive (Escarole)

Many people think that endive is a sort of lettuce, but it is not. Lettuce is an annual, only slightly frost hardy. Endive is a biennial relative of chicory and very hardy compared to lettuce. Freeze-out on most lettuce varieties is about 21 degrees, with some exceptional strains hardy to better than 19. Endive has overwintered in my garden in a very leaky cold frame, surviving 7-degree temperatures without sign of damage. I don't know at this time how much hardier it is than 7 degrees, but I do know that there are significant varietal differences in hardiness. The bitterness of endive becomes much less noticeable after some good frosts have worked the plants over a few times. Cold-frame-overwintered endive is nearly as sweet as lettuce when used in March and April.

Supermarket consumers of endive or escarole never discover its potential sweetness, because commercial production is done in California or Florida.

Culture

Though endive can be grown as a summer vegetable from sowings in spring or early summer, we only sow it unprotected in August for fall harvest. I also sow a cold frame of endive in September for harvest during early winter, and sow another large frameful in early to mid-October to overwinter for harvest during March and April. Sow seeds 1/2 inch deep, two to four seeds per inch, in rows 12 to 16 inches apart. Thin gradually and *carefully* to 12 inches apart in the row, so the beautiful rosettes develop fully. Good garden soil will release plenty of nutrients for endive sown late in summer, and frame-grown stuff is much better grown slowly so as to be as hardy as possible. In very poor soil, 1/4 cup of complete organic fertilizer per 5 row feet banded below the seed might be helpful.

Garden Planning

Good salad greens are scarce by November. Unprotected August sowings of endive often remain in good condition into December. Usually it is not cold that ends their life in winter, but rain and damp-induced mildews and rots. The rosettes gradually rot back, leaving a dying stump. Some varieties, particularly European selections, are more resistant to these stresses and to cold, but none seem able to take an entire rainy winter without the protection of a cold frame. Even the leakiest frame, which will hardly increase nighttime temperatures at all, will overwinter endive if it keeps off the rain. So, plant more endive than it might seem is needed. Frames full of endive can be started in beds that grew melons, cucumbers, corn, tomatoes, or other hot-weather crops.

Insects and Diseases

Not a problem if kept dry in winter.

Harvest

In winter, when harvesting most types of salad greens, it is usually more sensible to cut individual leaves, permitting the plant to continue production. Sometimes the outer leaves are pulled up and tied in a bunch to blanch the heart. It takes about one week and makes the center pale yellow and milder.

Saving Seed

Endive is a self-pollinated biennial. Plants that survive the winter will bolt to seed in April. Place the mature seed heads in a paper bag to finish drying, rub out the seed, and clean as best you can without milling equipment. Endive seed has a long life, usually three to four years.

Varieties

Two basic types of endive are grown. One is frilly with lacy, curled leaves, like Salad Bowl lettuce. The other is called Batavian endive and has thick, broad leaves and juicy, blanched inner leaves. Batavian endive is sometimes called escarole. Most endive seed sold in the United States is intended to be grown in California or Florida and is not as cold hardy as it could be. Stokes Full Heart Batavian is a European import and may be hardier. Territorial Seed Company brings in all its endive seed from Holland and sells only the hardiest, most bad weather-resistant types, especially good for maritime conditions.

Lettuce

Lettuce is a slightly hardy annual green that can be harvested from late spring through late fall. Looseleaf types are the easiest to grow; bibbs, romaines, and butterheads are fairly simple; and crispheads or iceberg types are somewhat difficult, requiring very rapid growth and correct nutrient levels to head out properly. The main trick to producing good lettuce is thinning. If crowded, shape, flavor, and succulence suffer. But if given ample room to expand rapidly, with enough water and nutrients to do so, the rosettes develop beautifully in any soil type.

A well-grown legume cover crop may release all the nutrients lettuce needs to grow well, or moderate amounts of complete organic fertilizer can be banded instead. Even ordinary manures or composts will usually grow decent lettuce. Iceberg types that are grown too slowly become bitter, but if given too much nitrogen are subject to blowing up (loose heads poorly shaped) or tipburn, which looks like thin, blackened leaves on the interior of the heads. Looseleaf types are not nearly as sensitive. Growing head lettuce may take a bit of experimentation to discover how much of what sort of fertilizer is compatible with the soil type being used.

Lettuce has a very dense root system that breaks down rapidly after harvest, leaving the soil in nice condition. Because it roots shallowly, attention must be paid to maintaining high soil moisture levels in the surface foot, or rapid growth will cease.

Culture

Use of cold frames can extend sowing dates by about one month, both earlier and later, but generally, sow outdoors from April through mid-August, though iceberg types won't head at Lorane if sown after mid-July. Sow 1/2 inch deep; sprinkle the seed thinly in furrows at least 16 inches apart; thin gradually *without permitting any crowding* so looseleafs stand about 8 inches apart; iceberg types and romaines should stand 12 inches apart. Up to half a cup of complete organic fertilizer banded below each 5 feet of furrow may help greatly, especially in poorer soils.

Garden Planning

Personally, I do not like iceberg lettuce nearly as much as some of the looseleaf or bibb types, or the romaines. Because we like small salads daily, even during the main garden fruit production period of August, I grow a continuous production bed of lettuce, allocating one 100-square-foot bed to it. Short rows of lettuce are sown across a raised bed about 24 inches apart, and when they are about one-third grown or about 3 inches in diameter, new rows are seeded in between the old. The mature heads do not shade out the rows of tiny seedlings coming up in between, and as the big heads are cut, the new seedlings are thinned gradually. By the time all the big heads are out, the seedlings are about 3 inches in diameter, and the cycle starts again; in subsequent sowings, I may sprinkle some compost between the rows and hoe it in shallowly before reseeding lettuce again. This way the bed keeps on making heads from the first sowing in April through the last harvests of October. I may well start another bed of cold hardy sorts in mid-August and put it under a tunnel cold frame by late September for harvest up to the time that a very cold night freezes the heads out (lettuce is hardy to about 20 degrees).

Insects and Diseases

We've never had any difficulties at Lorane.

Harvest

Cut heads as needed. Many varieties become bitter quickly after maturity, so successive sowings two to three weeks apart are wise.

Saving Seed

Lettuce is an annual that rarely cross-pollinates, so little or no isolation between varieties is needed. Commercial production of lettuce seed is done in California because the seed forms in late summer from early spring sowings, so it is nearly impossible to grow mature seed in the maritime Northwest unless the plants are started very early in cold frames, or the seedlings are transplanted out very early, or the seedlings are sown in October and overwintered in frames to begin rapid growth very early in spring. Some very mild years, lettuce will overwinter at Lorane. To harvest seed, cut the mature flower stalks, which become feathered out like dandelions, and dry indoors or under cover. Shake the stalks in a drum or big bag to gather the seed. Sometimes tight heads of iceberg lettuce must be scored with a sharp knife about 2 inches deep in an X to permit the seed stalk to emerge.

Varieties

Just about any type of looseleaf lettuce will do fine in the maritime Northwest, though a few varieties bred for southern latitudes bolt prematurely. Some of my personal favorites are Prizehead, Salad Bowl, and Grand Rapids. The best Grand Rapids strain is Slobolt, also excellent in cold frames during late fall and winter. Of all the romaines, I find the best grower to be Valmaine, which also has excellent flavor. Buttercrunch is a fine sort of bibb lettuce, having thick, juicy, sweet leaves as though a butter lettuce were crossed with romaine, keeping the shape of the butterhead with the crunch of the romaine heart. On my continuous bed, I mix the seed of all these sorts mentioned so far and thin the rows to allow a more or less even mixture to remain. Because the spread of maturity runs from Salad Bowl (earliest) to Valmaine several weeks later, the bed doesn't become bare all at once and the supply is more even. I've had good luck with most of the common sorts of butterheads, though some special varieties from Europe such as Merveille des 4 Saisons (TSC) are uniquely wonderful. Little Gem is another unique variety (TSC) that is a miniature romaine whose hearts are considered by Europeans to be the finest gourmet lettuce in existence. Winter Density (TSC, JSS), a small, fine-flavored romaine, is somewhat more hardy than other varieties, and is a good candidate for fall harvesting and standing into early winter in frames. Ithaca is the best adapted general-purpose head lettuce and is sold by most seed companies.

Mustard

Mustards are an easy-to-grow member of the cabbage family grown only for their leaves or stalks. Mustards are less prone to infestation by the cabbage root maggot. Highly photoperiodic, most mustard varieties go to seed under the influence of long days, and so must be sown early in spring to mature before mid-May or sown after the days shorten in July. I consider mustards to be an essential part of any year-round, maritime Northwest food production plan. They are much more delicious than most people realize. Stir-fried in the tasty fat from a single strip of bacon or in a tablespoonful of dark sesame oil, there is nothing better!

Culture

Light soils with coarse particles naturally hold a lot of air and have a low amount of retained water compared to the amount of solid particles they contain. This type of soil warms up quickly in spring. Heavy soils hold huge quantities of moisture and consequently have a much higher density. This means there is more material to heat up and their temperature is much lower in spring. Since biological processes, such as nutrient release and root development, occur more rapidly as soil temperature increases, getting mustards to grow rapidly in spring is easier in warmer soils. Heavier soil types will be better for this crop if first they are well amended with organic matter, lightening them up and causing their spring temperatures to be higher.

Mustards also need high levels of available nitrogen in spring if large plants are to be produced before they bolt. Midsummer sowings will usually grow adequately in decent garden soil with little or no fertilization. In spring, I add some blood meal to the complete organic fertilizer blend and band 1/4 to 1/2 cup below each 5 feet of furrow. Sow mustards in March, seeds sprinkled thinly in furrows 1/2 inch deep, rows 12 to 18 inches apart. Do not thin too rapidly as there will be large losses of seedlings to slugs, flea beetles, and general bad weather. Covering the mustard bed with a cold frame during March/April will greatly increase the yield. For fall and winter harvest, sow about August 1 to 15. For overwintered production and early spring harvest, sow mid- to late September and do not fertilize until spring regrowth begins in February, when a side-dressing of blood meal will spur a much larger harvest. For well-developed plants, take the time to thin gradually and completely so mature plants stand 3 to 5 inches apart in the row. Less hardy varieties of mustard that would not likely survive the winter unprotected will often overwinter in a cold frame. The hardiest varieties, which normally overwinter without protection, are much more productive if grown in a frame.

Garden Planning

Ten row feet is usually enough.

Insects and Diseases

Flea beetles are hard on slow-growing seedlings in spring. The best solutions are lots of fertilizer, extra seedlings to be eaten, and cold frames that induce more rapid growth. Rotenone will kill flea beetles for a few days after spraying if the rain doesn't wash it off immediately.

Harvest

In spring, pick off leaves as needed or cut plants off at the base. In fall, it is better to harvest individual leaves to conserve the patch. When mustards go to seed, it may seem that production is over; but actually, the plants are putting out their best food! Unopened flowers and the tender stalks below are the sweetest and fullest-flavored portions. After the main stalk is cut off, many smaller side flowers will appear for harvest.

Saving Seed

Mustards are bee pollinated and freely cross, producing many interesting and often not-too-edible progeny, so do not grow more than one variety for seed. Mustard seed lasts up to seven years with good vigor, so a seed saver could produce one variety each year, destroying the other plants before they open flowers. The clusters of small yellow flowers form little pods containing several seeds. When the pods are dry, cut the flower stalks, finish drying on a newspaper, thrash out the seed, dry fully in a paper sack, and store carefully. Allowing the flower stalks to fall on the ground will result in a self-sowing, perpetual mustard patch that needs only an occasional covering with compost or manure to maintain fertility.

Varieties

I believe all mustards originated in the Orient, and many varieties are amazingly beautiful examples of the plant breeder's art, with frilly leaves on long, graceful stalks. Others are rather plain. Only a few have become part of the conventional assortment available in America, such as Green Wave and Southern Giant Curled, which are hot and mustardy. Green Wave is slightly slower to bolt in spring, making it a better candidate in our climate. A much finer, mustardy mustard is Miike Giant (TSC) with reddish leaves and broad, thick stalks. Not only is it hot, but also distinctively sweet and good flavored. Miike is also much hardier than the others and will often overwinter at Lorane, while Green Wave freezes out. Tendergreen or Mustard Spinach is a plain-looking, broad-leaved sort, having virtually no pungency or flavor, and American selections have deteriorated badly. Late Komatsuna (TSC) is the original Japanese variety that, while still mild, has good flavor and retains uniform selection. Tai Sai (TSC, JSS) has long, white, celerylike stalks and broad, green, spoon-shaped leaves, a very mild flavor, and is essential to oriental cookery. Chinese Pac Choi (TSC, JSS) has shorter stalks than Tai Sai, but is the only mustard variety I know of that will not bolt during midsummer and so may be planted April through August. It is also fairly winter hardy. Kyona (Mizuna) (JSS, TSC) is a variety so mild and sweet that it is good in winter salads and has been bred for exceptional cold hardiness, often overwintering at Lorane. It bolts readily in early spring, and is good for fall/winter harvest only. Green-in-Snow (TSC) is a variety recently discovered in China that, as its name implies, is extraordinarily hardy. Sown for fall or winter harvest, it usually survives unprotected at Lorane to bolt in March. Because it is low growing and vigorous in winter, Green-in-Snow is a good frame candidate. Some of the new hybrid mustards recently coming from Japan like Tendergreen II are amazingly vigorous growers.

Some other greens that culture just like mustard but that are not actually mustards are Santoh, Edible Chrysanthemum, Tyfon, and Raab. Santoh is a type of Chinese cabbage that does not head and is slow to bolt. The outer leaves of heading Chinese cabbage varieties are tough and of poor eating quality, but Santoh has tender, mild leaves, good even in salads. Santoh is best grown as a fall/winter crop and in frames, though in a garden that warms up fast in spring, a good crop of greens can be had before it bolts in early May. The unopened flowers are particularly good. Raab is a type of turnip used for edible greens. It makes the most rapid growth of any type of green in spring, often in production several weeks ahead of mustards sown at the same time. It also bolts earlier. Raab has a mild flavor, but is not as choice fare as mustards. I'd consider growing it when a severe winter froze out most of the overwintered crops. Tyfon, mentioned before as a green manure, has leaves that are as palatable as Tendergreen mustard, but being biennial, will not bolt in summer. If well grown and carefully thinned, Tyfon will also make nice turnips. Tyfon is hardy to about 10 degrees and can be eaten from May through March. Edible Chrysanthemum is actually a small-flowering member of the chrysanthemum family used as a stir-fry green in Japanese cookery. It is easy to grow, cultures like mustard, and may be sown from April through August. It should be harvested before the flowers begin to open, at which time it becomes very spicy. For a continuous supply, successive sowings of Edible Chrysanthemum should be made every three weeks.

Parsley
See Roots.

Spinach
Spinach is a natural maritime Northwest crop—our long, cool periods in spring and fall make large, tasty plants. In fact, spinach is so well adapted that much of the world's spinach seed is grown in the Skagit Valley. Remarkably cold hardy, spinach almost always overwinters successfully, though it won't make nearly as much new growth as mustard or endive under low winter light levels. Spinach is very nitrogen-demanding, and in spring fertilizers are essential. Spinach is also very sensitive to day length, and most varieties bolt as soon as the days lengthen.

Culture
Sow most varieties of spinach early in spring for harvest during May, and then sow again about mid-July for harvest in late summer, fall, and winter. Sowings made after August 1 won't achieve much size before low light levels check their growth and will be harvested the following spring. Overwintered spinach tends to bolt a bit earlier than spring-sown, but overwintered plants sometimes can be harvested starting in March. A few types are so slow to bolt that they may be sown April through June for summer harvest. Spinach seed germinates better in soils between 50 and 60 degrees, and it can be a bit difficult to get a good stand of seedlings in midsummer. Sow the seeds thickly, 1/2 inch deep in rows 12 inches apart. It's a good idea to delay thinning until the seedlings get a true leaf because there will be many losses. Gradually thin to 3 inches apart in the row. In poor soils or early in spring, banding 1/4 to 1/2 cup complete organic fertilizer below the seed can be very beneficial. In very poor ground or in chilly, wet springs, substituting some blood meal for seed meal increases nitrogen release. I'd not fertilize midsummer sowings. Overwintered plants should be side-dressed with blood meal as soon as regrowth begins, usually in late February, using about 2 tablespoonfuls of blood meal per 5 row feet, sprinkled close to the plants.

Garden Planning
Twenty to 50 row feet of spinach will make salads or cooked spinach for even the heartiest of spinach admirers. A March sowing might be followed with a mid-April sowing of a late-bolting variety for a continuous supply from May through June. Dedicated spinach salad fanciers might try broadcasting several

ounces of seed atop a raised bed in March, chopping it in lightly, and without thinning, cutting off handfuls of succulent leaves as soon as they are the size of a quarter, sawing off plants at ground level with a sharp knife. Rows of seedlings about 12 inches apart may be left unharvested to develop full-sized plants. Carefully washed, these tiny leaves make the best of salads during April. I'd plant a spinach bed where an overwintered legume green manure was chopped in and sow midsummer beds following peas or favas.

Insects and Diseases

Symphylans seem to prefer spinach, and even thickly sown stands gradually disappear before maturity if symphylans populations are large. Densely sown broadcast plantings solve this difficulty by providing lots of root for symphylans to eat.

Harvest

Since you're not shipping spinach to market, there is no reason to cut entire plants. Snip off individual leaves as needed, and when the plants bolt, small leaves on the seed stalks can still be used.

Saving Seed

Spinach is a biennial, overwintering and forming seed the next summer. Spring sowings still bolt, though a bit later. Spinach is wind-pollinated and readily crosses, so varieties must be isolated by at least one mile. The species is sexual, having male, female, and hermaphroditic plants. The first bolters will be an undesirable type called dwarf males, and these should be rogued. The male plants open small pollen sacs and the female plants form seed. The seed stalks ripen unevenly, so delay harvest until the stalks are brown. Cut the stalks, dry indoors fully, and thrash out seed between the palms. Seed yields are very high.

Varieties

Bloomsdale is the basic home garden sort. There are many strains of Bloomsdale—Winter, Wisconsin, Virginia, etc.—and the gardener usually doesn't know which is being sold. The strains vary somewhat as to disease resistance (which doesn't usually affect garden production), bolting date, and cold hardiness. Winter Bloomsdale, sometimes called Cold Resistant Savoy, is the best all-around bet for sowing in spring and for fall/winter and overwintered harvest. Bloomsdale has curly, thick, sweet leaves and the best flavor of any garden spinach. Nobel is an old-standard, fine-flavored, thick, flat-leaved type and usually a bit later to bolt (by a week or so). Indian Summer (JSS) and Mazurka (TSC) are slow-bolting, flat-leaved types of good flavor that will permit summertime harvests from April through June sowings. Flat-leaved spinaches are popular with canneries because they're easier to wash, but don't usually have the best flavor. A promising new savoy-leaved, late-bolting summer variety is called Tyee, which is immune to all known races of blue mold. This disease retards growth during winter, so Tyee will permit much heavier cutting from late fall to spring.

Swiss Chard

Chard is a member of the beet family, bred for large, succulent leaves instead of root development. It is frost hardy and stands through many Lorane winters without freezing out. Chard cultures like beets and will grow fine in soils of only moderate fertility without fertilizer. Using some complete organic fertilizer banded below the seeds helps accelerate regrowth after cutting.

Culture
Sow between April and June, eight to twelve seeds per foot, 3/4 inch deep, in rows at least 18 inches apart. Thin gradually to 10 inches apart in the row.

Garden Planning
Ten row feet should supply a large family for nine months from a single sowing. It is a good strategy to locate chard in the same bed with parsley and leeks, as both will be in the ground for a long time, too.

Insects and Diseases
We've had no problems at Lorane.

Harvest
Cut individual leaves as needed. If regrowth is too slow, side-dress with blood meal—1 teaspoonful per plant every four to six weeks, sprinkled close to the base of the plant.

Saving Seed
A member of the beet family, chard crosses with beets and the procedure is identical to saving beet seed.

Varieties
Fordhook seems to be the hardiest, though most varieties available in the United States are produced in the Skagit Valley by overwintering, and are consequently fairly hardy. Some European types available from "gourmet" seed companies don't handle summer heat well. Ruby or Rhubarb tends to bolt prematurely from early sowings.

Brassicas

Brassicas are one of the best-adapted groups of vegetables a maritime Northwest gardener could grow. They like cool weather, are frost hardy—some extremely so—and may be depended on to produce even during those damp, cloudy summers that have been traditionally called "cabbage years." Brassicas are also very nutritious food and it has been said that the labor that built the Great Wall of China was fueled not on rice, but on cabbage.

Included in the family are all the coles—kale, rutabagas, cabbage, cauliflower, broccoli, brussels sprouts, collards, and Chinese cabbage. Mustards and turnips are close relatives. The brassicas have amazing potential to be "grotesqued" by the breeder, so terminal buds have become cabbages; lateral buds are now brussels sprouts; flowers are broccoli and cauliflower; stems have thickened into rutabaga and kohlrabi. Unfortunately, the more a single aspect of the plant's genetic potential has been emphasized, the more the line has lost vigor. The coarse brassicas like kale, collards, and Purple Sprouting broccoli will grow lustily in soil of only moderate fertility. More refined rutabagas and brussels sprouts take higher fertility levels, while the intensely inbred cabbage, cauliflower, and broccoli demand the finest soils and lots of fertilizer; though the less refined types of cabbage are much more vigorous than the others and can almost be considered "field crops" like corn or beans.

Brassicas tend to demand little phosphorus nutrition compared to vegetables that make edible seeds, but do require high levels of nitrogen and potassium and are heavy feeders on calcium, growing much better when soil pH is above 6.0. And even in fairly neutral soils, additional lime in the furrow can cause a marked growth improvement.

The cabbage fly seems to prefer some types of brassicas to others. For example, Chinese cabbage and turnips are the most attractive, while rutabagas seem the least. The fly's preferences and the variety's inherent root system vigor seem to determine how damaging the larvae will be. Cauliflower is usually very poorly rooted and a little root loss can be fatal, while brussels sprouts have much more vigorous root systems that can tolerate a lot more damage. Kale plants are almost never noticeably damaged by the maggot on our trial grounds or gardens at Lorane. The fly is not uniformly a pest throughout the maritime Northwest. Washington State has a higher level of infestation than Oregon, and the Skagit Valley has the worst in the United States. The chapter entitled "Diseases and Pests of the Maritime Northwest" outlines handling the cabbage root maggot, as well as a few other brassica pests.

Brassicas are also troubled by a soil disease called clubroot. Each type of brassica is affected somewhat differently by the disease. The infected root swells grotesquely and root efficiency is inhibited. Healthy soil can be infected from purchased bedding plants, from composts made from infected plants, and from gardener's feet and tools. Once clubroot is in the soil, it can be completely eliminated only by growing no member of the brassica family, as well as by religiously removing several types of host weeds for a period of seven years. However, even three or four years without brassicas in the soil will greatly reduce the level of infection, so gardeners with infected plots might consider a four-year rotation. Liming soil to a pH of 7.0 to 7.5 will also greatly inhibit the disease. Mysteriously wilting or stunted plants with swollen, knobby roots are sure indications of the presence of clubroot. If it is present, one should take care not to spread the disease by composting infected plants. They should be burned. Non-disinfected tools, even the gardener's shoes, can spread the organism from infected plots to healthy soil. The Extension Service prints a fact sheet about clubroot (EM 4205) free for the asking. A few types of brassica carry resistance to one or more strains of the disease, but resistance to one strain does not mean resistance to the strain in a particular plot.

Brassicas differ in their nitrogen requirements. Cold soils don't release high levels of available nutrients, so fairly healthy quantities of organic fertilizer laced with blood meal can make a significant difference in how spring-sown brassicas grow. Late spring or early summer sowings can use some nitrogen, but more will be supplied by natural nutrient release in better garden soils. Levels of available nitrogen should be allowed to decrease later in summer as soil temperatures drop, naturally permitting growth to slow down. The plants then toughen up and better withstand the frosts of winter. A moderate amount of complete organic fertilizer banded in June or July will mostly be gone by September, providing correct nutrient levels without fuss. Brassicas for fall/winter harvest should have made most of their size by the end of September. Varieties to be overwintered are sown mid- to late summer and should not be fertilized much so they will be as hard and tough as possible, and then side-dressed heavily with blood meal or other immediately available nitrogen when regrowth begins in early spring.

Though most brassicas adapt well to transplanting and most gardeners think that transplants must be raised or purchased when cabbage, cauliflower, broccoli, or brussels sprouts are grown, this is not so. If vigorous, fresh seed is sown outdoors when weather conditions are favorable to its rapid growth, and if the soil is welcoming to seedlings, direct-seedings will grow faster than transplants, and will mature only ten days to two weeks later than six-week-old transplants set out at the same time. The basic strategy for direct-seeding the more delicate coles is to put the potting soil outdoors instead of in a pot. Though it would be much too much work to make 8 inches of coarse, loamy soil out of heavy clay, gardeners with less than optimum vegetable ground can use raised beds, incorporate organic matter mainly in the surface 2 inches, and thus create a medium very favorable to the growth of brassica seedlings. Another similar approach is to mix up a bucket of light, humusy potting soil such as is recommended for raising transplants, and to set a pint of this in a little hole in the bed, spacing each specially prepared spot 18 by 18 inches or 24 by 24, and then sowing brassica seeds in the potting soil. All the cultural directions that follow suggest sowing dates and techniques for direct-seeding brassica crops.

Hybridization of brassica varieties has become a seed industry standard, and consequently many of the older, open-pollinated types of cabbage, broccoli, and brussels sprouts are no longer good quality selections, as well as being much less vigorous. As of this date, the reds and pointed-head cabbages are still not usually hybrids, nor are the European overwintered sorts, though the Japanese have developed round-headed, overwintered, hybrid varieties, which may soon replace the traditional English types.

Saving seed from fancy open-pollinated brassicas does not adapt itself well to most gardening situations. Except for Chinese cabbage and most broccoli, brassicas are biennial, having to overwinter without freezing out or rotting—something accomplished more easily in the seedling stage than as a mature plant. In the Skagit Valley, stock seed of high purity is planted in late summer, and the tiny seedlings (hardier than mature plants) overwinter to bolt in spring without ever having made a fully developed plant. The fields are not rogued and this sort of cheap production is called "seed-to-seed." To obtain high-purity stock seed, mature plants must be carefully selected for trueness to type and then dug and overwintered in cellars, pits, or occasionally protected right in the field by covering them with soil. These plants are then uncovered in spring or replanted under extreme isolation to prevent random outcrossing. Annual broccoli seed is produced in California by sowing in late fall to flower in early spring.

Overwintered cauliflower, kale, winter-hardy brussels sprouts, Purple Sprouting broccoli, and other very hardy open-pollinated types that make mature plants which usually survive winter unprotected, lend themselves best to home garden seed production. To prevent most crossing with other flowering brassicas, half a mile minimum isolation is required. In spring, overwintered brassicas put out a seed stalk covered with small, yellow flowers that are bee pollinated. Each flower produces a small pod containing four to six seeds. As summer progresses, flowering tapers off, and eventually the majority of the pods contain mature, dried seed, though some new flowers continue to form. At this stage, the huge masses of pods are cut, windrowed on tarps, fully dried (and protected from dews and rains), thrashed, cleaned, and stored. The seed will last four to seven years, depending on how well it dried down and whether it was cut at the right point. Getting seed of high vigor can be a specialist's art, but most gardeners can grow seed of acceptable vigor and sow larger quantities of lower germination seed if necessary. Each plant may produce upwards of an ounce of seed.

Broccoli

This is one of the easier garden vegetables to grow. Broccoli is frost hardy, has large, vigorously sprouting seeds, and may be direct-seeded. Broccoli will produce in soils of only moderate fertility, but to get big heads like those in the supermarket, high nitrogen levels are required from sprouting to the initiation of flowering. Heavy clay soils will also have to be well amended with organic matter if really husky plants are to be grown.

Culture

The earliest broccoli is grown by overwintering Purple Sprouting from midsummer sowings. Next in succession comes early spring-sown transplants of annual types. Seeds may be started indoors as early as February for setting out mid-March under small paper hot caps or in cold frames. These will flower by June at Lorane. Outdoor conditions permit direct-seeding to begin from mid-March to mid-April, depending on the spring weather patterns that year. These sowings mature by July. The last sowing of annual broccoli should be made before mid-July, and in cool areas, perhaps by July 1. The latest sowings mature in October or early November. Plant annual broccoli in little clumps of ten to twenty seeds over a spot where 1/4 to 1/2 cup complete organic fertilizer has been worked into about a half-gallon of soil, spacing the clumps 18 by 18 inches. Sow the seeds about 1/2 inch deep; thin gradually to the best single plant without permitting light competition. Thinning should be completed by the time the seedlings have two true leaves. If growth slows, side-dress the plants with a highly available nitrogen fertilizer. If a side-dressing is done just when the central flower first begins to form, it will be somewhat larger and side shoot development will be much faster and better.

Overwintered Purple Sprouting broccoli is a biennial bred from a family of brassica native to England. (Annual broccoli comes from less hardy Italian wild brassica stock.) It has smaller flowers but is much hardier. Purple Sprouting seeds are usually even more vigorous sprouters than annual broccoli, and grow about like kale. Because it should not be heavily fertilized until spring regrowth, I usually start Purple Sprouting in mid-July by sprinkling the seed thinly in an unfertilized furrow about 1/2 inch deep, in rows about 18 inches apart. The seedlings are gradually thinned to stand 12 to 18 inches apart. The plants are about 12 inches tall when winter checks their growth in late November. Larger plants are less cold hardy, especially if they grow rapidly under conditions of high fertility. Smaller ones may not produce much in spring. I think that if one's soil will not grow 12-inch tall plants from mid-July sowings without fertilization, the grower might be better off to start the plants a little earlier rather than fertilize and consequently have softer plants to overwinter. Then when spring regrowth begins, which is usually late in February at Lorane, side-dress the plants with about a teaspoonful of blood meal per plant. This provokes rapid March growth and larger, more abundant flowers.

Garden Planning

By sowing several different uniformly maturing, hybrid annual varieties simultaneously, half a dozen plants will keep our family in fresh broccoli for about a month, cutting first the central flowers and then the side shoots. So I make successive sowings monthly from April through mid-July (the last one). The Purple Sprouting matures during March/April when there is not much else to eat. At that season, we make whole meals of broccoli stir-fries almost daily, mixed with scallions or leeks. Where six plants a month will handle our needs in summer or fall, two 100-square-foot raised beds or about 150 row feet of Purple Sprouting seems to be required.

Insects and Diseases

We have noticed in our trials that some annual broccoli varieties have more vigorous root systems than others and consequently are better able to withstand the root maggot. Usually, a sawdust collar is sufficient protection, even for delicately rooted types. Purple Sprouting seems to be unbothered at Lorane. The flea beetle will make hash of direct-seeded broccoli in spring if weather conditions or fertility are not conducive to rapid growth. Planting ten to twenty seeds per clump gives plenty of material for the beetles to eat while the seedlings await their opportunity to burst into rapid growth.

Harvest

The central head should be cut when the "beads" begin to fatten, but before they begin to open into yellow flowers. With all sorts of broccoli, side shoots form after the central head is cut. These smaller flowers may be quite substantial on taller stalked varieties. Short-stalked varieties bred for once-over mechanical harvest usually make few side shoots. If side shoots are carefully cut off where they emerge from the main stalk, the plants will make fewer, larger side shoots that are much tastier. If any leaf axials are left growing on side shoot stalks after harvest, each axial will develop tiny side shoots that sap the plant's energy, reducing the overall size of the remaining side shoots. Purple Sprouting broccoli has been bred to not open its flowerettes quickly, permitting them to fatten up, getting sweeter as they swell, so unlike annual broccoli it should not be harvested quite as promptly.

Saving Seed

Annual broccoli flowers late and won't mature seed until late summer or fall, making collection difficult because the rains have usually begun, and resulting in low-quality seed. If the open-pollinated varieties like DeCicco or Waltham 29 are to be grown for seed in the maritime Northwest, they should be started at the earliest possible date and transplanted out. Overwintered Purple Sprouting is usually in full bloom in May, maturing seed nicely in midsummer.

Varieties

The old open-pollinated sorts like Waltham 29, DeCicco, Italian Sprouting, and Spartan Early aren't much good any longer, producing smallish heads, though of good flavor. Avoid hybrids intended for commercial production, as most of these produce few side shoots, unless the gardener intends to can or freeze broccoli and wants a highly concentrated harvest. The ubiquitous Premium Crop is currently the most popular commercial variety in the North but produces few side shoots, though it does grow excellent central flowers. Hybrid varieties change frequently, so exact varietal advice is hard to give. Stokes catalog currently suggests Goliath and Cleopatra for the home gardener. Harris has the bedding plant grower and commercial producer in mind when it sells broccoli seed—and unfortunately, the bedding plant grower is often much more interested in seedlings that have stocky stems that stand up straight in the tray and that size out fast and look good at four weeks old than in the type of harvest that results. Green Valiant (JSS, TSC), Bravo (JSS), and Southern Comet (TSC) are all excellent garden hybrids. The Purple Sprouting (TSC), which overwinters, is not anything like the other purple broccoli/cauliflower that is in many United States garden seed catalogs. The United States sort is a cross between annual broccoli and cauliflower that happens to produce a large, purple flower. Overwintering Purple Sprouting comes from England and only grows well in the maritime Northwest.

Brussels Sprouts

This very hardy member of the brassica family was bred to emphasize a natural brassica tendency of forming tight buds at the growing point and leaf axials. Cabbages sometimes make smaller sprouts along their stems, too, especially when overmature, and some brussels sprout varieties tend to make a cabbagelike head at the top. Early maturing varieties are usually compact, with the sprouts close together for the highest yield. Later varieties, bred to withstand rain and frost and sometimes even severe freezing, have their sprouts spaced out on taller stalks, which prevents trapped water between the sprouts and reduces rots and disease on the sprouts. Sown too early, sprouts either mature too early or grow too tall before forming sprouts, which gives the unstable plants a tendency to fall over or "lodge." Sown too late, the sprouts mature too late on short, lower-yielding plants.

Many people do not realize how good brussels sprouts are to eat because they've only tasted supermarket sprouts that come from California. With many brassicas, sharp frosts cause sugar development and improve the flavor greatly. Locally grown sprouts, especially those maturing from November through March, can have a very good flavor. We like to cook them slowly on the woodstove, a single layer of sprouts browning in butter on a cast-iron frying pan at low heat for an hour or more.

Sprouts also have a somewhat lower nutrient requirement than do cabbages, broccoli, or cauliflower, and in England this crop was traditionally reserved for heavier soils not rich enough for other, more lucrative crops.

Culture

Brussels sprouts like good soil, well limed with a pH above 6.0, and need a steady supply of nutrients and water to make continuous slow growth during their long season. Sprouts have much less tendency to lodge in heavier soils. Too much nitrogen makes plants too tall and, worse, makes the sprouts tend to "blow up" or get loose and take winter weather poorly. A soil that recently was dressed with organic matter and moderately enriched with complete organic fertilizer is usually perfect. Growers on light soils might want to stake up their later, tall-growing plants to prevent lodging, or start them a few weeks later so they don't get quite so tall.

We sow sprouts about June 1, though early varieties may be sown as early as May 1—but who wants to eat sprouts in August when there are tomatoes? Sprouts are vigorous growers and are easy to grow from seed. Transplants are not usually necessary. Besides, sprout varieties available from most nurseries are very early maturing ones more suited to eastern gardens. Space brussels sprouts 24 by 24 inches. Work 1/4 to 1/2 cup complete organic fertilizer into about a half-gallon of soil and sow a pinch of ten or so seeds 1/2 inch deep over the fertilized spot. Thin gradually to the best single plant per clump by the time the seedlings have developed two or three true leaves, without allowing competition. Then, if kept watered and weeded so growth is continuous, the plants pretty much care for themselves.

Garden Planning

If transplant trays are sown June 1, the seedlings can be plopped into beds that grew peas in spring by about July 10. Sprouts allow a fair amount of light to reach the ground below, and the sprout bed is a good spot to sow Crimson clover in September. The clover is noncompetitive with the sprouts all winter and then proceeds to take over in March. I want to begin eating sprouts about November and use them increasingly through winter, so the earliest varieties have little appeal to me. A couple dozen mid- to early plants hold us through Christmas, and three to six dozen more of the latest types are usually barely enough to handle our family from January through March.

Insects and Diseases

If sprouts are sown in June, the worst of the cabbage maggot infestation is avoided, and by the time the fly population is peaking again in late summer, the large, well-rooted plants don't seem much bothered at Lorane. Aphids can be troublesome. Colonies on the leaves can be hosed off and do little damage. Aphids on developing sprouts can ruin them or make one peel off half the outer layers before eating. Safer's Soap will reduce this damage, but the easiest solution is to concentrate on varieties that mature the buttons after summer ends so that there is nothing on the stalks to appeal to aphids until after cold weather has reduced their population.

Harvest

Sprouts will mature first at the base of the plant and can be snapped off starting at the bottom and working up over a period of several months. Commercial growers often cut the growing tip a month before harvest, which prompts the plant to fatten up all its sprouts simultaneously; but this practice has little use in the garden. I used to advise breaking off lower leaves (permitting at least a foot of leaved upper stalk to remain untouched) to allow more light into the lower areas and fatten lower sprouts. Now, however, I think there may be much value in allowing all the leaves to remain. The leaves form a sort of tent which protects the sprouts from weather. If the stalks are permitted to remain in the ground and don't freeze out over the winter, the flowers that form in April make delicious "broccoli."

Saving Seed

Sprouts are among the hardiest of biennial brassicas and usually overwinter to make seed. Harvesting the buttons reduces the seed set, but still, a plant will make half an ounce even if completely picked during the winter. Select seed-making plants for large, clean, compact sprouts with nice, green color. There is considerable variation in flavor and selections could be made for sweetness.

Varieties

There are few decent open-pollinated varieties left in commercial trade. Catskill or Long Island has deteriorated badly and is too early for the long growing season of the maritime Northwest, forming sprouts in August that have poor field-holding qualities. Early Dwarf Danish (JSS) is also very early and so short that it is low yielding. Territorial Seed Company sells later-maturing varieties. Their Harola matures late September and holds through Christmas, while Roodnerf Late Supreme is a classic Dutch winter-hardy sprout, forming buttons in November that mature in December and hold until April most years. Roodnerf is not an extremely uniform selection compared to the hybrids now available, though Harola (an open-pollinated variety) still retains good breeding as of the date of this writing.

Hybrids have virtually eliminated open-pollinated varieties in commercial trade. Eastern United States seed companies offer Jade Cross strains and now have a new one called Prince Marvel. These are Japanese hybrids, and the Japanese plant breeders never seem to forget that the ultimate destination for a vegetable is someone's mouth. Their varieties usually taste very good. However, Jade Cross strains and Prince Marvel are mature by September and aren't very hardy. Territorial is selling Dutch and English commercial types at present, offering Fieldstar F1 for winter and Asmer Aries for late winter, reknowned in England for its amazing hardiness. Unfortunately, Aries also has a very high dry matter content and not exceptional flavor, though it is the most dependable when winter lows drop below 8 degrees. Recently, the Japanese have developed late, hardy varieties to export into the European sprout market. Trial reports from England indicate they have very good flavor (as would be expected), but their hardiness has not been established as yet. These are under trial at Territorial this winter (1984–85) and may prove better than the English/Dutch varieties.

Cabbage

Cabbage is one of the most dependable and productive vegetables in the maritime Northwest garden. Year-round harvests can be had from May until April; certain less-refined types are fairly well adapted to growth on relatively poor soils; and more food per square foot can be had from a cabbage than just about any other vegetable except the root crops. Cabbages are also much more nutritious than lettuce. One can just about live on them, especially when the weather is not conducive to hot-weather crops. This kind of summer is traditionally called a "cabbage year" with good reason.

Culture

There are three basic types of cabbage: early, late, and overwintered (or spring, as the English call this type). Their culture is somewhat different, though generally, cabbage is grown much like broccoli. Other sorts of cabbage, like reds or savoys, are also either early or late.

Early cabbages are fast-growing sorts that have not much cold tolerance compared to the really sturdy late varieties. They also tend to be smaller in size and are grown on closer spacings. The varieties found in the supermarket are almost inevitably early sorts. The more hardy of the earlies can be set out as transplants in March and do better this chilly month if small hot caps are used. They may also be direct-seeded from April through June at Lorane, and it might be possible to extend their sowing to mid-July in warmer areas or along the Oregon coast. Most earlies are best grown on about an 18-by-18-inch spacing, and otherwise cultured like broccoli, though without need to side-dress them. Direct-seeded, most early types take about three months to mature.

Late types are slower to mature. The standard types offered in eastern

United States seed company catalogs usually take 120 or so days to mature from direct-seeding, and are grown for either kraut making or cellar-type storage all winter. They are intended to be sown about June 1 and harvested in October. Lates are usually grown better on a 24-by-24-inch spacing—and for big heads, I've used 24-by-36 inch spacings. Sometimes late types are grown closer together, somewhat stunting the plants and reducing head size. These are harvested for fresh market in October in northern areas. (The cabbages that appear in supermarkets from November through July are from southern cabbage production areas and all are early types.) The English and Dutch have developed even slower-to-mature varieties that match their maritime climates (and that match ours, too). These very late varieties still must be sown about June 1 at Lorane, but head up during November, December, and January. Often, they have excellent field-standing ability and can hold until April, even withstanding low temperatures below 10 degrees while freezing solid for days at a time, then to thaw and resume growth. Many of these are very large cabbages.

Late types are best cultured by provoking rapid growth in summer and allowing that rate to taper off in September so the plants harden off and can better withstand frosts. One-quarter to 1/2 cup of complete organic fertilizer located below seeds or transplants will usually create just the right levels of nutrients through the entire growth cycle of the plant.

Overwintered cabbages are grown exactly as seed-to-seed brassica production is done in the Skagit Valley. Seeds are sown in early September without much fertilization—none is usually needed in decent garden soil. The idea is to get the seedling to grow six to seven true leaves and be 6 to 8 inches tall before cold weather and low light levels check their growth in early winter. However, instead of immediately bolting to seed in spring, these varieties have been bred to be very slow to bolt and consequently, if well fertilized when spring regrowth begins, will make good heads in April or May, depending on the variety grown and the weather that year. Overwintered cabbages still have a strong tendency to bolt, especially if they get too big before their growth is checked by winter. Fall weather can make a big difference in growth rates, so planting dates are critical and hard to judge from year to year. In England, many years the spring cabbage crops fail due to bolting before heading, and overwintering cabbage is jokingly referred to there as a gambler's crop. However, good salad greens are scarce in April/May, making overwintering cabbage well worth the gamble. Generally, overwintered cabbages are fairly small, and their final spacing may be 18 by 18 inches. I've also had good luck growing spring cabbages sown in October in cold frames, then dug up and transplanted in March when they're about 8 inches tall. Gardeners in northwestern Washington State, where winter freeze-outs are common, might use this type of culture profitably. It can also work with the earliest sorts of cauliflower if European Alpha varieties bred for this purpose are grown.

Garden Planning

I depend on cabbage, so I usually start a dozen overwintered plants in September. If I miss that, I start them in the October cold frame and transplant them in March for harvest in May. Then, another dozen early variety transplants go outside in March. Some years, March weather is fair and warm and these get going well. Other years, they're stunted badly and chewed by flea beetles. Usually, I direct-seed another twelve plants early in April. These three sowings have me covered from May through July. To avoid eating too many cabbage salads in August or September, I only start half a dozen or so quick-maturing early sorts along with my main cabbage planting in early June; but June 1 remains the date when the main cabbage patch goes in. Some years I direct-seed it, but when I'm doing cabbage trials in the poorer soil of my trial grounds, I get more reliable results by sowing in bedding plant trays and transplanting out in early July. This main sowing consists of a succession of winter salad cabbages, some reds, and a few big, sweet heads for October kraut making—usually six to eight dozen plants in all.

Incidentally, though many seed catalogs sell special kraut cabbage, some of these are poor for home kraut making because they've been bred to be tough and withstand canning after being sliced very thin—something not necessary for home kraut making. Decent kraut can be made from almost any variety of cabbage, and in fact, the tender, early types often make the sweetest kraut, and freshly made kraut is much, much better than kraut that has been in storage for several months in the cellar or garage. I plan to make a bit from time to time as the season goes on.

Most varieties of cabbage require pretty good ground, so the main sowing always goes into a plot that was well manured and put into green manure the previous fall. I've had good luck scattering Crimson clover seed in the late patch during September, and if the autumn is a wet one, it thrives. The clover doesn't compete with the cabbage, but takes over the patch in March.

Insects and Diseases

Flea beetles often make hash of direct-seedings of cabbage, but sowing ten to twenty seeds for every plant desired supplies ample food for both man and bug. If the beetles are ruining such a well-seeded stand, it's because the seedlings are growing too slowly. Putting a pint of potting soil in a little hole and starting the seeds atop that small, enriched spot lets seedlings outgrow predators. Root maggots can be troublesome, especially to half-grown early varieties in May. Mulching with sawdust is a very effective organic control. Cabbage worms are very easily controlled by spraying Dipel every few weeks.

Harvest

Early varieties tend to burst quickly after maturity; later types hold for months because growth rates slow dramatically by October. Bursting occurs because as the inside enlarges, the outer leaves become tough and woody and lose their ability to stretch. Some early varieties are much less prone to bursting than others. In winter, the outer layers of the head may become somewhat unappetizing, but when peeled off leave a fine inner head. Overwintered types tend to bolt readily after heading, so must be picked promptly.

Saving Seed

As with brussels sprouts. Some tight-headed varieties should have their heads cut with a 2-inch-deep X in early March to permit the seed stalk to emerge. Often the stumps in the field will put up seed stalks. Saving seed from early varieties can be done by the seed-to-seed method, giving poor-quality seed, or by carrying over in root cellars heads that matured in October. The plants are dug, roots and all, cellared over, and replanted early in spring. In Denmark, where winters are too frosty for reliable overwintering, mature heads are sometimes buried under a few inches of soil in October to prevent their freezing, and then uncovered in spring, the tops X'd, and seed grown.

Varieties

The earliest, quickest-growing varieties are pointed-head types like Early Jersey Wakefield or its variants like Wakker (TSC) and Golden Acre types. Golden Acre strains are small, green, round-headed cabbages, usually with pale yellow/white centers, sweet flavor, and tender texture. Harris sells no open-pollinated round-headed earlies any longer, recognizing that truly high-quality selections are no longer in existence. Stokes, Johnny's, and Territorial still sell fairly decent open-pollinated strains. Some of the better Golden Acre hybrids are Tucana (STK) and Princess (TSC, STK). Harris hybrids are geared for the commercial grower because they are bred for yield over field-holding ability or flavor. One popular bad-for-the-garden variety is Stonehead (STK), sold by many seed companies. It is preferred by the commercial grower because of its excellent field-holding ability and small, highly uniform head size; however, it has poor flavor and a tough texture. Salarite (STK, TSC), Savoy King (HAR, TSC), and Savoy Ace (HAR) are all excellent-flavored, early-maturing savoy types from Japan that make much better salads than do Golden Acre types. All have good field-holding ability as well.

Danish Ballhead selections, both hybrids (Harris has two) or open-pollinated (Johnny's has three), are sure-growing, all-purpose late sorts that mature in September or October and will often stand in the field until Christmas in the maritime Northwest. Custodian (STK) is an excellent hybrid of this sort. The English have bred smaller market-sized heads of this sort of stock that are well protected by wrapper leaves to retain good appearance when cut for market in November/December or later. Remember that England has no southern cabbage-growing area like California, Florida, or Texas and so must produce its own cabbage or import it. Territorial sells one or another of these types, later to mature than the Danish Ballheads of eastern seed companies.

For late salads, Chieftain Savoy is becoming a rather poor selection these days, though still it is decent, matures in October, has good field-standing ability and cold tolerance, and often holds until Christmas. Savoy Monarch (TSC) is a late hybrid savoy in this class, much more uniform and equally tasty. These savoys, as well as Salarite, Savoy King, and Savoy Ace, are all bred in Japan. The European savoys are much tougher and of poorer quality, from an American point of view, so I'd not grow them for fall/early winter use. This removes from consideration Johnny's Blue Max and Stokes's Ice Prince and Ice Queen. However, certain of these European savoys are able to withstand late winter conditions, so for harvest after New Year's, there is no other choice. Territorial offers two—an open-pollinated type called Ormskirk Extra Late, and a fine, even hardier hybrid called Wivoy that is the industry market standard in Europe at this time. The English also have a late type that is a European savoy/green cabbage cross called January King (TSC). Smaller in size, more like Golden Acre types, January Kings head out in November and often hold into February. They make excellent salads.

Most reds grow well in the maritime Northwest. The late-maturing types have good cold tolerance. For the best flavor, I like Ruby Ball, a Japanese early hybrid. Most seed companies carry this variety. The late-maturing, storage reds are very tough and often not too sweet, though they'll withstand bad weather almost as well as late savoy types.

As mentioned in the introduction to this section on brassicas, most cabbage varieties are highly inbred and thus do not possess much vigor, requiring the most fertile soil with the best tilth. However, I have noticed that the larger red types, particularly the late-maturing varieties and the savoy cabbages, have remarkable vigor and ability to grow. For this reason I recommend especially the savoy types for the home gardener, as well as because they possess the best flavor and make the finest slaws and salads.

Chinese Cabbage

Like its close relative mustard, Chinese cabbage is an annual with a strong tendency to bolt if it experiences long days. This makes growing early in the season very difficult. Bolt-resistant hybrids do permit late spring sowings, but generally the group grows better when sown after midsummer for fall harvest. Chinese cabbage is not an easy crop in an organic garden, because the cabbage fly seems to prefer this plant above most others and its larvae cause devastating damage easily. Chinese cabbage also requires very rich soil.

Culture

Heavy soils must be well amended with organic matter far in advance so that preliminary decomposition will have occurred before Chinese cabbage is sown. Light soils aren't so fussy. Band 1/2 to 1 cup complete organic fertilizer below each 5 feet of furrow. Sow the big, strongly germinating seeds about one per inch, 3/4 inch deep, in rows 18 to 24 inches apart, depending on the size of the variety being grown. Thin gradually *without permitting any crowding* so the plants stand 18 inches apart in the row. Do not transplant, as Chinese cabbage does better if its taproot is unbroken, though hybrid varieties are not quite as fussy. Keep the plants well watered, as they have very shallow root systems and must make very rapid growth to head successfully.

Garden Planning

Early varieties barely head before bolting. Late types will stand for a month or longer before putting up a seed stalk. Four to six good-sized heads will make a gallon of kim che (Korean sauerkraut).

Insects and Diseases

Slugs do not do any damage, except perhaps to the sensibilities of the gardener washing them out of the outer leaves. Root maggots attack in an unusual way. Instead of invading the roots, they seem to prefer going up the thick, juicy stems, cutting the vascular system and causing the leaves to collapse, which ruins the head. Early varieties are not bothered as much as late ones at Lorane, but after August, the maggots do increase and give late-maturing heads a bad time. Some varieties, like China King, seem better able to handle a few maggots than other types. The maggots are usually confined to the lower inch or so of head and may be trimmed off. Because I am a fanatic kim che fancier, Chinese cabbage is the only vegetable that tempts me to spray the very effective chemical insecticide Diazinon. Instead, I spray twice weekly (and sometimes more often) with rotenone or rotenone/pyrethrum, quitting only a week before harvest. Thinning early and then growing the plants under a screen house or a new product called Reemay (which is a combination cloche/screen) might be a better solution.

Harvest

Heads should be cut promptly when filled out, before they either bolt or are infested by maggots. Bolted heads in fall put up *delicious* flower stalks that, if cut before the flowers open, are excellent in stir-fries and salads.

Saving Seed

I have not found any reliable open-pollinated strains, and the seed-making process starts too late in the North.

Varieties

There are many high-quality varieties available from Japanese seed companies. Johnny's and Harris keep changing so fast I cannot keep up with their current choices. Spring A1 (TSC, JSS) is very good for mid-May through July sowings, very bolt-resistant and easy growing. Springtime (STK) is equally fine. I've had good success growing Summertime and Wintertime (both late types) from Stokes, and China King (TSC) is also good sown about mid-July for fall harvest. Matsushima is an old, open-pollinated variety (JSS) that has good maggot tolerance, though it is a bit ragged compared to the hybrids currently available.

Cauliflower

It took me many years to learn how to produce cauliflower reliably. I studied this difficult vegetable because I love to eat it, and really fresh ones are much sweeter than those from the market.

If a cauliflower has its rapid growth stopped or "checked," as professional growers say, the plant may well not form a decent curd later on. So to culture this vegetable, careful attention must be paid to ensure that nothing interferes with its rapid development. If transplanting is done, the seedlings must not become pot-bound in the least. This means that commercially purchased seedlings must be examined very carefully and homegrown ones must be set out promptly. Buying cauliflower seedlings is doubly dangerous because if hothouse grown, they may be big and beautiful but very tender, and if set out before summer weather is really "on," may be shocked. A shock checks growth. Because of this difficulty, I've tried to direct-seed cauliflower and discovered that when seeded this way, it is a fairly easy-to-grow plant—if the correct varieties are used.

Culture

Direct-seeding usually won't work until about mid-April and may continue through June for harvest from June through November. If you wish to attempt the earliest possible harvest, start seedlings about March 1 for transplanting out mid-April. These may mature about two to three weeks ahead of those seeded in April if spring weather is gentle. Space cauliflower 18 by 24 inches, and when direct-seeding, grow like broccoli. However, most United States varieties have been bred for the specialist California grower operating on ideal soil types—usually a light, silty loam that retains water fairly well and that is irrigated and chemically protected from the cabbage root maggot. Under these conditions, root systems develop easily and can be rather small, permitting the plant to direct most of its growth into leaves and later the curds. For the gardener operating on heavier soil types without pesticides, this means that the soil must be well amended with organic matter in a manner timely enough that it will have broken down well before the plants are grown; otherwise, root development and overall growth will suffer badly. Underdeveloped root systems have little ability to "scratch up" much water, so the grower must keep the soil moisture high and pay close attention to fertility levels. It may even be helpful to side-dress the plants when about 8 inches tall with a bit of blood meal or liquid fertilizer because the "program" of the cauliflower seems to be that it will produce a certain number of leaves and then flower. If those leaves are big and husky, the curd will be large. If the leaves are smallish from slow growth rates, the flower will be small and often of poor flavor. And, if the growth was checked badly, the plant may "button," producing a tiny curd, despite the size of the plant.

Overwintered cauliflower is easier to grow. Sow this about August 1 with lower levels of fertility and grow much as Purple Sprouting broccoli, though it demands slightly more nutrients. The 8- to 12-inch-tall plants overwinter and can survive lows below 10 degrees and sometimes below 6 degrees if they're hardened off well by the fall weather and not overly fertilized in summer. In spring, they should be fertilized well with highly available nitrogen, such as from blood meal or liquid fertilizer, as soon as the regrowth begins, which is usually about late February at Lorane. The plants grow rapidly and head out from April through mid-May.

Garden Planning

The maritime Northwest is a good climate for a long supply of cauliflower. The harvest begins in April and May with overwintered cauliflowers; the earliest transplants come on in early June, followed by cutting direct-seeded curds from late June through November. I save my best, most fertile beds for cauliflower. Cauliflower has been bred to mature very uniformly. Though it is possible to use only one or two varieties of annual cauliflower for continuous summer and fall harvests by sowing every few weeks, I've found it much more reliable and less time consuming to start two or three early types in mid-April that have successive maturity dates, and then about June 1, start these same three earlies with other four or five late-maturing types. This June 1 sowing can produce curds from August through November as each of seven to eight varieties matures in succession.

Insects and Diseases

Cauliflowers tend to have delicate root systems, easily ruined by the cabbage root maggot—especially the Snowball varieties and their derivatives, which have been bred for growing in the irrigated fields of the Salinas Valley, where most of this nation's cauliflower is produced. European varieties bred for English and Dutch farmers are not usually grown under irrigation and possess vigorous root systems in many cases, though their greenhouse or very early market garden varieties have very small, fibrous roots. Unless the gardener is willing to use soil pesticides to protect the cauliflower's root system, European varieties should be grown. Well-rooted types can be adequately protected by sawdust collars; the best of them have a high survival percentage without any protection on our Lorane trial grounds. Otherwise, cauliflower is bothered by the same insects as broccoli and cabbage and should be handled similarly.

Harvest

Cut the flower when the curds are just beginning to get ricey or separate a bit. This is a trifle later than when commercial crops are cut, but results in much larger yields. Cut this late, however, they don't store as well.

Saving Seed

Regular types are annuals, but even the earliest spring sowings tend to go to seed on the late side for reliable maturity and high-vigor seed production as far north as the maritime Northwest. If started early enough, they will produce seed. Saving seed from overwintered cauliflower is as easy as with any other biennial brassica.

Varieties

For spring sowings and quick maturity in summer sowings, use the European Alpha types and avoid Snowball types. Some good Alpha varieties are Alpha Begum, Alpha Balanza, Alpha Paloma (TSC), Alert (JSS, STK), and Andes (STK). Snow Crown is a hybrid that seems to be carried by all seed companies, because its amazingly vigorous, rapid growth and healthy root development make it an almost sure thing for an early garden variety. Good later types are Dominant (JSS), White Fox (TSC, STK), and White Rock (TSC, STK). Territorial sells some very late types that mature October/November from a June 1 sowing that will only produce in the maritime Northwest, and is as well a supplier of quality Dutch overwintered cauliflower varieties.

Collards

Grown for leafy greens during fall and winter, collards are unrefined members of the brassica family that retain good vigor and are easy to grow.

Culture

Sow June through mid-July for harvest in fall/winter. Direct-seed. Sow the seed thinly, 1/2 inch deep, in rows 18 to 24 inches apart. Thin gradually so the plants stand 12 to 18 inches apart in the row. Fertilizer is not usually needed in decent garden soil.

Garden Planning

Collards may be grown on poorer plots in the garden with a little fertilizer. Ten to 15 row feet will allow weekly harvests all winter.

Insects and Diseases

Not usually a problem for these vigorous plants.

Harvest

Cut leaves or whole plants during winter.

Saving Seed

Like any other biennial brassica.

Varieties

Vates is hardier than Georgia. Johnny's has a new Vates selection called Champion. The Japanese seed companies are now offering hybrid collards that may appear on the United States market.

Kale

Kale is one of the most vigorous and easy-to-grow brassicas. The leaves and stems of some varieties are of salad quality, especially if cut and shredded finely. It develops much more sweetness after some good, heavy frosts, while quickly becoming tough and inedible if not used shortly after harvest. Consequently, the supermarket product that comes from California is very inferior.

Culture

I grow kale about like Purple Sprouting broccoli, sowing in midsummer, sprinkling the seed thinly in 1/2-inch-deep furrows, in rows 18 inches apart, and then thinning gradually so the plants stand about 12 inches apart in the row. Kale grows well, needing little or no fertilizer in decent garden soil. Additionally, it should be grown without too much nitrogen so the plants will be a bit on the hard side and thus more frost tolerant.

Garden Planning

Fifteen to 25 row feet usually provide plenty to supplement salads and for an occasional stir-fry. Sowing Crimson clover under the kale plants in September won't cause competition, and the clover will take over in March after the kale has begun to make seed.

Insects and Diseases

Kale rarely has any trouble with the cabbage root maggot at Lorane, nor with other common brassica pests.

Harvest

Cut individual leaves as needed. A midsummer sowing will grow big plants by late October, when low light levels and chill check further growth. The plants can be gradually harvested back, but permit a few leaves and the growing point to remain intact, because spring regrowth starts early and makes an abundance of new greens. Very hardy, kale may be the only survivor in a hard winter. To increase spring harvest, side-dress with high nitrogen fertilizer as soon as regrowth begins. Most strains of kale bolt fairly early, but the flower stalks are particularly sweet and good in stir-fries.

Saving Seed

Like any other biennial brassica.

Varieties

I've found the Siberian types more hardy and sweeter flavored than the "curled" or "Scotch" types. All varieties are well adapted to maritime conditions.

Kohlrabi

This peculiar member of the brassica family has been shaped to make a swollen stem or bulb that grows above ground. Located there, it is safe from the cabbage root maggot. The flavor is mild, like a sweet turnip. Kohlrabi is vigorous and fairly easy to grow.

Culture

In hot weather, kohlrabi makes tough, hot, woody bulbs, so avoid growing for harvest during July/August. Sow the seed in April for June harvest, and sow again mid-July through mid-August for harvest late September through fall. Sow seed thinly, two to four seeds per inch, 1/2 inch deep, in rows 18 inches apart. Thin very carefully as the seedlings become established so the bulbs stand 3 inches apart in the row. In soils that have been manured recently, kohlrabi often requires no fertilizer. In less fertile situations, 1/4 to 1/2 cup complete organic fertilizer per 5 row feet banded below the seed is enough. Very early production can be had by sowing in frames during March or by raising transplants and setting them out 3 inches apart.

Garden Planning

Because spring sowings mature very rapidly and quickly get woody, small sowings one week to ten days apart are in order at that time. However, there is much less tendency to become woody when harvested in fall, particularly with some varieties, so as much as 25 to 50 row feet sown at once might be in order.

Insects and Diseases

Kohlrabi is bothered by the usual brassica pests, but rarely do the plants at Lorane become stunted or wilt due to the root maggot. The bulbs are much more likely to be edible than turnips, and just as good or better.

Harvest

In early summer, harvest while small. Though the bulbs will become as large as tennis balls, they're better when eaten half that size. Egg-sized kohlrabi may be used in stir-fries, tops and all.

Saving Seed

Overwinter late-summer sowings by burying the bulbs and most of the leaves under a few inches of soil, which is hilled up over the mature plants in November. In early spring, uncover and permit to make seed like other biennial brassicas.

Varieties

The Early White Vienna and Early Purple Vienna found in most American seed catalogs are usually inferior generic selections grown only for the home garden market. Often these will not make round bulbs. Instead, large percentages of them will develop tall, pointed, swollen stems of poor quality. Grand Duke hybrid is a good selection for more southerly climates and very popular these days, but not particularly good in the maritime Northwest. Winner F1 (TSC) retains good eating quality amazingly long without becoming woody, as does Lauko (TSC). Johnny's choices are good commercial-quality selections from Europe.

Rutabagas

Rutabagas keep well in the ground all winter at Lorane, remaining in good eating condition until late March. They produce amazing yields of flavorful roots that make a fine, nonstarchy potato substitute and are much less troubled by brassica pests than turnips.

Culture

Vigorous growers, rutabagas will usually grow fine in soils manured recently, though in less fertile locations, banding 1/4 to 1/2 cup complete organic fertilizer per 5 row feet below the seed is helpful. Sow the seed during July, sprinkling thinly in furrows 1/2 inch deep, in rows 18 to 24 inches apart. Thin gradually to 8 inches apart in the row. Later sowings won't make large roots and should be thinned accordingly.

Garden Planning

Rutabagas yield prolifically. A true fancier or someone really trying for winter self-sufficiency might want as much as 50 row feet or half a large raised bed. The rutabaga bed or row is a good site for spring peas, while spring pea beds are a good place to sow rutabagas after the peas have been harvested.

Insects and Diseases

At Lorane, the root maggot seems uninterested in our rutabagas, though slugs do like to dig cavities in some of the roots. Sometimes mice do, too. This is quite a different story than we have with turnips.

Harvest

If winter gets freezing cold for a short spell, the roots will freeze solid and then rot afterward—if not protected. So during November, we cover the row or bed with flakes of straw and bury the roots 2 to 3 inches deep. This is enough protection for a three- to five-day snap of minus-10 degree weather, which we get about one winter in three.

Saving Seed

After overwintering under straw, rutabagas go to seed like any biennial brassica.

Varieties

Most Purple Top or Laurentian selections available in American seed catalogs will produce good-quality, uniform roots. There are some especially good selections like Stokes Altasweet and Best of All (TSC), an English home garden variety. A few types like Marion (TSC) also have clubroot resistance.

Turnips

Turnips are a biennial brassica that grow like radishes, but that require more fertile soil (which is why radish culture is discussed in the section on roots). Sometimes root maggots leave the gardener a few not completely ruined. In the maritime Northwest, turnips are easier to grow for greens than for roots!

Culture

Turnips need fertile soil so they can grow fast enough to "outrun" the cabbage root maggot. If they mature quickly enough, the maggots will have barely hatched out before the roots are plucked from their grasp. Below each 5 feet of furrow, band 1/4 to 1/2 cup complete organic fertilizer. Sow the tiny seed fairly thinly, four or so seeds per inch, 1/2 inch deep, in rows at least 12 inches apart. The larger varieties like Purple Top White Globe can stand 18-inch row spacing. When the seedlings are established, thin *carefully* to 2 to 3 inches apart. Keep them well watered, and if flea beetles are causing much havoc with the leaves, spray them or growth will slow and the roots become maggot bait.

Garden Planning

Because turnips must be harvested promptly, small sowings made every week to ten days are in order. Turnips grow quickly, and their space may be followed by other crops.

Insects and Diseases

Flea beetles like turnip greens as much as they do radish tops. Rotenone will keep them under control. Sowing the seed under a sawdust mulch will prevent the cabbage fly from gaining access to the soil until the swelling roots push the sawdust aside. This is fully discussed in "Diseases and Pests in the Maritime Northwest." Growing the roots under a screen cage or Reemay cloche is something a dedicated turnip fancier should consider seriously.

Harvest

On the small side, both for milder flavor and to avoid the maggot.

Saving Seed

Like rutabagas, though the roots are less hardy and will require careful mulching if they are to overwinter intact.

Varieties

Purple Top White Globe and its variants like Milan and Strap Leaf are the fastest-growing varieties and seem to be somewhat less attractive to the root maggot than are the many tasty, all-white hybrid varieties that originate from Japan. The new Purple Top hybrids are more uniform and vigorous than the old open-pollinated types. For greens, any variety is edible, but Shogoin is the best for this purpose.

Roots

A number of vegetables produce edible roots. Though they have no close botanical relationship, root crops grow similarly. Their basic pattern is to put down a taproot (or feeder roots in the case of potatoes) and then fill up the root with stored food. If the soil is soft and friable, the roots swell up easily and uniformly, producing shapely and tasty carrots, parsnips, beets, potatoes, parsley root, or chicory. If the soil is hard and compacted, the roots develop poorly or not at all. Such sensitivity makes uncompacted, raised beds especially helpful on heavier soil types. Commercial root crops are grown on coarse-textured soils.

Most roots are adapted to growth in relatively infertile soils. Wild carrot (Queen Anne's Lace), for example, is a nuisance weed in poor pastures, while it is smothered by grass in rich soil. The basic survival strategy of most root-developing crops is to store up a large supply of food one year and then use it early in spring the next year for making seed. Instead of having to outgrow neighboring plants by using the current input of light, water, and nutrients more efficiently, roots can wait until a time when their neighbors can barely make any food, choosing this auspicious moment to make seed. The grower should not encourage roots to make too much vegetative growth by heavy use of nitrogen fertilizers, but instead should maintain high levels of phosphorus and potassium and make soft soils.

Creating good soil for root crops is not always simple, especially when the gardener has to work with heavy clays. Softening up heavy soils is usually accomplished by manuring or adding composts, but these materials often contain significant amounts of nitrogen. In the presence of very much nitrogen, most root crops produce small roots that tend to be hairy. This is even somewhat true of potatoes. The solution to this dilemma is to prepare the bed a year in advance, growing a highly demanding vegetable when large amounts of organic matter have been worked into the soil, and planning to follow that with a rotation into roots the next year, without further additions of organic matter or fertilizer.

Thinning can be very important when producing good root crops. Carrots will not develop well unless carefully thinned, nor will parsnips or radishes. Most varieties of beet have highly variable vigor, and if left crowded, some will overwhelm their neighbors. But still, beets do much better if spaced about 2 to 4 inches apart in the row when the seedlings are very well established.

Roots need large quantities of water to be succulent, sweet, and large. This is particularly true of radishes.

Hybrid beet and carrot seed is available these days. Though there doesn't seem to be much improvement in vigor when using hybrid seed, there is much more uniformity in carefully selected hybrid strains than in the cheaper open-pollinated home garden varieties.

Beets

Beets are native to Mediterranean climates, where soils are usually alkaline. Any soil that isn't too acid will grow good beets, though when grown on heavy soil types, the crop does better if the bed has been well amended recently with organic matter. Beets grow best when temperatures are moderate and soils are warm, though some early varieties can be started in midspring. Spells of cold weather or periods of low soil moisture result in the formation of rings of white interior material or "zoning," but zoning does not usually affect flavor much.

Culture

Forming roots as beets do on the soil's surface, it is not usually necessary to work the beet bed deeply when growing them on raised beds that contain decent amounts of organic matter. Beets have a low to moderate nutrient requirement, and except on very poor soils, or those that have not been manured in the past few years, fertilizer is unnecessary. If fertilizer were needed, I'd try only 1/4 cup complete organic fertilizer per 5 row feet, banded below or beside the furrow. Sow from April through mid-July. Make early sowings 1/2 inch deep, later ones 3/4 inch deep. Each seed is actually a fruit containing several embryos, but germination rate is often low. Plant two to three seeds per inch in rows 18 inches apart. Many beet varieties, especially those sold to gardeners, are highly variable, so more vigorous individuals crowd out weaker plants and careful thinning is not absolutely necessary. However, better roots will be had if the row is thinned when the seedlings stand about 3 inches tall and are firmly established. Seedlings should stand as far apart as the mature roots are going to be. For baby beets, that could be 1 to 1½ inches apart; canners run 3 to 4 inches in diameter; winter storage varieties can grow 6 inches across.

Garden Planning

Unthinned home garden selections of table beets can yield for a long time, because as large roots are pulled, smaller plants that had been shaded out begin to grow rapidly and make new roots in the same place. I've found that a 4-foot-square patch can keep our table supplied for over a month. For winter use, half a 100-square-foot bed or about 50 row feet is enough for us.

Insects and Diseases

Mexican bean beetles will chew on slow-growing seedlings in spring. The solution is to plant lots of seed and wait until the soil warms before sowing. Leaf miners can ruin a stand of beets. Their larvae tunnel through the leaves, killing the plant. There is no organic insecticide that works on the leaf miner; the only solution is to grow beets in a screen cage or under Reemay. When grown under a screen, light levels are reduced 15 to 25 percent, depending on the type of screen being used. This can make the plants get "toppy" with poorer root development. When using screen protection, increase row spacing to 24 inches, leaving several inches between each mature root to permit more light to reach each plant.

Harvest

Mature beets will stand a long time awaiting harvest, though in very hot weather they may become woody. Winterkeepers and some of the Detroit selections can hold from October to March, while retaining good eating quality. Protect overwintering beds of beets from freezing (and then later rotting) by covering the roots with 2 or 3 inches of straw in late November.

Saving Seed

Beets are wind-pollinated biennials. Their light pollen can carry a mile and more downwind. Beets also freely cross with chard. Beet seed can last three to four years, so different varieties could be produced in different years. For a seed crop, sow mid-July and harvest carefully in November. Select perfect roots for replanting and eat the rest. Replant the beets 12 inches apart in rows 24 inches apart, with the crowns just above the soil line. Cover with 3 to 4 inches of straw or soil and overwinter. Early in spring, remove the covering and allow the roots to put up seed stalks. (The roots may also be overwintered in a cellar and set back out in early March.) Harvest the seed stalks when they are dry and grown. Strip off the seed by hand and dry fully before storage. Seed yields are huge.

Varieties

Early Wonder is a fine table variety for the garden. Most Early Wonder selections have tall, tasty tops and variable maturity, which doesn't require perfect thinning. Early Wonder types also make better growth in cool weather than most canners. Detroit types (including Ruby Queen) are numerous and grow better when sown to mature in midsummer to fall. Some of the new hybrids are very carefully selected Detroit types. Little Ball (TSC) and Little Miniball (STK) are varieties bred for dense plantings to form small roots to can whole or to eat as "baby" beets. Usually, they are very tender and sweet. Cylindrical beets like Formanova, Cylindra, and Forono were bred for canneries and slice into lots of nice rings. These varieties also cook very quickly. Winterkeepers, sometimes called Lutz (the same variety), are large roots that tend to be somewhat irregularly shaped, with thick, tough skins that protect the root all winter in storage. Winterkeepers also have a high sugar content and are delicious and tender even when 8 inches in diameter. Albina Vereduna (TSC) is a winter storage variety from Holland that has absolutely no red color at all. The white meat is very sweet. Stokes also sells Albino White Beet, though I'm not certain it is a quality selection, and Burpee's Golden, an old home garden variety with yellow flesh and little flavor to recommend it. The gardener should feel free to experiment with beet varieties, as the only type we've ever grown in our trials that did not perform well was Detroit Short Top. Short Tops are bred to allow higher density stands on very rich soils.

Carrots

The poorer soils around Lorane are covered with wild carrot. This should convince anyone that carrots are well adapted to the maritime Northwest. In fact, wild carrot is so abundant in our region that carrot seed must be grown east of the Cascades to avoid crossing with wild plants. If the carrot rust fly maggot can be avoided and if wireworm damage is minimal, carrots can be one of the easiest-to-grow crops and produce amazingly high yields.

Carrot seed does not germinate rapidly, often taking twelve to fourteen days to sprout. The shoots are weak and cannot force their way through crusts or puddled soil, and the seed must be sown shallowly. Plantings started before the heat of summer usually germinate well because the soil stays moist and uncrusted naturally. However, sowings made after May are more dicey. I've found that covering the seed in the furrow with a finely sifted horse manure or compost, or mixing a bit of sphagnum moss into the soil that covers the carrot seed, retains moisture and prevents crusting. This technique is useful when sowing parsnip seed as well and on any midsummer sowing done under conditions of high heat and dryness.

Culture

What the carrot seedling encounters during the first six to eight weeks of its life determines the quality of the root it will produce. Immediately upon sprouting, a carrot begins to put down a taproot. If that root does not encounter any impenetrable clods or zones of high nitrogen concentration (such as might come from pieces of undecomposed fresh manure or fertilizer granules), it will grow straight down without forking, crooking, or becoming hairy. Then, if the soil remains soft and moist and the roots don't compete with each other, the upper 4 to 12 inches of the root will swell up with stored food. So, to grow good carrots, one should have manured the soil well the previous year, which eliminates any need for fertilizer as well as improves the water retention and tilth of the soil, thus allowing good root formation. The only hard thing to do is grow carrots in heavy, hard soil. Clayey types must be especially well amended with organic matter, and then only short varieties like Chantenays should be grown. *In well-tilled soil*, sow the seed from mid-April through mid-July; sprinkle seed thinly in furrows 1/2 inch deep, with rows 12 to 18 inches apart. *Thin carefully* before the tops are 3 inches tall to 1 to 1½ inches apart in the row, depending on the final size of the variety being grown. Mature roots should not touch. Keep the bed well watered so the roots swell up rapidly and taste sweet. Suddenly increasing soil moisture after periods of growth in dryish soil can cause many varieties to split and then rot.

Garden Planning

About 50 row feet of carrots sown in spring keeps our family supplied during summer. I then start at least 200 square feet of raised bed or 200 row feet of carrots between late June and mid-July for maturity in early fall. These are put under straw for harvest all winter. The main sowing often follows crops of early brassicas or other greens that have removed much of the nitrogen from the soil.

Insects and Diseases

Carrot maggots and wireworms burrow into carrots, causing rotting and leaving a bad flavor. Handling maggots is discussed in "Diseases and Pests in the Maritime Northwest." I cannot offer good remedies for wireworm infestations, though it is thought that high humus levels decrease wireworm damage. Damage to the roots can be so severe that in-the-ground winter storage becomes impossible.

Harvest

At Lorane, carrots will hold in the ground all winter with only minor insect damage. We cover the carrots with 2 to 3 inches of straw in November to protect the roots from freezing in the event of a severe cold snap. Covering the mulch with a sheet of clear plastic increases the protection, keeping the bed dry, but also makes a haven for field mice that may eat the roots.

Saving Seed

Carrot seed is produced essentially like beets. Grow mature roots. In fall, dig and examine them for trueness to type. A good nonsmoker's nose can smell sweetness. Replant the roots immediately about 12 inches apart in rows about 24 inches apart, mulch them well to protect against winter freezing, and then remove the mulch in March to allow the flower stalks to emerge. The flowers are insect-pollinated. Cut down wild carrot (Queen Anne's Lace) as much as possible to a distance of a mile. (It may be that decent carrot seed cannot be produced in the maritime Northwest unless done in a clearing in the woods with only fir trees for a mile or more in any direction.) Crosses with wild carrot result in whitish roots of poor texture and flavor.

Varieties

Almost any variety will grow excellently in our climate, though the long Imperator types preferred in supermarkets require coarse-textured, deep soils to develop well-shaped roots. Nantes varieties are best for summer or early fall use, having tender texture and good sugar content. Danvers and Flakkee types make pointed roots 6 to 7 inches long, with higher fiber contents, that hold well in the ground during winter. Chantenay types are short and broad, developing better in heavier soils than other kinds of carrots. Different varieties have highly different tastes and textures, so the gardener should experiment until he or she discovers the most pleasing choice. Hybrid carrots tend to be more uniform, though not much more vigorous.

Chicory

The various chicory selections are actually biennial root crops that make edible tops. They grow in relatively infertile soils, as do carrots. In the case of chicory, I am writing about a vegetable I am only now beginning to learn about and with which I have not had actual experience, so reader, beware. The information which follows was taken from *Leafy Salad Vegetables*, by Edward J. Ryder, who is a world expert on commercial production of lettuce and a famous lettuce breeder.

Culture

Nonforcing types are sown in June. Plant seeds 1/2 inch deep, in rows 12 to 15 inches apart; thin gradually 8 to 12 inches apart in the row. In fall, the top is cut off and used for a salad green or the overwintered root resprouts in spring, producing tender greens very early in the season. Fertilizer is not needed in soil manured within a year or two. Forcing types are commercially grown in coarse-textured, fertile soils. The shape of the root is important, so deep tillage and all the precautions that must be taken to grow good carrots also apply. Excessive nitrogen makes plants too leafy, with thick crowns, and thus, undesirable for forcing. Start forcing types in May; sow seed 1/2 inch deep, in rows 12 inches apart; thin carefully to 6 inches apart in the row. Obtaining uniformly sized and shaped roots is vital. Overly dense stands produce too small roots. Stands too spaced out produce overly thick, coarse roots. Neither extreme produces good chicons. Ideally, roots should be 6 to 8 inches long. The roots are harvested commercially from September to December and may be kept in cold storage until spring. If the tops are still green, the roots are laid in rows outside for several days and then the tops are cut and the roots put into storage. The tops are cut, leaving about 1/2 inch of stalk above the shoulder of the root to avoid damaging the growing point. It is probably a better garden practice in the maritime Northwest to allow the tops to die back and the roots to go into dormancy, while you harvest roots as wanted, as long as they don't rot.

Chicons are forced from the roots by packing them in a box or pit 16 inches deep, the roots held upright, and spaces between the roots filled with fine, light soil, the tops all on one level. Usually all roots are trimmed at the bottom to 8 inches long. Then the roots are covered with 8 inches of fine soil and the soil covered with straw. The box is then heated to 65 degrees, and in about twenty-two days the chicons have sprouted and are ready for harvest. Forcing can be done from 40 to 71 degrees, but at low temperatures the process is slow, while at higher temperatures, the rapid forcing makes tough and bitter chicons. At home, a room in the high sixties would probably be perfect if the forcing were done in a large wooden box.

Garden Planning
Slow-growing chicory will be in the ground a long time.

Insects and Diseases
We have no test results on this vegetable at this time.

Harvest
Sugarhat will stand for weeks in autumn, like endive. Treviso is best over-wintered under straw or with soil hilled up over the row to protect from freezing. It resprouts in early spring.

Saving Seed
Same as for endive.

Varieties
A commonly available nonforcing type is Sugarhat. Stokes also sells Catalogna, San Pasquale, and a forcing type. Catalogna is like a wild dandelion and is an annual whose flowers are picked before they open. Catalogna is very bitter. Treviso overwinters for spring use.

Parsley
Most people buy transplants unnecessarily for this easy-to-grow crop, when the only trick to getting parsley seed to sprout is to start it early.

Culture
Parsley seed germinates slowly and better under cool conditions, taking two to three weeks to sprout. If sown in April, naturally cool conditions and damp soils

will enhance germination; but if sown after mid-May, it must be watered almost daily when the sun shines, a demanding chore that is often an invitation to failure. But once the seed is up, it is a vigorous grower that produces on relatively infertile soil, much as do carrots. To grow leaf parsley, sow seed 1/2 inch deep, in rows 12 inches apart; thin gradually to 3 inches apart in the row. If leaf production is too slow or falters, side-dress with a high-nitrogen fertilizer such as blood meal or chicken manure. To grow root parsley, work the bed carefully as though growing carrots. Sow seed 1/2 inch deep, in rows 16 to 18 inches apart; thin carefully 4 to 6 inches apart in the row.

Garden Planning

Four or 5 row feet of leaf parsley will produce all the garnishes and seasonings a family could use. Root parsley is similar in flavor to parsnips, though it grows better in heavier or shallower soils than parsnips. It holds in the ground all winter, so a large patch might be in order.

Insects and Diseases

Neither leaves nor roots seem bothered by anything on our trial grounds.

Harvest

Snip leaves as needed. Dig roots from late September on. Cover the roots with straw to prevent freezing after November.

Saving Seed

Parsley is an insect-pollinated biennial like carrots, and saving seed is a similar process. I do not believe that there is any danger of crossing with "wild" parsley. Leaf varieties need not be dug because there is no need to select for root shape. Instead, put the plants under straw to protect the root from freezing in winter and uncover in early spring to permit the seed stalks to emerge easily. Seed for root varieties should be grown from hand-selected, replanted roots.

Varieties

There is not much difference in varieties of curly leaf parsley, though we've noticed a range of flavors in our trials and cannot agree on which tastes better than which. Flat-leaf types are strong flavored, good for drying. The root varieties offered in American catalogs are of indeterminate quality and, I suspect, obtained from a different European supplier every time a bag is purchased. Most of those I have tested are fairly long, needing 8 or more inches of light soil to perform well. One variety, Toso (TSC), develops a shorter root that may do better in heavier soil types. I'd grow parsley root over parsnips in heavy soil types. The flavor is very similar.

Parsnips

Culture

Growing parsnips is very similar to carrot culture, though parsnips are even more prone to becoming hairy in strong soils and demand light soil if well-formed roots are to be grown. Work up the bed deeply—12 inches minimum with a spading fork. Sow seeds from May through mid-July. Sowing on the earlier side produces very large roots; sowing in July makes supermarket-sized roots. Sow 3/4 inch deep, three to four seeds per inch (poor germination, usually), in rows 18 inches apart. Thin carefully to 3 inches apart in the row.

Garden Planning

The roots mature late in summer and will hold in the ground all winter. The bed should be sown to a green manure or to garden peas in spring.

Insects and Diseases

At Lorane, parsnips seem invulnerable to everything except field mice, who prefer the sweet roots to carrots during winter.

Harvest

Protect from freezing by storage under straw after November. Dig as wanted until spring, when they begin to make seed.

Saving Seed

Like carrots. The seed tends to fall from the flowers very easily, something like dill, so harvest promptly and then dry fully indoors. Parsnip seed tends to be short-lived, lasting at best two years with good vigor, and also tends to germinate at low percentage.

Varieties

Harris Model was originated by the Joseph Harris Company, who still grows a quality selection that is the industry standard for what little United States commercial parsnip raising is done. Other seed companies offering Harris Model do not usually buy their seed from Harris, but offer cheap stuff grown from seed-to-seed instead of root-to-seed. Stokes says their Harris Model is grown from selected roots. Territorial buys its seed from Harris.

Potatoes

Potatoes are not a biennial root crop like carrots, beets, parsnips, and parsley root, but are actually in the same botanical family as tomatoes. However, they do not demand high levels of fertility, nor are they heat-demanding like the other solanaceae. The most important cultural aspect of potato growing is having light-textured soil so the tubers can swell up easily and prolifically.

Culture

In light-textured soils, 1/4 to 1/2 cup of complete organic fertilizer per 5 row feet sprinkled into the row below the seed potatoes will provide abundant fertility. In heavier soils, the bed should be well amended with manure or compost. I've had best luck growing potatoes in a bed enriched with 2 inches of horse manure/sawdust bedding the previous fall. This manuring may be enough fertilizer as well. Feeding too much nitrogen fertilizer tends to result in big, lanky vines with few tubers at harvesttime. Potatoes can be grown under mulches of hay or sawdust, in old tires, and from sprouting potato peelings emerging from compost piles. However, I've generally grown them in soil and had the best luck doing so. I make two plantings. The first is done about St. Patrick's day (mid-March) if the soil can be worked, or as soon after that as possible. This planting matures midsummer. A second sowing made in early June matures in September and is used for winter storage.

I dig a trench about 8 inches deep, lay one seed potato per foot in the bottom, sometimes sprinkle in a bit of fertilizer, and then fill in the trench. If the bed wasn't manured heavily the previous year, I like to incorporate some compost into the trench as I fill it back up, to keep the soil light and enhance tuber formation. I prefer to use small potatoes whole as seed, but I've also had good success cutting larger ones up into 1½-inch-sized chunks and leaving them out on a tray for a week or so in bright light to skin over, green up, and start sprouting before planting. Two trenches fit nicely down a 4-foot-wide bed, run the long way. If frost burns back the spring sowing, it is of no consequence as new shoots emerge within a week or two. Other than that, the bed should be kept moist until the tubers have formed and then, when the foliage starts to die back, the soil should be allowed to dry out completely, giving the potatoes a tough skin that stores well. Sometimes the weather doesn't cooperate late in summer, which is why the larger commercial potato-growing areas are located in irrigated districts where fall rains are few and rare.

Garden Planning

Fifty feet of trench yields about 100 pounds of potatoes in my heavy, silty clay soil. Much higher yields are possible in lighter ground, and with more intensive cultural methods, such as hilling up soil in tires or hilling up soil atop the vines as they grow (which keeps the soil light and fluffy for the tubers to swell up easily). I've had excellent growth of overwintered cauliflower and Purple Sprouting broccoli sown following harvest of early potatoes.

Insects and Diseases

Flea beetles do like to chew on potato leaves, and their larvae are supposed to damage the skin on the tubers; but I've had little significant trouble with them. One thing I've done about the flea beetles is to broadcast an ounce of radish seed atop the potato bed immediately after filling the trenches. The radishes are mostly harvested by the time the vines cover them over, but the flea beetles seem to prefer radish tops to potato leaves. A few radishes remain growing among the potatoes, but do not seem to reduce the yield while continuing to detour the beetles.

Scab is a disease attacking the skin of the tubers. It makes tough, scabby patches, lowering eating quality and storage potential. Scab is supposed to be enhanced by higher soil pH and liming is supposed to be *verboten* in the potato bed. But I've never paid attention to this, have grown potatoes in beds recently limed, and have had no significant amount of scab.

Harvest

Begin digging early potatoes once the blossoms form, digging a plant or two at a time as needed. Withhold further watering when the vines begin to deteriorate to try to dry up the bed completely and thus produce tough, long-storing skins. When the vines are fully dead and the soil dried out, dig the tubers. I store mine in buckets in an unheated shed and surround the buckets with straw or blankets to prevent them from freezing in a cold snap. The tubers remain in good condition until the end of April.

Saving Seed

Certified seed potatoes purchased from a garden center or seed company are guaranteed free of virus diseases that can greatly reduce yields. However, if the potatoes in your garden grow all right, there is no reason to assume they have any diseases or will "catch" them. I'd sort out the smaller potatoes at harvesttime to use for seed next spring. Some people believe in using the largest and finest-looking tubers for seed, cutting them up in chunks, each of which contains an eye or two. After you cut them up, allow time for the tubers to scab over or heal before sowing. When I cut up large portions, I leave them cut side up on a newspaper in bright light in the house for a week or so until scabs form and the tubers begin to sprout (if they haven't already). Usually my June sowing is done with sprouting, shriveled-up roots, but even if the sprouts are several inches long, everything works well.

Varieties

I've conducted potato varietal trials with the old standards as well as with many heirloom varieties, and I've never grown a variety that performed really poorly. Some good common varieties are Netted Gem, Norgold, Russet, Red Pontiac, Nordland, Red LaSoda, and Nooksack Cascadian (which is the variety grown commercially east of Bellingham, Washington). More and more gardeners are beginning to discover the superior flavor of the yellow potato and today, Yellow Finns are available as seed in some garden stores. Finns can usually be found in health food markets that sell produce, and though not "certified," these still make good seed potatoes. For several years now, I've only grown yellow potatoes. Another yellow variety of extraordinarily good flavor is the German Fingerling available from Gurney's (a mail-order seed company). However, Fingerlings are very low yielding.

Radishes

Technically, radishes are an annual brassica, but I classify them as roots because they have a high water requirement, need soft, humusy soil to grow properly, and have little use for the high nutrient levels demanded by most other brassica crops. Fairly easy to grow with a bit of knowledge, radishes can be harvested from late April until late October. If protected by a simple cold frame, harvests can be extended a month or so on either side of the season.

Culture

The single most important thing in producing successful radishes is rapid growth. The plants have shallow root systems, and though they'll survive and go to seed in droughty soil, good root formation will only occur with more than adequate moisture. Where most crops will allow soil moisture to drop considerably from capacity, radish crops should be held above 70 percent at all times, and for really succulent radishes, 80 percent or better would be a good idea. For this reason, most commercial radish growers have extensive and expensive sprinkler systems so they can water every few days. The best way to make light soil retain moisture and heavier soils light enough to permit good rooting of this crop is to add organic matter. Usually, manures that are not all sawdust or bedding, or ordinary composts, will provide more than enough nutrients for the crop as well.

Sow the seeds from March through September outdoors, and in February or October in cold frames. Radish seed usually germinates at nearly 90 percent outdoors. Carefully place one seed per inch, 1/2 to 3/4 inch deep, in rows 12 inches apart. Radishes cannot stand crowding. By the time the seedlings are developing a true leaf, they should stand 1 to 2 inches apart, or root formation will suffer. In early spring plantings which grow slowly, flea beetles may be thick and sowings might be a bit thicker, but be sure to thin promptly once the seedlings are growing well.

Garden Planning

Radish crops must be harvested promptly—usually a single sowing is harvestable for only ten days at best, so successive sowings are required for a continuous supply. Radishes are a good crop to sow between rows of other slower-growing crops because they'll be harvested and out of the soil before the surrounding plants begin to shade them. I've found that interplantings with onions or garlic tend to deter flea beetles.

Insects and Diseases

Two insects make radishes hard to produce. The flea beetle chews holes in the leaves, slowing growth and retarding root formation. Slow-forming roots tend to be hot, woody, and become bait for the other insect pest, the cabbage root maggot. Flea beetles may be sprayed every few days with rotenone, and/or varieties of radishes that make large tops should be grown. With a larger ratio of top to root, the plants can tolerate more damage. Short-top varieties were bred for intensive commercial culture where all pests are chemically eradicated, and in those circumstances, can produce the highest yields by allowing closer spacing without competition for light.

Infestations of cabbage root maggot can be reduced by harvesting rapidly growing roots promptly, before the fly larvae have had an opportunity to hatch out and invade the root. Allowing sized-up roots to remain growing is an invitation to infestation. Sowing the seed on the soil's surface instead of in a furrow and then covering it with about a 1-inch-thick by 4-inch-wide band of soft, fine sawdust allows the sprout to emerge through the sawdust, while preventing the fly from gaining access to the soil at the base of the plant. If the fly cannot find the soil, it won't lay its eggs. Enlarging roots may well push aside the sawdust, exposing soil, but by then harvest is approaching sooner than the eggs can hatch out. This technique works with turnips as well.

Harvest

Pick radishes before they become pithy (which they do rapidly), split, get hot, or maggot-infested. There are two other edible parts of the radish most people are not familiar with. The tops make acceptable stir-fry greens, especially in early spring after a severe winter has frozen out overwintered crops. The seed pods that form after bolting are tender as little pea pods and have a mild, radishy flavor if picked before seed formation gets too far along. They are excellent in salads.

Saving Seed

Because it is an annual crop, growing seed is easy. Allow spring-sown roots to remain in the ground, bolt, flower, form seed, and mature. Harvest the stalks when much of the seed has dried out and thrash. However, growing quality seed is not so easy. It takes constant maintenance to keep a strain bulbing with a high percentage of well-formed, uniform roots. To do this, carefully harvest mature roots, pick out only the best ones, clip the tops back somewhat to reduce transpiration, and replant selected roots about 8 inches apart in rows 12 to 18 inches apart. Radishes cross freely with each other, so varieties must be isolated by over 1,000 feet. Radish seed can remain vigorous four to seven years after harvest.

Varieties

Most varieties grow well spring through fall. Champions are the best in early spring and late summer plantings, but will not do well during summer's long days, when they grow huge tops and do not form good bulbs. Avoid short-top varieties. Also avoid both the larger white oriental radishes that the Japanese call *daikon* and the Koreans call *mu*, and the big winter radishes like Black Spanish. Slow to form, these inevitably are riddled with maggots before maturity, unless screen cages or pesticides are used.

Cucurbits

Cucurbits are a family of annual vining plants that make fruits. Included are cucumbers, melons, and squashes. All cucurbits are sensitive to frost and poorly adapted to cool, damp conditions. It seems the family originated as desert plants growing along stream banks or where there was subsurface moisture—many cucurbits still develop very deep taproots. When exposed to high humidity, especially when cool, cucurbits fall prey to powdery mildew diseases that cover the leaves, preventing photosynthesis and rapidly killing the plant.

In order of hardiness, curcurbits run: squash, cucumber, cantaloupe, and watermelon. Squash and cucumber will grow vigorously during warmer parts of our frost-free season, except directly adjacent to the coast, where conditions are extremely cool, damp, and cloudy most of the summer. Cantaloupe can be grown throughout the Willamette, along the Columbia as far north as Longview, and if mollycoddled, can be raised even at higher elevations in Oregon at places like Lorane. Watermelon will only produce in the warmer portions of the Willamette most years, but is fairly reliable south of Yoncalla, Oregon.

Cucurbits never stop making vegetative growth as long as weather conditions permit. Fruit is ripened concurrently. So the vines have a high need for fertilization. The vines are hard to side-dress and are best fertilized with slow-release organic materials banded below the seedlings. Besides using complete organic fertilizer, I've had excellent results blending a large shovelful of chicken manure (without bedding) into a hill below the seeds or transplants.

Getting cucurbit seed to sprout requires an understanding of the family—and a little luck when sprouting them outdoors. Like the vines, the seedlings are very sensitive to powdery mildew diseases (and others) when exposed to damp, cool conditions—especially when sprouting. Ideally, the large seeds are planted deep so that the roots will find adequate soil moisture and so the sprout will come up through relatively dry soil, emerging healthy and undiseased. This is accomplished by allowing the soil to dry out after sowing; by the time the sprout emerges from the seed coat, the soil above it is quite dry, but farther down, it remains damp. A gardener must hope it won't rain after sowing! Rain both increases moisture and, worse, lowers soil temperature. Gardeners who try to help cucurbit seed sprout by watering it frequently experience poor germination. Sandy soils, which dry out very rapidly, may have to be watered between sowing and emergence, but they also tend to be warmer than clayey types, which encourages sprouting.

It's a sound practice when sprouting cucurbit seeds outdoors to resow if it rains very much before emergence. In the event both sowings sprout, the later one can be thinned out. When the spring weather is wet and unsettled, I like to sprout cucurbit seeds indoors in small peat pots, using fairly dry soil that will just barely form a soil ball. Then I seal the pots in a plastic bag to prevent moisture loss, thus eliminating any need to water them. These pots are kept at 70 degrees and the seedlings emerge within four to five days. Once sprouted, the pots are transferred to the cold frame for about two days while roots develop. Then they are transplanted. Though peat pots are supposed to permit roots to penetrate while they rot in the soil, theoretically allowing transplanting without any root damage at all, I've found that they don't always allow the roots through. It's a better practice to carefully peel away the pot as much as possible from the root ball before transplanting.

All cucurbits make separate male and female flowers. The male flowers appear as a simple flower containing stamens. The female flower is easily recognized because it forms at the end of an ovary, which resembles a miniature fruit. The ovaries must be pollinated, usually by insects, though it can be done easily by hand simply by inserting the stamen of a recently plucked male flower into a recently opened female flower (usually done first thing in the morning). Unpollinated ovaries wither and fall off within a few days. To grow prizewinning giant squashes or pumpkins, simply remove all female flowers after the first one has been successfully pollinated, and the vine will put everything it has into a single fruit.

Obtaining mature melons or winter squashes in the cooler districts of the maritime Northwest may demand rapid fruit-set. As a young vine grows, it has to make a certain number of leaves before female flowers first start to form, often as many as fifteen. I call this period of the plant's life "early vine growth." Usually the first flowers that form are male flowers, and the vine will produce five or more male flowers before it finally begins alternating male/female flowers. Practically, this means that until the vine has grown fifteen or so leaves, it will not make a female flower and cannot begin to develop fruit. To get early production, early vine growth must be hastened. This is not always simple, because early vine growth of cucurbits is greatly retarded by cool, damp conditions, but proceeds very rapidly under warm, dry ones. In cooler areas, the grower often must use black plastic mulches and/or cloches to create the correct environment, or the fruit forms too late to mature properly.

Cucumbers

Cucumbers are as intolerant of cool conditions as cantaloupes, but mature so quickly that they can be grown successfully almost anywhere in the maritime Northwest. The key to success with this vegetable is to wait until conditions outdoors are favorable before sowing seeds or setting out transplants. At Lorane, summer comes on for "real" about June 15 most years, and cucumber seed will not germinate well before this date, nor will transplants grow. In fact, transplants set out before nights stay warm usually die rapidly after getting powdery mildew diseases. However, once the seeds are up and growing, the vines develop rapidly. We usually can harvest cukes from August till the last part of September, when the vines break down as the weather cools and humidity rises.

Culture

At the same time that tomato seedlings are set out, make planting hills for the cucumber vines. To make a "hill," work a cup of complete organic fertilizer into about two gallons of soil. A shovelful of strong chicken manure is equally as good. Locate the hills 24 inches apart, in rows at least 6 feet apart. A single row of hills down a raised bed is ideal. About two weeks later (mid-June at Lorane), the soil will be very warm, and nighttime lows will probably remain above 50 degrees. This is the time to sow the seed. In the center of each hill, plant six to eight, 1½ to 2 inches deep. Do not water unless the soil is very dry, and if so, try to water only one time when the seeds are sown, because irrigation (or rain) lowers soil temperatures and increases soil humidity. If a spell of bad weather should come before the seeds sprout (usually about ten days after sowing), it is good insurance to resow immediately after the weather settles. If the earlier sowing makes it, fine. If it has died in the soil, the second sowing will have started to sprout. Once the seeds are up, water if needed. When the seedlings have a true leaf, thin to two seedlings per hill. Cucumber vines will grow better if watered fairly deeply and less frequently, because every irrigation makes the damp vines more susceptible to mildew. Try to water when the weather will be warm and sunny to dry off the vines immediately.

Garden Planning

I usually grow a single, 100-square-foot bed of cucumbers each summer. This requires about ten hills on a 4-foot-wide by 25-foot-long bed. The production gets so enormous that we pick a bucketful every other day during August and early September. The vines will almost certainly be falling apart by late September, making the bed available for a green manure like Crimson clover.

Insects and Diseases

I've not had insect problems with cukes, but they are vulnerable to powdery mildew in the maritime Northwest. Cucumber seeds can get it as they sprout if the soil is damp and chilly. The vines will get it as soon as weather conditions turn unfavorable. Though some varieties are resistant, this resistance seems to mean little more than that the variety will get the disease a day or two later than a nonresistant variety.

Harvest

If seeds are allowed to develop in any of the cucumbers, fruit-set slows or stops altogether. So keeping the vines picked keeps them productive. Large cukes make good chicken food or compost. Oversized cukes do not make good eating.

Saving Seed

Cucumbers do not cross with other cucurbits, but are bee pollinated, so different varieties must be isolated by at least 1,000 feet for purity, or they must be pollinated by hand. This is accomplished early in the morning when new flowers have just opened, but before the bees become active. A hand-crossed flower is protected from bees inside a brown paper sack until the fruit is developing, at which time it should be flagged with a ribbon or twine around its stem. When the fruit is overly mature and turning yellow or golden, the seed is ripe. Remove the seed and pulp and ferment in a bowl at room temperature, stirring daily. After three to six days, the pulp will liquefy. Pour it off and wash and dry the seeds completely at room temperature on a newspaper.

Varieties

The best open-pollinated types for the maritime Northwest are Marketmore (slicer) and SMR 58 (pickling). Unfortunately for the seed saver, Suyo Long, an open-pollinated burpless type, tends to be unusually late and grows poorly under cool conditions, so the only well-adapted burpless types available are hybrids.

Most hybrid burpless cucumber varieties grow well at Lorane. I prefer burpless types (actually Japanese) because their thin skins need no peeling and the flavor is usually very sweet. Some of the new slicing and pickling hybrids are gynoecious, meaning they make only female flowers and, to be pollinated, must be grown with a small percentage of another variety that produces male flowers. Having only female flowers results in slightly earlier fruit-set and higher production. However, gynoecious types should be avoided when only a few cucumber plants are being grown. At our trials, most hybrids come on only a few days earlier than the standard open-pollinated types and are slightly more productive. I think open-pollinated varieties are adequate in the garden. Another type of cucumber is the seedless greenhouse variety, which produces only female flowers and which must not be pollinated or the fruits become inedible. These should not be grown outdoors. Apple or Lemon cucumbers are an old home garden delicacy that makes lemon-sized fruit with deep green flesh that has a remarkably sweet and crisp texture like some exotic fruit from the tropics.

Melons

Melons are so poorly adapted to cool, humid conditions that they can only be grown in the warmer areas of the maritime Northwest. Gardeners north of Longview, Washington, and along the coasts rarely have any success growing cantaloupe; watermelons are even more delicate, and only the hotter parts of the Willamette and the banana belts of southern Oregon can raise them successfully most summers. Oregon State University has been doing melon trials at Corvallis and Canby for a number of years and their trials indicate that one must not only culture them exactly right, but also must be very selective about varietal choices.

Culture

Melons prefer a light soil that warms up quickly and permits early rooting. Heavier soils will do all right if well amended with organic matter. Sugar production of melons is closely related to the amount of magnesium available, so use of dolomitic lime in their complete organic fertilizer is very helpful. So might be spraying the leaves with epsom salts every few weeks if dolomite is not used. Epsom salt is magnesium sulfate and is absorbed right through the leaf. Mix it at 1 tablespoonful per pint of water. Make and space hills as though growing cucumbers, about the time tomatoes are set out, and work in complete organic fertilizer. However, the more heat-demanding melons virtually *require* a black plastic mulch, except in southern Oregon, and even there mulch will improve early vine growth. Lay a sheet of black plastic that is 3½ to 4 feet wide down the melon row, atop the hills, and anchor along the edges, leaving as much plastic as possible exposed. Cut a small hole over each hill. The plastic warms soil temperatures a few degrees and reradiates heat at night. Start transplants late in May. Germinate the seeds in individual peat pots about 4 inches in diameter, and after emergence thin to three plants per pot; in a week or so, thin again to the two best plants. About mid-June, the transplants should have grown about four to seven leaves. Drafty cold frames may not be warm enough for melons in late May if nights turn cold. I grow mine in a hot frame. About mid-June, transplant one pot of two vines per hill, peeling off as much of the peat pot as possible without damaging the root ball. After that, water thoroughly but infrequently to avoid damp leaves.

Garden Planning

I've never gotten a watermelon to ripen at Lorane, nor to grow a fruit larger than a grapefruit. Cantaloupe is much easier, and I've harvested as many as ten good-sized melons from each hill in a hot summer—as few as three in a poor one. Folks in the Willamette do better.

Insects and Diseases

Resistent varieties might not come down with powdery mildews during a short spell of unsettled weather during summer, but by September the weakening light and cooler conditions weaken all varieties. Once weather turns rainy, even for a few days, they come down with the disease. After the leaves are mildewed, all ripening of fruit stops permanently. Ripe melons may as well be harvested, the vines pulled out and composted, and green manure sown.

Harvest

Cantaloupes will slip the vine (detach easily) when ripe. They do not ripen after harvest! Only the leaves putting sugars into the fruit makes them ripen. Some exotic types of muskmelons (similar to cantaloupes) will not slip the vine at all, but must be judged by slight color changes or smell. Some of these types will ripen slightly after harvest. Watermelons do not ripen after harvest either, and must be knowledgeably thumped to judge maturity.

Saving Seed

Generally like cucumbers, though cantaloupes don't cross with muskmelons and neither cross with watermelons. When the fruit is fully ripe, the seeds are mature.

Varieties

A few old, well-adapted, open-pollinated cantaloupe varieties still are cultured by home gardeners, though the seed is not readily available, nor are these varieties nearly as productive as the hybrids. They include the Oregon Delicious and the Spear melon. Iroquois (STK, TSC) has done fairly well at trials here. Not all the early hybrids will produce under cool conditions, though they may be earlier under warm ones. I'd stick to Harper Hybrid (STK, HAR, TSC), which makes fruits of excellent quality and is as reliable as a melon can be in a region where melons hardly grow at all. Harper Hybrid outyields the few open-pollinated varieties that can mature here by about double. Honeydew doesn't mature usually, and Earlidew doesn't have the flavor or yield of Honey Drip (TSC) when the summer is on the cool side. I'd advise caution when experimenting with melon varieties. During cool years at Corvallis, I've seen hundreds of row feet of hybrid early cantaloupe varieties not ripen anything, with only a few of many varieties producing at all.

Watermelon varieties that will produce as well as watermelons can are Crimson Sweet, Sugar Baby, and Sweet Meat II Hybrid.

Squashes

Of the cucurbits, squash is the most tolerant of cool conditions. Because of its vigorous growth, almost any gardener in almost any soil can produce some summer squash. However, some care is required to get winter squash to mature in the cooler microclimates west of the Cascades.

Culture

The only hard part of getting squash to grow is getting the seed to sprout. Like all cucurbits, squash seed will not germinate in cold soils. However, where cucumber seed needs soil that remains at a temperature over 65 degrees, and melons need soil above 70 degrees to germinate, squash will sprout in 60-degree soil, though it does much better at higher temperatures. If at all possible, plant the seed at the beginning of a spell of sunny, hot weather and do not water after sowing to avoid lowering soil temperature. And, if weather conditions worsen before emergence, be prepared to resow. Summer squash matures rapidly, so should the first sowing fail, replanting is no problem. However, in cool areas like Lorane, winter squash varieties usually need every possible day of good weather to mature fully. Because a failure to sprout outdoors might prevent full maturity of a second sowing, I've taken to germinating winter squash varieties in small peat pots indoors where moisture and temperature are carefully regulated, growing them in those pots for only a day or two after emergence in the cold frame, and then transplanting. Traditionally, squash is grown in hills. Make a hill by working a cup to a pint of complete organic fertilizer or a shovelful of chicken manure into a few gallons of soil with a shovel, and then sowing or transplanting above that enriched "hill." Space summer squash 2 feet by 4 feet; small vining squashes 2 feet by 6 feet; the extensive vines of the larger winter squash plants need 3 feet by 10 feet. At Lorane, we sow squash about June 1. Sow four to six seeds per hill, 1½ to 2 inches deep. When the seedlings have developed a true leaf, thin to two plants per hill. If the seed has not sprouted within a week (especially if there has been poor weather since sowing), resow again as a precaution.

Garden Planning

Two or three hills of summer squash will supply most families with all they want. Winter squash vines will usually produce about 30 to 50 pounds of squash per hill. Big varieties only make two to three 10- to 15-pound squashes, small-sized ones may produce eight to ten squashes of 3 to 5 pounds each. Winter squashes are best located at the outer fringe of the garden, and the vines may be allowed to run on the lawn or outside the cultivated area.

Insects and Diseases

Like all cucurbits, squash gets powdery mildew when the weather gets cool and damp at summer's end. Mildew ends the ripening process of winter varieties and indicates harvesttime. Squash can also get powdery mildew shortly after emergence if the weather is not warm and sunny. Should that occur, sow again, because mildewed seedlings rarely resume proper growth.

Harvest

Summer squashes are best harvested on the small side, having the tenderest skins and most delicate flavor at that stage of development. Permitting large squashes to remain on the bush initiates seed formation, and once this occurs further set of new squashes is reduced or stopped. Winter squashes usually need all the days they can have to mature fully. Unripe squashes have light-colored, flavorless flesh and light, thin seeds. When fully mature, the flesh usually becomes deep orange and the seeds are fat after drying down. A fully mature winter squash will also have a shriveled, brown stem that no longer transports nutrients into the fruit. At Lorane, most varieties of winter squash are barely mature, at best, by the end of September. Once the weather has gotten poor and the vines develop powdery mildew or have been frosted back, winter varieties should be harvested immediately. Allowing them to remain in the field will greatly lower their storage potential. Leave a few inches of stem on the squash, bring them indoors, and cure the skin at room temperature for a week or so. Before storage, sponging off the skin with a disinfectant-strength solution of household bleach will kill mold spores that may later rot the squash. Squashes store best at 55 to 60 degrees and low humidity. I've successfully kept ours in a back bedroom closet and also under the sink in the kitchen, both allowing squash to last until April or early May. While the squash is being cured and while in storage, allow dry air to pass freely around the entire squash.

Saving Seed

There are four basic families of squashes: *Cucurbita pepo*, *Cucurbita maxima*, *Cucurbita mixta*, and *Cucurbita moschata*. Each family will cross freely with other members of its family as well as outcross with other families in some cases. *Pepo* will not usually cross with *maxima*. *Moschata* will cross with both *pepo* and *maxima*. *Mixta* is a tropical sort not usually grown in the maritime Northwest, and is known to some southern gardeners as cushaw types of squash or pumpkins.

Pepo includes the summer squashes, most pumpkins, and certain winter varieties like the acorns, Delicata, Vegetable Gourd, Vegetable Spaghetti, Gem, or Rolet. *Pepo* varieties can usually be recognized by their small seeds. *Pepos* are also the fastest to mature, usually requiring about 90 warm, sunny days from emergence to maturity of seed or fruit. Gardeners in cool areas can reliably save seed from *pepo* types and should concentrate on these for winter squash too.

Maxima squashes include the large, hard-shelled winter types such as Sweet Meat, Buttercup, and the Hubbards. Their seeds are much bigger than *pepo* varieties and require slightly more heat to sprout well. *C. maxima* needs about 120 good, warm, sunny days from emergence to full maturity of seed. If they don't fully mature, the seed will be low germ and low vigor, and the flavor of the flesh will be less full. One hundred twenty good growing days is all there is, at best, most summers in the maritime Northwest, except in the warmer areas of the Willamette and south.

Moschata varieties consist of butternut types. They, too, are longer growing, requiring about 120 to 130 good growing days.

The best bet for the seed-saving gardener is to grow only one type of *pepo* and one *maxima*, or to hand-pollinate selected flowers. Squashes are bee pollinated naturally, and require isolations over 1,000 feet for fair purity. The seed is removed from the mature fruit, washed free of the pulp by rubbing in water, and then dried fully. The usual life of fat, well-filled seed that was dried well can be over seven years.

Varieties

Butternut types do best in the warmer areas of the maritime Northwest, and cool area gardeners should try Ponca, which is a much earlier, smaller-fruited butternut type. Some years, we cannot get Ponca to be fully mature at Lorane. I've had fairly good success maturing many of the *maxima* winter squash varieties at Lorane, though I prefer the flavor and keeping qualities of the Buttercup and Sweet Meat. Delicata (*pepo*) is an early-to-mature winter squash of superlative flavor and storage, but it makes very poor vine growth under cool conditions. All summer squash varieties do well. One unique squash is Gem, sometimes called Rolet, which is used either as a summer squash or allowed to mature fully and used as a small winter squash. It is much earlier and makes better quality winter squash than the currently-in-vogue Kuta, also touted as a dual-purpose variety. Hybridization of squash seems to produce no more vigor, though the varieties are more uniform.

Alliums

Included in this group are leeks, shallots, onions, scallions, and garlic. All are frost hardy, some remarkably so. Bulbing alliums that overwinter and mature in summer are better adapted to maritime conditions than those that are spring sown and mature late in summer, because it is hard to cure the skin on a bulb under damp conditions, and poorly cured onions don't store for long.

Alliums are highly photoperiodic, so regardless of sowing date, they'll bulb when day length dictates. Very much like cauliflower, the size of the plant when bulbing commences determines the size of the onion or garlic head. This means the plants have to be grown fast to become as large as possible before vegetative growth stops. Alliums have weak root systems, best adapted to coarse, light soils. Growing husky plants on clayey soil types can be difficult, because adding large quantities of organic matter to loosen soil enough to permit good rooting also tends to tie up nutrients until the organic matter breaks down somewhat. If I have any fully broken down compost, I save it for the onion patch. Alliums can use good quantities of fertilizer when making vegetative growth, but when bulbing starts, very little nutrient uptake is needed. So early fertilization to spur rapid seedling growth is essential.

Getting seed of the allium family to sprout and grow initially has discouraged many gardeners. Consequently, growing bulb onions from sets has become popular, even though these are of poor quality compared to seed-grown bulbs. Allium seed is weak-sprouting and takes up to two weeks to germinate. Because it is small and shallowly sown, the seed must be kept moist during spells of hot, sunny weather, *and* the soil must be free of crusting or puddling. So direct-seeded bulb onions are easiest sown in late spring when weather is usually moist and cool. Later sowings of scallions and overwintered bulb onions, if made in raised beds with high surface humus contents, usually germinate well, especially if watered daily during sunny weather. I've found that covering the seed with finely sifted compost or aged horse manure during midsummer holds in moisture and absolutely prevents crusting.

Alliums transplant very easily, even when the roots are completely bare of soil. This facility makes it easy to avoid the difficulties of field germination by starting seedlings in a nursery or greenhouse and transplanting them out when sized up. To facilitate transplanting, the tops are clipped so the plants are only 3 to 5 inches tall, reducing transpiration.

Some alliums have been propagated from bulbs for so long that they have lost the ability to make viable seed. Included in this group are garlics and some shallots. Other types of shallots (which are usually called multiplier onions when grown from seed), scallions, onions, and leeks do form seed and grow as biennials when they do so. Allium flowers are insect pollinated and varieties have to be isolated by several hundred feet for fair purity. Commercial seed crops are separated by a mile or so. Allium seed is lightweight and short-lived—two to three years at best. Getting high-vigor seed with long storage potential is also dicey. High temperatures at seed formation can kill seed, as can molds and various diseases of the seed head. Crop failures or seed too weak for sale are typical setbacks in the commercial onion seed business.

Garlic and Shallots

Garlic and shallots are excellent keepers, because they form bulbs during summer when soil is dry and their skins cure out well. The delicious aroma of freshly harvested garlic drying in the kitchen is a treat to anticipate each July.

Culture

Break a head of garlic into separate cloves. Sow them during September, root side down, 1 inch deep. Grow the plants in rows at least 12 inches apart, 3 to 4 inches apart in the row. Use no fertilizer at sowing, but for good bulb formation the following spring the soil must not be too heavy. Clayey soils should be well amended with organic matter 4 to 5 inches deep before planting garlic so it remains loose until next July. Shallots, which bulb on the surface, aren't so fussy. For the largest bulbs, side-dress overwintered plants late in February with about 3 or 4 tablespoonfuls of blood meal per 5 row feet. In cold, rainy springs, an additional side-dressing may be helpful if made mid-April.

Garden Planning

Remember that the bulbs won't be mature until midsummer.

Insects and Diseases

We've had no problems at Lorane.

Harvest

Some types of garlic put up a seed stalk. When the seed is mature, so are the cloves—though the seed rarely is viable. Some types brown off at the top like onions. One type of garlic makes miniature bulblets on top, each of which will grow a separate garlic. I've found it optimal to remove this flower stalk before bulblets form and to propagate from cloves. Doing so produces much larger cloves by redirecting the plant's energies to bulb formation below ground. The cleanest garlic is dug before the outer skin has dried out. The dirty outer skins are peeled off and the head allowed to dry indoors or under cover in a braid or clump. If allowed to remain in the soil too long, bulbs split apart and soil enters between cloves. Shallots usually brown off like onion tops and are ready to harvest when fully dried out. A single clove forms five or six the next spring.

Saving Seed

Use the largest cloves for replanting next year's crop. Larger cloves make larger plants. Varieties of garlic do not cross, nor do they make viable seed. Some types of shallots or multiplier onions do make seed, though these also may be best propagated from cloves.

Varieties

The best varieties are usually not found in seed catalogs, but in ethnic specialty stores or occasionally in supermarkets. The garlic variety that makes bulblets is called variously Italian Silver Skin or Rocambole. One unusual kind is called Elephant garlic because its bulblets are as large as a normal head of a regular variety. Many local gardeners grow it and a few mail-order seed companies sell it.

Elephant garlic can be recognized by the large, bluish seed balls it forms, which stand over 5 feet tall in July. Many gourmets think Elephant garlic has poor flavor and is more a relative of the leek than a true garlic. There are many types of shallots with various flavors and skin colors. Some authorities classify certain types as "multiplier onions" and others as true shallots. Other authorities state that all these are in the same family.

Leeks

Most types of bulb onions are not an easy crop for the maritime Northwest gardener. Those wonderful, sweet, and easy-to-grow overwintered bulb onions don't keep for more than three or four months, giving out by summer's end. Storage and Sweet Spanish types often don't cure well and so have limited storage potential. Bulb onions also do not grow well on heavier soil types. Leeks, on the other hand, do grow well in heavy soils, and can be harvested from the garden from October until April. For this reason, I no longer struggle to grow storage onions on my silty clay soil, but have come to depend on leeks instead.

Culture

When grown on heavier soil types, leeks do better if the soil is amended with organic matter at least 3 inches deep. This permits the shafts to enlarge readily. Leeks also need a fairly good amount of nutrition, and soils high in organic matter will supply a good portion of that without much fertilization.

The planting date is determined by when leeks are to be harvested. If sown in very early spring and transplanted out during May, they will be table-sized by late September and may become absolutely gigantic if fall weather is conducive to even more growth. Some very hardy leek varieties may also be direct-seeded from mid-April through May and will size out from fall to late winter, remaining in table condition until spring. Directions for raising leek transplants are found in "Raising Transplants."

Later-maturing leek varieties may be direct-seeded where they are to be harvested, or started as transplants in a nursery bed. I prefer the nursery bed method, because leeks are slow growing and the tiny seedlings are hard to manage when spread out over large spaces. But concentrated in a small space, they are easy to sprout and tend. I also think transplanting is a much easier way to blanch the stems than hilling up soil and results in cleaner leeks with less soil in the stem. Leeks are also incredibly tough and easy to transplant. I make a small nursery by amending a small part of a raised bed heavily with well-aged compost 3 or 4 inches deep, which permits both easy germination and digging the seedlings without root damage. One cup complete organic fertilizer per 4 square feet is also broadcast and worked in with the compost. Furrows 1/2 inch deep and about 8 inches apart are sown with about eight seeds per inch. The seedlings should be thinned so they stand 1/4 to 1/2 inch apart in the row when they are well established.

The rate of growth of these seedlings will depend on soil fertility and the weather, but generally by sometime in August the seedling leeks will be over 1/4 inch in diameter, crowded, and demanding transplanting. Growing crowded in a nursery, they develop longer shafts. Dig the seedlings, shake off the soil from the roots, taking care not to unduly damage the root systems, and clip the tops back to about half their length. This reduces transpiration and makes transplanting a snap. Make deep furrows about 18 inches apart across a raised bed and sprinkle in about 1/4 to 1/2 cup complete organic fertilizer per each 5 feet of furrow. Set the transplants 2 to 3 inches apart into the furrows up to the first leaf joint and bury the stems, taking care not to get soil into the first leaf notch. Water well, and if the weather is hot and sunny, water every day or two for a week to ten days. Seedlings started in early spring and transplanted from flats or trays in late spring are set out the same way.

The tender, white portion of the shaft is the best eating. Leek varieties have been bred to have long shafts, but they will be white only as deep as they are buried. Burying the shafts by hilling up soil as the leeks grow has a liability. If soil is allowed to get stuck in the leaf notches, it will remain there at harvest. Raising lanky transplants by crowding them and then burying them deeply when transplanting blanches the stem without hilling up soil.

Garden Planning

Leeks may be in the soil from spring to spring. Consider this when locating them. Twenty to 50 row feet keeps us well supplied from November to April.

Insects and Diseases

We've had no problems at Lorane.

Harvest

Dig them when the shafts are over 1 inch in diameter. If winter-hardy varieties are sown early in spring and are sized up by October, they'll become gigantic and raggedy appearing by late winter, though if the outer layers of the leek are peeled, the inner shaft will still be in prime eating condition. When sown earlier, varieties which overwinter tend to bolt a little earlier, so for harvest in spring do not sow before mid-May.

Saving Seed

Leeks are biennials like onions. In spring, they bolt, sending up a seed head. The balloon-shaped flowers will eventually show the black seeds they contain. Cut off the stems at this time and allow the flowers to dry fully for several weeks on a tray indoors. Then, rub the heads between your hands and the seeds will fall out. Leeks are insect pollinated and require at least several hundred feet of isolation between varieties. Leeks do not cross with onions or scallions. For quality seed, dig the plants before bolting (best in fall) and select for straight, long, white shafts without bulbing at the bottom and replant these selected specimens.

Varieties

Autumn leeks are fast growing, sizing up by late summer—but they are not very hardy and won't survive hard frosts well. So autumn varieties like Tivi (HAR), Supreme (TSC), Titan, Elephant (STK), King Richard, and Inverno (JSS) are better for the commercial grower who wants to dig his crop for sale in fall or keep it for a time in cold storage. Truly hardy varieties like Alaska, Unique, Musselburgh (STK), and Electra (HAR) are better for winter harvest. Durabel (TSC) is a remarkable winter variety that has been bred to overwinter and be dug in spring. Durabel is later to bolt than most varieties.

Onions

It is said of knowledgeable people that they "know their onions." There is something to this old saw, for bulb onions are a tricky and hard-to-produce crop. However, scallions are fairly easy, and leeks make excellent, easy-to-grow onion substitutes.

Onions may be grown from sets or seed. I have not encouraged people to use sets, because set-started bulb onions are usually not the best keeping varieties, and the percentage of bolters and doubles that occurs when using sets is usually high. However, sets do solve one problem many gardeners find difficult in growing onions, which is getting the seed to sprout at all. Yet, I've never experienced a germination failure with onions, growing them on humusy raised beds and covering the seed with pure, sifted humus in midsummer sowings of scallions or overwintered bulb onions.

There are three types of bulb onions grown from seed, and two (or more) sorts of scallions. Each requires different handling.

Sweet Spanish onions are large, slow-growing types best adapted to latitudes slightly south of the maritime Northwest, and are cultured commercially in Utah, New Mexico, and California. The day length that triggers their bulb formation and maturity occurs on the late side at our latitudes, making it hard to cure them well in the maritime Northwest. Even the earliest of the Sweet Spanish types won't be tops down before mid-September at 45 degrees latitude. If Sweet Spanish onions don't get big, they usually don't get sweet either, so they are best started early as transplants.

Storage onions are faster growing and some varieties mature on the early side. I've had varieties ready to cure and put into storage by September 1 at our trials. Other varieties are much too late to cure well, so maritime gardeners producing their winter's bulb onion supply really do have to know their onions. Storage onions may be transplanted if very large bulbs are wanted. If direct-seeded a little later in spring when conditions suit them outside, the yields per area used will be as large, though the bulbs may be smaller.

Overwintered bulb onions have been grown commercially for a long time in southern California and the most southerly parts of Texas and New Mexico. However, the Japanese have developed varieties hardy enough to overwinter reliably in the maritime Northwest. These types are sown in late summer and are mature in June. Overwintered bulb onions are the easiest to grow, particularly in heavier soils, though care has to be taken to achieve good germination should August or early September be hot and dry. Overwintered varieties are not good keepers, being very soft and extremely sweet with little pungency. We've had crops last till October from a mid-June harvest.

Scallions are of two general types. The Sweet Spanish derivatives are very late-bulbing Spanish types that are harvested before bulbing begins. These have been bred for a thin outer skin, sweetness, and tenderness. If sown in spring, they'll make good size by midsummer and can be used until late September. The other group is composed of several overwintering types that share a common trait—they don't bulb under the decreasing day length of late summer. Lisbons are an overwintered type that bulbs in late spring, though they have not been bred to make large, usable bulbs. Welsh onions are another overwintered type that does not bulb at all. Both Lisbons and Welsh onions may multiply during winter if they are of good size by fall. Welsh onions bolt in March/April. Overwintered types of scallions are best for the gardener, because they can be sown from spring till midsummer and can be held for harvest until the following spring.

Culture

Sow Sweet Spanish onions in early spring indoors in a greenhouse or frame and raise to be transplanted in May. (See the section on raising transplants for details.) Set out transplants 3 to 4 inches apart in rows at least 18 inches apart, with 1/4 to 1/2 cup complete organic fertilizer banded below each 5 feet of row. Sow storage onions late April to mid-May. Earlier sowings make larger bulbs, but weather and soil conditions usually will not permit it. Sow seed 1/2 inch deep, three to four seeds per inch, in rows 18 inches apart. Band 1/4 to 1/2 cup complete organic fertilizer below each 5 feet of furrow. Thin gradually so the seedlings stand 2 to 3 inches apart. Yields will be larger if the bulbs are a bit crowded, though the bulbs will consequently be a bit smaller. Sow overwintered onions mid-August to early September, depending on how fast they grow at your location. Plant them as though they were storage onions, but do not use much fertilizer, if any. These onions must be tough and hardy and should not grow too fast. However, they should be the size of a pencil before winter checks their growth in December. Do not completely thin before spring, because there may be a few losses during winter, and seedlings may be easily dug and transplanted in February to fill in the gaps. When regrowth begins in spring—usually about the same time the crocus comes up—fertilize by side-dressing about 2 tablespoons of blood meal per 5 row feet close to the seedlings. Also thin and weed carefully at this time. Side-dress again late in March and, should March be particularly rainy, do so again early in April. Bulbing begins in May, and once that occurs there is little point to further fertilization.

Sow scallions like storage onions from mid-April through mid-July, depending on the variety, and when well established, thin to about 1/2 inch apart in the row. Sowings intended to overwinter should not be heavily fertilized.

Garden Planning

A foot of well-grown storage onion row makes a pound or two. Because I can rarely get storage onions to cure up well at Lorane, I like to use leeks instead for winter, but do grow a big bed of overwintered onions, producing at least 50 pounds for summer use. We also usually sow a big bed of overwintered scallions during summer for use in fall/winter/spring. Scallions are delicious in stir-fries, especially with Purple Sprouting broccoli in March/April. Overwintered Lisbon onions remain in good condition a month longer in spring than do leeks. Because storage varieties cure better in dry soil, it is best to locate the onion bed on the edge of the garden where irrigation may be withheld as the tops begin to go down.

Insects and Diseases

We've had no problems at Lorane.

Harvest

If bulbing types divide into two separate parts (called doubles), they will not store long. Eat these first. Usually we harvest doubles before maturity as giant scallions. Onions that put up a seed stalk will not bulb properly (bolters). When the stalk appears, the plant should be pulled and used as a scallion. Usually only a small percentage of a crop bolts before bulbing. Once the bulbs are well formed, the tops dry out, as the nutrients they contain are transferred down into the bulb for storage. It is helpful if the soil also dries out at this time, promoting formation of a hard, tough skin that protects the bulb during storage and that enhances keeping. However, it is not always possible to dry down the soil in a climate where late summer rains are frequent. For this reason, the earliest-maturing varieties have a better chance to cure well. When about half the tops have naturally fallen over, break over the remaining tops, wait a week or so, and then dig the onions.

Lay them out in the sun in windrows and cover at night to protect from dews. If it should rain, bring them inside and cure indoors. After they are thoroughly dry, keep them in onion sacks. If not well ventilated, they may rot, so hang the sacks up to allow air to circulate freely around and through the bulbs. Best storage for bulb onions is *dry* and cool.

Saving Seed

Sweet Spanish and storage types have to be kept in storage and planted back out in spring to bolt and make seed like leeks. Overwintered bulb onions have to be stored all summer, and then the last-to-sprout ones (the best keepers) are replanted in September to overwinter again and bolt. Onions that bolt before bulbing should not be allowed to make seed. The seed formation and handling procedure is like that for leeks.

Varieties

Open-pollinated Sweet Spanish types are going out of vogue, so the selections are getting a bit raggedy. Yellow Sweet Spanish Peckham (JSS, TSC) is my favorite. Hybrid Spanish varieties like Fiesta are usually a bit earlier and more likely to cure well. When selecting storage onions, buy the earliest-maturing variety. Usually seed catalogs recommend later-maturing types for longer storage potential, and this may well be true in other growing regions; but if the variety does not cure well, it has little storage potential anyway. I'd choose Early Yellow Globe or Early Yellow Globe Hybrids or other hybrid varieties maturing in less than one hundred days. Red storage onions tend to be late and consequently poor keeping. Overwintered onions are available only from Johnny's and Territorial Seed Company. Mini-onions or pickling onions are simply quick-maturing types grown as storage onions that are row spaced like scallions and have thin, tender skins.

The Japanese type of scallions are Welsh onions, often hardy enough to winter over in the East. Johnny's sells three types; Stokes and Harris offer them, too. I think Welsh onions are coarse and hot compared to the mild, tender flavor of Lisbons, which are plenty hardy enough to winter over at Lorane.

Miscellaneous Vegetables

Asparagus

Asparagus is a perennial that stores a lot of food in its root system to use early in the year to put up tall, lacy, fernlike shoots very rapidly in spring. However, unlike biennial root crops, asparagus demands very deep, rich soil. Commercial production of asparagus is done on very well-drained soils that stay fairly dry in winter, because the roots are prone to various diseases that occur under damp conditions. Most soils west of the Cascades are too wet in winter to allow asparagus to live more than a winter or two. Only very light and deep soils will grow it in our region, though I have seen a few successful plantings done in large boxes about 2 feet tall set atop the ground and filled with sandy soil.

Culture

Asparagus can be started from seed, but this adds two years to the time one has to wait for the first harvest. Most gardeners buy two-year-old roots from a garden center. Plant the roots in April or early May. Make trenches about 12 inches wide and at least 12 inches deep; the trenches should run at least 4 feet apart if more than one row is being planted. Put 2 to 3 inches of well-aged manure or compost into the bottom of the trench with lime and rock phosphate (bone meal may substitute for phosphate rock) at about 10 pounds per 100 row feet. With a shovel or spading fork, work the organic matter and rock minerals into the bottom of the trench, trying to break up the soil another 8 to 10 inches down. Then, spread another equal quantity of organic matter and rock minerals on top of the soil that was removed from the trench and blend it in as the trench is gradually filled up. Spread out the roots on the bottom of the trench, locating one root about every foot, and cover them about 1 inch deep. As the root sprouts and puts up a shoot, gradually cover it up, leaving about 1 inch of the shoot exposed. By summer, the shoot will have emerged completely from the trench and the trench will have been completely filled in.

When the tops turn brown, cut them down and compost them. Every fall, cover the bed with an inch of manure or compost, and every few years add as much lime as the rest of the garden is given. If the ferns are cut back before the seeds begin to fall, thousands of little asparagus plants will not begin to sprout atop the bed. Beds that become crowded with too many plants produce small shoots.

Garden Planning

The bed is perennial, needs as much water in summer as any other part of the garden, and may last over twenty years if limed and manured regularly and not allowed to become too thick with seedlings. Unless heavy freezing or canning is intended, 25 row feet should be enough.

Insects and Diseases

Well-drained soil avoids subsequent loss of the planting.

Harvest

After transplanting two-year-old roots, there will be no harvest that season. Only a few small shoots will come up. If the bed survives the winter, next year there will be many more coming up in spring. It's a good idea not to harvest these, allowing all the energy to remain in the root for further rapid growth. The second spring after transplanting, the bed should be thick with shoots, and these may be cut off for a number of weeks until the size of the shoots begins to decrease, at which point the bed should be allowed to develop ferns and recharge the root food storage supply.

Saving Seed

The seeds may be collected when the pods are dry but before they shatter and fall to the ground. These may be sown in fertile soil in spring, 1/2 inch deep, in rows 18 inches apart, and thinned to about 10 inches apart in the row. After two years, the roots may be dug early in spring before they sprout and are transplanted into trenches.

Varieties

Well-drained, fertile soil is more important than varietal choices. Mary Washington or California 500 are recommended by Oregon State University. I've never gotten a bed of asparagus to live on my heavy soil, though I did have a good one in California back in the early seventies.

Sweet Corn

Though truly fresh sweet corn is a wonderful treat, it takes up more space and time than it's worth in most gardens. If I were not in the seed business, I'd never grow corn. But since sweet corn is one of the most popular garden vegetables, I conduct moderate-sized trials and grow a succession of familiar and unfamiliar varieties each summer.

Corn is easy to grow if properly fertilized and will adapt to most any soil type. However, though easy to grow, it is not always certain to mature. Let me relate a short story about how interestingly corn can "misbehave" in the maritime Northwest. At the suggestion of an urban acquaintance who grew a summer privacy hedge of a corn variety he said was "tall," I included a patch of Trucker's Favorite White in my corn trial one summer. Trucker's White is listed in the Park Seed Company catalog as taking 67 days to mature and as growing 6½ feet tall. I'm sure that is true—in South Carolina where Park is located. At Lorane, however, the corn kept growing and growing vigorously, and by September 20 (110 days after sowing), it was 12 feet tall with stalks nearly 2 inches in diameter at the bottom, and was just beginning to put up a tassel. I'm sure if the summer had continued into November, the corn might have been ripe. What happened is that growth of sweet corn is regulated by heat, and though we had enough sun for Trucker's Favorite White to make vigorous vegetative growth, its internal heat "clock" hadn't collected enough calories to inform the plant to start making seed until late September.

Plant breeders understand this phenomena well and have developed a measure of heat called a *heat unit*, similar to the "degree day," which is another measure of energy used to figure how much energy it will take to heat houses in different climates. A heat unit is a numerical expression of the amount of time and number of degrees the average temperature is above 50 degrees from the last frost of spring to the first frost of autumn. Vegetable varieties that regulate their growth by heat accumulation, such as corn, beans, and peas, are listed in professional catalogs by the number of "HU" they take to mature. In the case of beans and peas, this is not particularly relevant to our region, because all are plenty early and mature readily. But sweet corn is more tricky.

The earliest maturing sweet corn varieties need about 1350 HU to ripen; the later types can require as many as 2200 HU. And, to go to fully dry ears, seed corn varieties start at about 2100 HU and can require close to 3000 HU. Now, the earliest sweet corn varieties needing around 1350 HU are usually listed in mail-order catalogs as maturing in 55 to 69 days. This is the case with Earlivee, which is listed by Stokes at 55 days and by Johnny's at 69 days. A later variety like Golden Jubilee is in Stokes' catalog at 84 days and in Johnny's at 87 days. Jubilee takes about 1750 HU. What their catalogs are telling the reader is that Albion, Maine, receives 1750 HU in about 87 days, while it takes slightly less time at Stokes's Ontario research farm. It would also appear that Ontario warms up much faster in early summer than Maine.

The Willamette Valley usually receives about 2000 HU in the entire summer, with some microclimates warmer, some cooler by a hundred or so HU. Puget Sound might be lucky to get 1500. At Lorane we probably get about 1800. Southern Oregon might get over 2200, while around Umatilla in eastern Oregon the HU accumulation might well exceed 3000. So a Umatilla gardener might grow two entire crops of early corn on the same plot in one summer, while a Puget Sound gardener might be lucky to ripen one crop of the earliest variety. At Lorane, we sow our corn variety trials on June 1 without fail. Earlivee usually matures early—mid-August—and Jubilee comes on slightly after Labor Day most summers. But in the very cool summer of 1983 the early varieties in our trials matured toward the middle of September, and Jubilee barely made it before frost took the field just about October 1. I bet Trucker's Favorite White takes close to 2500 HU—which it gets in 67 days in steamy South Carolina.

Culture

Corn is wind-pollinated, and if the ears are not well pollinated, they do not become well filled. To achieve good pollination, plant corn in large blocks at least four rows wide by 10 feet long. For this reason, corn does not lend itself to culture on raised beds. Rain or irrigation when the pollen is flying will also prevent good ear fill, so don't sprinkle when the tassels are dropping pollen.

Corn seed doesn't germinate well in soils below 60 degrees, though it is slightly more tolerant of cold soil than bean seed. Corn is also sensitive to frost, so it should be sown no more than a few days before the last anticipated frost date. At Lorane, we sow sweet corn June 1. In the Willamette, this might be pushed back as much as a month. Make at least four adjoining 3-inch deep furrows about 30 inches apart with a stout hoe or trenching tool. Sprinkle 4 to 10 pounds of complete organic fertilizer down each 100 feet of furrow and mix it in somewhat with a light hoe or cultivator. Sow about four seeds per foot, and cover them so the seeds are from 1½ to 2½ inches deep. Do not water the seeds after sowing, if at all possible, because watering lowers soil temperature and causes much more seed to rot. Hope for warm weather and quick sprouting. Within a couple weeks of sprouting, thin the rows so the seedlings stand 8 inches apart. Keep the weeds hoed out thoroughly until the corn is knee high and then stay out of the patch to avoid compacting the soil between the rows.

Garden Planning

Hybrid corn varieties mature very uniformly and remain in good eating condition at best for ten days. Simultaneously sowing three or more varieties that have a spread of maturity dates will produce a continuous harvest. Our corn patch always seems to grow an excellent crop of Crimson clover after it is tilled in early in October. I first broadcast the clover seed in the standing corn and then till in the corn shallowly.

Insects and Diseases

Earworms can be handled with BT if sprayed when the tassles first drop pollen and again about ten days later. However, I've seen very few in the maritime Northwest.

Harvest

The ears will be ripe when the wrappers are slightly browning off, or sometimes the ears will lean out when ready. Each variety has slightly different indicators.

Saving Seed

Five hundred feet of isolation between varieties will make fair purity. However, open-pollinated sweet corn varieties produce, at best, half the yield of hybrids. Seed may be saved from the smaller second ears, allowing the grower to stomp over any stalk that doesn't produce a well-filled, large primary ear, thus making it easy to select plants for desirable traits.

Varieties

Golden Jubilee is the most popular main-season variety in the Willamette, and it often matures in warmer Washington microclimates. Harris's Wonderful should have about the same maturity and is listed in their catalog at 82 days. I would not grow anything taking longer to mature, except in southern Oregon or in the banana belt immediately around Portland. Many of the new shrunken-gene, supersweet corn varieties need isolation from other normal types or the corn will not come out extrasweet. Additionally, supersweet varieties achieved with the shrunken gene are very poor germinating types and are not well adapted to cool May soils. Other types of extrasweet corn that don't use the shrunken gene are now available.

Corn takes time to store up enough food to make big tasty ears. Thus, in choosing early varieties, the alternatives are big or tasty. I prefer smaller yields of superlative flavor. The plant stores its food in the stalk in the form of pure glucose. Cut a stalk just when tasseling starts and bite into the pith. It's sweeter than sugarcane. Boil it down and you can make your own corn syrup. All that glucose is rapidly translocated into the ear as the seeds form, and by the time the ear is ripe, the stalk is tasteless.

Dill

Dill is a very easy-to-grow, frost-sensitive annual that any serious cook or pickler should grow fresh themselves. There is nothing like fresh dill in the garden.

Culture

Sow dill about the same time that beans or tomato plants are put in. Plant it in rows at least 18 inches apart, 3/4 inch deep, seeds about 1/2 inch apart. Thin when established to about 8 inches apart in the row. Dill does not require rich soil to make a crop and is almost a weed; but the plants will be larger if the ground is rich.

Garden Planning

I like to make a second sowing about the third week in June, which flowers later, toward the end of summer. If the plants are allowed to make seed, dill is likely to establish itself as a naturalized "weed" in the garden, coming up all over in following years.

Insects and Diseases

Insects and diseases are not a problem.

Harvest

The best, most aromatic seasoning comes from plants just beginning to flower.

Saving Seed

Easy as pie. Allow the seed heads to mature and cut before the seed shatters from the head. Dry the heads in a large paper bag or on a newspaper until the seed is fully dry.

Varieties

Long Island Mammoth makes large seed heads, as do many other varieties. A few types have been bred to make more leafy material and have smaller seeds and lower seed production. However, the difference between the two types is minimal. I've grown many varieties in our trials and prefer Aroma for best flavor and most leaf.

Index

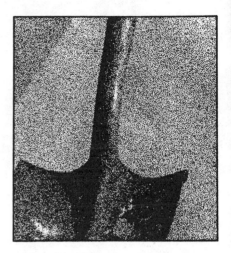

Notes

Selected Books from Pacific Search Press